BOOKS BY ILAN STAVANS IN ENGLISH

Fiction

The One-Handed Pianist and Other Stories

Non-Fiction

Bandido: Oscar "Zeta" Acosta & the Chicano Experience
The Hispanic Condition:
Reflections on Culture and Identity in America
Imagining Columbus: The Literary Voyage

Editor

Tropical Synagogues:
Short Stories by Jewish Latin American Writers
Growing Up Latino: Memoirs and Stories
(co-edited with Harold Augenbraum)

Translation

Sentimental Songs, by Felipe Alfau

OSCAR "ZETA" ACOSTA

THE
UNCOLLECTED WORKS

Edited by
ILAN STAVANS

Arte Público Press
Houston, Texas
1996

hrough grants from the
a federal agency) and the

Recovering the past, creating the future

Arte Público Press
University of Houston
Houston, Texas 77204-2090

Cover design by James F. Brisson

Acosta, Oscar Zeta.
      [Selections. 1996]
      Oscar "Zeta" Acosta, the uncollected works /
edited by Ilan Stavans.
            p.   cm.
      ISBN 1-55885-099-6 (pbk.)
      1. Acosta, Oscar Zeta. 2. Mexican Ameri-
cans—Biography. 3. Mexican American authors—
Biography. 4. American literature—Mexican
American authors. I. Stavans, Ilan. II. Title.
CT275.A186A25   1996
973'.046872'0092—dc20   95-33398
      [B]   CIP

The paper used in this publication meets the requirements
of the American National Standard for Permanence of
Paper for Printed Library Materials Z39.48-1984. ∞

For José Antonio Burciaga

CONTENTS

INTRODUCTION
by Ilan Stavans

Oscar "Zeta" Acosta (1935-1974) is one of the most enigmatic and compelling figures in Chicano history, as well as a profoundly puzzling writer. Born in El Paso, Texas, he became a legendary Legal Aids attorney in Modesto, and later on, after wandering around the country in search of a vision, assumed his calling as political activist in Los Angeles at the height of the Civil Rights Movement. He unsuccessfully ran as an independent (with an anarchist platform) for the office of sheriff of L.A. County in 1970, befriended Hunter S. Thompson and accompanied him to Las Vegas in what would be known as "a mythical journey to the heart of the American Dream," and shortly after writing a couple of autobiographical novels (*The Autobiography of a Brown Buffalo* and *The Revolt of the Cockroach People*), he disappeared, mysteriously and without trace, in Mazatlán, Mexico.

Numerous questions remain regarding his whereabouts. Was it a suicide? Was he involved in drug trafficking? Were his actions, monitored by F.B.I., considered a threat to national security, which could have resulted in some form of political assassination? Is he still alive somewhere, Central America perhaps? My fascination with Zeta dates back to 1992, when I edited *Growing Up Latino*. I requested permission to reprint a segment of one of Zeta's books and, during a conversation with his son Marco, a lawyer and musician in San Francisco, he directed me to his father's archives at the University of California-Santa Barbara and mentioned the existence of various boxes of unpublished material eclipsed in closets and basements. The result was *Bandido*, a book-long essay of detective journalism about his life and legacy, published in 1995. But while researching, it became clear to me that to satisfy the public's interest and mine in Zeta's, his correspondence, legal and creative writings needed to be made available. That, then, is the sole purpose of this volume: to make the private public, to offer a sample of the primary historical sources he shaped and produced, which serve as map to his odyssey.

Much of Zeta's writing was autobiographical. His main concern was identity, individual and collective, and in that he foresaw the climate to flourish a decade after his disappearance, obsessed in "minority" memoirs. I have not mingled with Zeta's literary style. Aside from occasional spelling mistakes, the material appears in its pure form. Since he was quite disorganized, I, with the help of Marco Acosta and the staff of the California Ethnic and Multicultural Archives at UCSB (particularly its director, Salvador Güereña, to whom I am greatly indebted), have tried, to the best of my knowledge, to date and when possible place each entry.

I have divided the content into seven sections. The first two are memoirs: the "Autobiographical Essay," written circa 1971, was used by Zeta as a promotional kit; and "From Whence I Come" is a loquacious piece probably used as draft in the shaping of *The Autobiography of a Brown Buffalo*. In them he offers insights into his experience in Panama, drugs, and his career as a Chicano activist. It should be noted that the second piece is incomplete. Zeta, it seems, intended it as part of a longer narrative, perhaps a novel, for which he contemplated a couple of working titles: "Are You Spanish?" and "O: The Brave and Agile Warrior."

Then comes a sample of assorted poems more or less about spring days, written in the late sixties. Zeta consistently wrote poetry since he graduated from Oakdale Joint Union High School, but his talent as poet was small. Thus, his verses are useful in shedding light into his moods and existential dilemma. The selection included here aims at being representative and is organized chronologically.

It was as an epistolary writer that Zeta was most prolific and copious. His archive at UCSB includes close to a hundred letters. Three of them were published in 1970 in the Chicano periodical *Con Safos*, but the rest remain unknown. Most were addressed to his first wife, Betty Daves, and were written between 1952 and 1960. (He divorced her in 1967). Apparently, he used the form with a multiple objective: to communicate to his beloved and acquaintances, to exercise his literary talent, and to unravel his labyrinthine self. Since they are repetitive and obnoxiously unpolished, I have selected a very small fraction, useful to understand his views on marriage, his difficulty in providing support for the family, and his desire to become a lawyer and writer. This section also includes letters to a judge regarding the education of Zeta's troubled brother Bob, a drug addict who engaged in criminal behavior; and to the personnel at the Doctor's Hospital in Modesto, where Zeta was hospitalized for a brief period. I have also included the only surviving letter to Hunter S. Thompson, with whom Zeta had a rocky friendship (Zeta is the 300-pound Samoan in *Fear and Loathing in Las Vegas*), but thanks to whom, according to historians, he was able to get contracts for his books with Straight Arrow Books in San Francisco, a publishing house linked to *Rolling Stone*. Finally, the section closes with a letter to *Playboy* magazine complaining about the use of the term "Gonzo Journalism"; a letter to Willie L. Brown, Jr., a black candidate in the 1970 state election, where Zeta explains his ambiguity, based on a racial argument, at running for the office of sheriff of Los Angeles County; and one to Zeta's friend, Douglas Empringham, about his plight as writer and his need for guidance.

Among Zeta's most memorable papers are four autobiographical short stories, three of which are published here for the first time: "To Whom It May Concern," an anti-utopian, science fiction tale subtitled "A Solicitation"; "The Worm Dieth Not"; and "The Little House." The last one was probably intended as a segment for a novel he began writing in the mid-sixties, *My Cart for My Casket*, to which "Perla Is a Pig," the only story published during Zeta's lifetime, in the 1970 anthology *After Aztlán*, also belongs. It announces many of the themes and obsessions that plagued his life and work: racial discrimination, ethnicity as a form of inferiority. Section five also includes two drafts of segments in *The Autobiography of a Brown Buffalo* and *The Revolt of the Cockroach People*: the former was published in 1971 in *Con Safos*, which promised to serialize the whole book but didn't, and it slightly varies from its equivalent in the book (cartoons of a humanized buffalo accompanied the text); likewise, the latter appeared in *La Gente*, was dedicated to Zeta's second wife, Socorro Aguiniga, and had a headnote that read: "Oscar Acosta, a lawyer and former author of *Brown Buffalo*, has a new book coming out next month entitled *The Revolt of the Cockroach People*. *La Gente* is supporting Acosta in his concern in reaching La Raza in our communities."

The next section is made of what is obviously a rough draft of Zeta's teleplay in two acts, "The Catalina Papers."

Although equally undeveloped as his three unpublished stories, the text, mentioned in the letter to Empringham, is valu-
able to understand his vision of the future in California. Its
science-fiction theme is the manipulation of race through psychological and mechanical devises.

Then come four invaluable historical pieces; they help
understand Zeta as lawyer, activist and writer. The first, published in *The Caveat* and fully titled "Challenging Racial
Exclusion on the Grand Jury: The East L.A. 13 vs. the L.A.
Superior Court," is a legal document detailing Zeta's anger
toward the state and local judicial system in California in
which he worked from 1968 to 1971. A headnote reads: this
periodical "is indebted to Attorney Acosta of the Mexican-
American Legal Defense and Educational Fund for permission
to print his important and provocative article. Proud of his
heritage, proud of his people, Oscar Acosta details in this article the exclusion of Spanish-speaking people from the Grand
Jury in Los Angeles over the years. The situation in L.A. is
only a manifestation of the problem throughout California,
and Attorney Acosta points out the growing militancy of
young Chicanos who will no longer tolerate injustice anywhere."

"*Una carta de Zeta al barrio*" is Zeta's only known text
written in (or probably translated into) Spanish. Designed to
attract a constituency that could help him become the L.A.
County Sheriff, in it he describes his goals as a political candidate and mentions his controversial career as lawyer and
activist. It is followed by his "Declaration of Candidacy," made
of a press release and a plea letter. And finally, the non-fiction
material concludes with Zeta's last will and testament, written in a hospital bed in early 1974, to his son Marco. It is his
last known document before his disappearance.

It would be easy to argue that Zeta's life after life is as
interesting as his time on earth. Since his vanishing more
than twenty years ago, his portrait, distorted and deconstruct-
ed numerous times, frequently appears in murals from Denver and Chicago to East Los Angeles. Indeed, it resembles
those religious images that keep on resurfacing even after
being repeatedly deleted. His writing, an essential part of the
curriculum in the Southwest, has been instrumental in shaping a new generation of Latino literati. He appears as ghost in
various Chicano novels. His anarchism has been glorified and

ridiculed, and his misogynist views have been consistently attacked by feminists. In short, Oscar "Zeta" Acosta has been turned into myth. His pathos, his tragic fate, are fertile ground to reflect on the past and future of Mexican Americans north and south of the Rio Grande. Again, since I have unraveled my own reflections elsewhere, my hope with this volume is to open up his life and work to a curious readership still avid for heroes and martyrs like the Brown Buffalo.

Amherst, Mass.

CHRONOLOGY

1935	Oscar Acosta is born on April 8 in El Paso, Texas.
1940	The Acosta family moves to Riverbank, now part of Modesto, California.
1942	The Sleepy Lagoon Incident takes place in Los Angeles, in which twenty-four Chicano youths are charged with gang killings. Seventeen are sentenced to prison until their convictions are reversed for lack of evidence and for civil rights violations.
1943	The Zoot Suit Riots, in which U.S. servicemen attack Chicanos, occur in Los Angeles, San Diego, Philadelphia, Chicago, and Detroit.
1949-52	Zeta attends Oakdale Joint Union High School. He has his first romance and soon becomes a fervent Baptist. He rejects a music scholarship to the University of Southern California, enlists in the United States Air Force, and is shipped to Panama, turning into a minister at a lepers' colony.
1956	As Operation Wetback, in which more than two millions Mexicans have been deported in three years, is terminated, Zeta is honorably discharged from the Air Force. He tries to commit suicide in New Orleans. Shortly after, he married Betty Daves, whom he met at a Modesto hospital.
1957	He begins a ten-year-long psychiatric treatment.
1959	His son, Marco Federico, is born. Soon after, Zeta suffers another mental breakdown. José Antonio Villarreal publishes *Pocho*, considered to be the first Chicano novel in English.
1962-67	The National Farm Workers Association is founded in Delano, California, by César Chávez and Dolores Huerta. Zeta divorces Betty Daves. He begins sending out manuscripts to New York publishers. Writes poetry, a two-act play, and some short stories, only one of which, "Perla Is a Pig," is accepted for publication. He begins studying law

at night at San Francisco Law School, passes the
California State Bar Exam in his second try, and
becomes an attorney for the East Oakland Legal
Aid Society, an antipoverty agency near Modesto.
In 1966 César Chávez and Dolores Huerta lead
farm workers on a three-hundred-mile march from
Delano to Sacramento, California. Rodolfo "Corky"
González founds the Crusade for Social Justice in
Denver, Colorado. At the end of this time period
Zeta quits his Oakland legal job.

1967   Zeta travels by car around the Southwest. Reies
López Tijerina and his supporters storm a court-
room in Tierra Amarilla, New Mexico, to free col-
leagues held as political prisoners. "Corky"
González publishes his militant poem "Yo Soy
Joaquín"/"I Am Joaquín."

1968   César Chávez begins the first of many fasts to
protest violence. Robert F. Kennedy is assassinat-
ed in Los Angeles, California. Zeta is put in a jail
in Ciudad Juárez, Mexico. He arrives in California
and acquires a new identity, becoming Buffalo Z.
Brown. He meets César Chávez, Angela Davis,
Rodolfo "Corky" González, and other Chicano and
civil rights activists. He represents poor Chicanos
in East Los Angeles, becomes a vociferous lawyer,
and challenges racial exclusion on the California
Grand Jury. Chicano teachers boycott and walk
out of schools, and nearly 3,500 students stay
away from classes for eight days.

1969   Protesting Chicano fatalities in Vietnam, the
Brown Berets organize the National Chicano
Moratorium Committee in Los Angeles. The La
Raza Unida party is formed in Crystal City,
Texas, under the leadership of José Angel Gutié-
rrez. Zeta meets his second wife, Socorro Anguini-
ga. His legal work and militant activities continue.
He takes part in the St. Basil's Roman Catholic
Church riot.

1970   The La Raza Unida Party becomes a national
independent party, with *El plan espiritual de
Aztlán* as its platform. Over 30,000 attend the
National Chicano Moratorium march in East Los

Angeles against the Vietnam War. Three people are killed by the police, including *Los Angeles Times* reporter Rubén Salazar. Zeta defends Mexican-Americans charged with setting fires at the Biltmore Hotel in Los Angeles while Governor Ronald Reagan delivered a speech. He declares his candidacy for sheriff of Los Angeles County as a La Raza Unida Party independent, running with an anarchist, apocalyptic platform that promises to abolish the police force. He is interviewed by Rubén Salazar for KMEX radio. The United Farm Workers Union signs contracts with California grape growers

1971   Reies López Tijerina is paroled after serving three years in prison for storming a courthouse in Tierra Amarilla. Tomás Rivera's ...*y no se lo tragó la tierra*/*And the Earth Did Not Part* wins an award and is quickly considered a Chicano literary classic. Disappointed with his career, Zeta gives up the practice of law. Soon after, he is arrested on charges for possession of drugs. In April he meets Hunter S. Thompson and travels with him to Las Vegas. He divorces his second wife.

1972   Publication of *The Autobiography of a Brown Buffalo* by Oscar "Zeta" Acosta, as well as *Bless Me Ultima* by Rudolfo Anaya and Rodolfo Acuña's *Occupied America: A History of Chicanos*. Rumors circulate that the FBI is after Zeta for political activism.

1973   Publication of *The Revolt of the Cockroach People*. He is last seen by his family at Thanksgiving.

1974   He is hospitalized for ulcer attacks in San Francisco. In June, Oscar "Zeta" Acosta disappears in Mazatlán, Mexico, and is never seen again. A year later, the United States officially ends its military involvement in Vietnam.

[Reprinted from *Bandido*.]

OSCAR "ZETA" ACOSTA

THE
UNCOLLECTED WORKS

AUTOBIOGRAPHICAL ESSAY

I, Oscar Zeta Acosta, who, in the beginning of 1971, was the only militant Chicano lawyer in the country, was born in El Paso, Texas, in 1935.

Because my family couldn't make a living during the Depression there, we moved to California so my parents could work as migrant field workers. We lived in Riverbank in the San Joaquín Valley. The towns there were all the same, built around the railroad tracks. On one side of them you had the Mexicans; on the other side you had the Okies and then further out you had the Americans. Where I grew up, the world was composed of that—Mexicans, Okies and middle-class Americans—and nothing else; no Jews, no blacks.

My father was a little different than the other people where we lived. He wanted me to compete more than anything else, so he pushed me into competition with himself. When I was five he encouraged me to argue and fight with him, which is unusual in a Mexican family. I guess that is where I became as nasty as I am.

When I got to high school, I was not like the average Chicano who, in the forties, would either drop out or go quietly off to the side. I became involved in sports and music and was president of my class. I got a music scholarship to the University of Southern California, but I was going with this Anglo girl whose parents didn't like me so I decided to get out of the way by going into the Air Force Band. We planned to get married when I came out. After a year of her visiting me and hiding around, she split and I was stuck in the service. I thought of going away but changed my mind. That's when I started smoking grass and taking bennies. I was a jazz musician, mainly.

Within months after her splitting—which was the first big trauma in my life—I thought that maybe religion had the answer for me. I started going to the Catholic Church pretty regularly and reading all kinds of religious literature. Then there was a guy in the band who started telling me about Baptists. I was stationed at Hamilton Air Force Base near San

Francisco, so he started taking me to his church in Petaluma, which wasn't far away. Everybody at the church saw me as being really different. I was a Chicano, a musician, a Catholic and a sinner. So all of the little chicks dug me and loved to hear me tell about all of my sins. This blew my mind and I started going to the church. Within a few months, I was converted. I saw Jesus coming down from a cloud one night. I got saved, really, Billy Graham style. Being the fanatic I am, I became a preacher immediately. I became the head of the student or youth Baptist group, whichever it was, and, within a matter of four months after my conversion, I had converted my entire family with the exception of my brother.

I was also holding noontime prayer meetings in the basement of the barracks of the band with about fifteen of the jazz musicians in attendance. It was unbelievable. It got so bad that the first sergeant asked me one day if I'd go easy on his Catholic boys. Being the idiot that I was, I said, 'They need God... You need God, too.' So, a few weeks later I was shipped out to Panama.

Between the ages of eight and eighteen, I hadn't spoken Spanish or hung around with the other Chicanos because, especially in high school, they stood off on the sidelines while I went ahead to do other things. Consequently, when I got to Panama I couldn't speak Spanish at all, so I took a class in it along with the other guys and then I became a missionary. In the two years I was there, I set up about five missions. I was still in the Air Force, but my only duty was band rehearsal in the morning and I had the rest of the time off.

When I had about six months left to do, I realized I was going crazy so I made a last, final study to see if what I was teaching was true. I made a study of the gospels and, on one side of the page, I put the things I felt good about, and, on the other, the things I felt bad about in comparing the life of Jesus. Within three months the bad side was about 20 times heavier than the good side, so I no longer believed in him. That caused the second big trauma in my life. Here I didn't believe in him and I had a hundred people believing in me in my congregations. I had Indians, Panamanians, servicemen of all races. They looked on me as their pastor. So for three months I had to go on preaching and teaching shit that I didn't believe.

That really affected my whole thing with the result that, when I got out of the service, I attempted suicide. Naturally, I chickened out like everybody else, but I ended up in psychiatry. I started school at San Francisco State and I started writing. I was majoring in creative writing and mathematics and I dug both of them. I had one more semester to go to get my degree in math but, by that time, I was halfway through a novel, so I dropped out to finish that and then intended to go back. I never did because by that time it was 1960, the Kennedy campaign and I got involved in that. I hadn't had a political thought up until then. I decided I didn't want to be either a mathematician or a professional writer after that involvement, but I did finish the novel and submitted it to three publishers, all of whom almost accepted it. They all said that I was great, earthy, poetic, the most brilliant unpublished writer in the world, but I was writing about Chicanos at that time—it was a Romeo and Juliet story of Okies and Chicanos in the valley—and that subject wasn't acceptable. So I decided I would write because that is what I am, a writer, but that I didn't want to have to write or to be a professional writer.

Since I was interested in politics and Chicanos, I decided to go to law school then work with Chávez and the farmworkers and be a union organizer. So I did it and got involved in the black civil rights movement for the next four years in San Francisco, but it wasn't really me. I told people that it wasn't just black and white, that there were Chicanos, too, and they laughed at me so I told them to go fuck themselves and they split. I graduated from San Francisco Law School, a night law school, in 1965. I was working at the *San Francisco Examiner* all of this time through college and law school as a copy boy, along with all of the political activity. When I got out, I took the bar exam and flunked it. It was the first time I had flunked an exam in my life and it was the third major trauma, so I ended up back with the psychiatrist. I studied for the bar again and passed it a couple of months later.

I became a legal aid lawyer in Oakland in a half-black, half-Chicano section. I hated it with a passion. I'd wake up in the morning and throw up. All we'd do was sit and listen to complaints. There were so many problems and we didn't do anything. We didn't have a direction, skills or tools.

After a year, I became totally depressed. I couldn't do anything, so I said fuck it to everything and I told the psychiatrist
to shove it and to stick the pills up his ass. I said I'd been with
him on and off for ten years and that I was still as fucked up
as when I began, just taking ten times as many pills. I took off
and ended up in Aspen.

I met some people who were pretty nice to me, including
Hunter S. Thompson, the writer, and I started dropping acid
and staying stoned most of the time and doing all kinds of odd
jobs—construction work and washing dishes—and, within
about three months my head was clear. I felt like I knew who
I was, what I was and what I was supposed to do. I stayed
there for about six months and then I was on my way to
Guatemala to smuggle guns to the revolutionaries down there
and to write about them. I got stopped in Juárez and thrown
in jail. When I got out I called my brother who suggested that
I go to Los Angeles. Well, I hated it. Being from up north, I
was subjected to this old prejudice between Northern and
Southern California, which was ridiculous. I asked my brother
why I should go there and about a newspaper called *La Raza*.
That was in January 1968. I arrived here in L.A. in February,
intending to stay for a few months, write an article about it
and then get out.

Then the high school walkouts occurred and I agreed to
take a few misdemeanor cases. Two months later, thirteen of
the organizers of the walkouts were busted on sixteen counts
of conspiracy which could have resulted in forty-five years in
prison for each of them. I agreed to take the case. It was my
first major case, my first criminal case and here I am three
years later. I haven't been able to get away and I don't think I
ever will leave. This is it for me because I've gone through
intensive changes in myself and my consciousness has developed about Chicanismo, La Raza, revolution and what we're
going to do, so it looks like I'm here to stay. It seems to me
that at some point in your life you have to make a stand, and
I've decided that I might as well be here as anywhere else.
This, East Los Angeles, is the capital of Aztlán, because there
are more of us here than anywhere else.

To understand where I am you have to understand how
the Chicano Movement has developed. In 1967 and 1968
young Chicano students, both in high school and college,
began to identify as Mexican Americans. The first issue was

what to call themselves. They began to organize coffee-houses and clubs but were mainly interested in the educational system. So, in March 1968, they had massive high school walkouts from four of the Mexican-American high schools in East Los Angeles. The result was numerous busts and that is when I became involved. Those walkouts were the first major activity by Chicanos as Chicanos in the history of this country. There had been labor groups and political-type groups, but there had never been any group organized to organize and politicize the community as Chicanos on broad-based issues. There are two million Chicanos here in Southern California. I think we're the largest ethnic minority in the Southwest—certainly here in Los Angeles we are. Statistically, we're the lowest in education, with an eighth-grade education being the median, and we're the lowest in housing and jobs. We have the problems here in Los Angeles and the Southwest that the blacks have throughout the country.

But the history of the Southwest is totally different from the history of the rest of the country, which is something that most people don't understand, and they don't understand that this historical relationship is what causes the attitudes that exist here today. They tend to see us as immigrants, which is absolutely wrong. We were here before the white man got here. The American government took our country away from us in 1848, when the government of Mexico sold us out. They sold not only the land, but they basically sold us as slaves in the sense that our labor and our land was being expropriated. The governments never gave us a choice about whether or not to be American citizens. One night we were Mexican and the next day we were American. This historical relationship is the most important part of the present day relationships, but it's totally ignored or unknown or rejected by the Anglo society.

In 1968, when we started making a movement toward attaining better education and schools, we wanted the literature to reflect our heritage and our culture. We started meeting with school boards and the city council and we began to know the enemy. At that point I think that most of us believed we could integrate into the society and get a piece of the action, since nobody denied that we had problems. But now, three years later, there have been few changes. Now there are two assemblymen in the California legislature, one Congressman, and one member of the school board who are Chicanos, and that is it for a class that constitutes thirteen percent of the population.

In 1968, our first problem was that of identity. As time went on we no longer questioned that. We had chosen a name—Chicano—whether we had Spanish or Indian blood, and we knew that we existed alone. That is, we relate to Mexico, but in a nostalgic way. We know that when the going gets rough, the Mexican government ain't going to do shit for us. And we know that no other aspect of the broad movement is going to do shit for us. They'll pay lip service, they'll condescend to us, but basically they're just as paternalistic to us as the white racist pigs. For example, I've spoken at numerous rallies for the Panthers, for Angela Davis, and every time I get the same bullshit treatment. I'm the last on the program with five minutes to speak and we get no offers of any real unity or working together.

I think that the Black Movement has been co-opted. Three years ago I used to know a lot of heavy blacks. They're just not around anymore. I'm talking about the Black Panthers. They're just rhetoric; they're just sucking in that money. They talk heavy as hell, but when it comes down to what they're fighting for I don't think even they know what they're fighting for because they're integrating into the society that they despise as fast as that society allows them to. I made this decision during Corky's trial.

Corky González is head of the Crusade for Justice, which is based in Denver. He is also a poet, a street-fighter, a theorist and an organizer, and he is recognized by a lot of Chicanos as the boss, the leader. Chávez is like a grandfather to the Movement. We respect him and love him and would help him anytime he asked, but we don't feel that his progress, his ideology, is Chicano enough. César used the white liberal population quite a bit and, more than anything, this offends the average Chicano. It is bad because they take jobs that Chicanos should be taking and using them is the easy way out. There were probably more competent white militants three years ago than there were available Chicanos, but we feel that he should have trained his own people more as we do now.

Corky was on trial on a weapons charge arising out of the August 29, 1970, police riot here, where three people, including Rubén Salazar, were killed by the police. Corky had been trying to get away from the violence with his two children when the police busted him for a traffic violation, suspicion of robbery and a concealed weapons charge. He was on a truck with a lot of people and we never denied that somebody on it had a loaded pistol, but it wasn't Corky. He wouldn't dare carry a goddamn gun around with him. He's a leader. He doesn't have to carry a gun for the same goddamn reason that Nixon doesn't have to. But we didn't stress that point at the trial for fear of alarming the jury and perhaps inflaming the press and cops. Why should we give them an excuse to shoot at Corky like they did at Rubén when they thought that he was a leader?

What I did stress in picking the jury was whether they would be prejudiced if Huey Newton testified for Corky. See, Huey had called and said he wanted to talk to me. I asked him if he'd come down and be a character witness for Corky. I thought it would be a great show of unity. Everybody said he would. Then, after I'd announced it all over town and picked a jury by hammering at that question, he wouldn't come or talk to me on the phone, so I have nothing more to do with the Black Movement. I'm talking about the professional revolutionaries, not the people.

I think in the past year or so the Chicano movement has begun to solidify. After the August 29th thing, there was the National Chicano Moratorium 'non-violent march for justice' on January 31, 1971. It was against police brutality and repression and was non-violent until the end when fighting broke out and the cops swarmed out of the police station with everything, including twelve-gauge shotguns firing buckshot balls straight into the crowd. After two hours, one person was dead, thirty seriously injured and there was about a half-million dollars worth of damage, including seventy-eight burned police cars.

Things have gotten heavier since then and Chicano consciousness is spreading. Everybody in 'El Barrio' is a Brown Beret. It's a concept, an idea. M.E.CH.A. (Movimiento Estudiantele Chicano de Aztlán): the Chicano-student movement is also growing. Aztlán is the land we're sitting on now. The land where my forefathers lived hundreds of years ago before they migrated to the valley of Mexico. The Aztecs referred to the entire Southwest as Aztlán. Now the Chicano movement has no need for anyone else's ideas but our own. We have a way of life that we've learned from childhood. The concept of *la fami-*

lia, the respect for elders is not Sunday-school bullshit with us. It's part of our culture. A Chicano can no more disrespect his mother than he can himself. Which means he can, but at great cost to himself. The concept of community—of La Raza—isn't a political term to us as I feel it is to black and white radicals. The term brother is a social term to us, one we learn before we learn about politics.

We don't kid ourselves anymore. We know we're headed for a head-on collision with the rest of society. We're absolutely convinced of it and we're not being paranoid or nothing. We know that the main thing we want now is not better education or better jobs or better housing, because we know that they are not possible to achieve. It is not possible as the result of the history of human nature and the animal instinct against the races integrating in the liberal sense of the word.

You can't be a class or a nation without land. Without it, it doesn't have any meaning. It's that simple. So we are beginning to see that what we're talking about is getting land and having our own government. Period. It is that clear-cut. As to what land, that is still in the future. We have to develop the consciousness of land as the principal issue, just as three years ago we had to develop the consciousness of identity as the principal issue.

The black man came here as a slave. He is not of this land. He is so removed from his ancestry that he has nothing but the white society to identify with. We have history. We have culture. We had a land. We do feel solidarity with the American Indians because we are Indians. We have a total unification in ideology but no unification organizationally. I look upon them as my blood brothers. It is the Indian aspect of our ancestry that gives meaning to the term 'La Raza'. We are La Raza. Of course there is Spanish and European blood in us, but we don't always talk about it because it is not something that we are proud of. For me, my native ancestry is crucial. This consciousness is beginning to develop now, symbolized in the word *tierra*. We want our land back and this is what we are going to be fighting for.

I don't think you're going to see too much more of demonstrations against education or things of that sort. I think that has petered itself out. A lot of kids have gotten into OEO projects and school projects as a result of the movement, so they've been in college for a few years now and they are as hip to what's being taught in the colleges as the white radicals have been for some years now. They think it is a waste of time, that it takes away what little you have of your identity.

A perfect example is the National La Raza Law Students Association, here in Los Angeles, which I am pretty much associated with. The very first day they started school here on some O.E.O project I went in and spoke and told them, 'Half of you will never be lawyers. Those of you that do are going to become so only because of your race. You got into these programs because you're Chicano. So you owe something to your Raza. Yet, I predict that in three years I'm going to be fighting fifty percent of you guys. You're going to be my enemies.' They laughed. But it is a fact. This past year I've been working on these major cases of importance to Chicanos not only organizationally but legally, and often I've been unable to get the assistance of the Chicano law students. My prophecy to them has come true, except I was wrong in one respect. It is not fifty percent I'm fighting. It is about seventy-five percent. This is why I'm no longer pushing for more school programs, more handouts, more welfare. I think that will destroy the movement. They are attempting with those to do the same things they did to blacks.

For example, with the law students when I was doing this judges thing in 1971, they didn't want to be associated with it because they were afraid that it might affect their future, their careers. That judges' thing was my third challenge to the Grand Jury system here. I was defending the 'Biltmore Six', six young Chicanos who were busted for allegedly trying to burn down the Biltmore Hotel one night in 1970, when Reagan was delivering a speech. They were indicted by a Grand Jury and I contended that all Grand Juries are racist since all grand jurors have to be recommended by Superior Court judges and that the whole thing reeks of 'subconscious, institutional racism'. I was trying to get the indictments squashed on that basis.

To prove my contention I subpoenaed all 109 Superior Court judges in Los Angeles and examined them all under oath about their racism. After almost a year of work on this, the judge on that case, Arthur Alacrón, who is Mexican American, rejected the motion. The way it looks now, I think we're just about finished with that whole legal game.

I'm the only Chicano lawyer here. By that I mean the only one that has taken a militant posture, to my knowledge, in the whole country. When I got here I decided that if I was going to become anything legal I couldn't use the profession as it was. Lawyers are basically peddlers of flesh. They live off of other people's misery. Well, I couldn't do that. I made a decision that I would never charge a client a penny. As a matter of fact, I end up supporting some of my clients. I get money by begging, borrowing and stealing. Sometimes I get a grant from some foundation like Ford. For a while I was under a Reggie program, although all I was doing was political, criminal work and they knew it. I don't even have an office. I'm in court practically every day.

I relate to the court system first as a Chicano and only seldom as a lawyer in the traditional sense. I have no respect for the courts and I make it clear to them from the minute I walk in that I have no respect for the system. That I'm against it and would destroy it in one second if I had the physical power to do it. The one thing I've learned to do is use criminal defense work as an organizing tool. That is my specialty. I organize in the courtroom. I take no case unless it is or can become a Chicano Movement case. I turn it into a platform to espouse the Chicano point of view so that that affects the judge, the jury, the spectators. We organize each case, set up defense committees, student groups, and use the traditional methods of organizing.

I think one thing I haven't mentioned enough yet, which is a very pertinent thing, is what drugs have done for me personally. I think psychedelic drugs have been important to the development of my consciousness. I don't think I'd have gotten to where I am without the use of these drugs. They've put me into a level of awareness where I can see myself and see what I'm really doing. Most of the big ideas I've gotten for my lawyer work have usually come when I am stoned. Like the Grand Jury challenge was the result of an acid experience. A lot of the tactics I employ I get the ideas for when I am stoned, which is not to say that I wouldn't get them if I wasn't stoned. A lot of my creativity has sprung from my use of these psychedelic drugs. And this doesn't just apply to me. When I got here to LA three years ago, I only knew one other guy who was taking acid. Guys were shooting heroin and they'd say to me 'You dope addict. Are you crazy?' Now, just about all of my friends have tried or are taking acid. I think the acid experience is part and parcel of the radical Chicano Movement.

I don't have much contact with many of the other radical lawyers here. I think a lot of them are still finding themselves. Consequently, they'll often chicken out of something at the last minute. I think it's chickenshit, reactionary, and that they're the enemies of the people. I like them; they're nice guys, but it's too late for these personal things. Too many of them aren't doing the work that has to be done.

Now some of the Chicano law students are thinking of organizing a collective, but I've disagreed because I think it is looking to the future as any other lawyer would do. They are thinking in terms of money to make, cases to take. They're thinking of business. For me, to think of the future is inconsistent with my thinking of the present. It is only the present that is important. I think you develop yourself much more if you don't think of those things, if you think only of the job: defending Chicanos and organizing around the case.

[Circa 1971]

FROM WHENCE I CAME

I

If I had it my way I'd just be O; but as it is, my name is Oscar and my father's name is Acosta. I was never given a middle name and don't ask me why I was given the name Oscar. I've asked my mother and all she ever says is, "I think it's a pretty name." I used to think that I should have been named Albert or Thomas. I think Albert was a saint and his name is celebrated on the date of my birth, 8th of April, but I'm not sure. I *am* sure that I will not look it up.

You may as well know right from the start that I have no intention of looking up anything. I will do not one hour's research for this purgatorial purge. Either it comes from the brain or it doesn't come at all. At most I will look up how to spell a word or two because I do know that I am an atrocious speller. It just doesn't make sense to me that men who write journals of their journeys either into or out of hell, and that is what all fiction is about, it just doesn't make sense to me that men should spoil it with facts. It is the feeling, the memory that matters. What's all this business about getting the account right. That might be fine for paying one's just debts, but it has no place and will have none in this little tidbit.

Why *was* I given the incongruous name of Oscar Acosta? And why has there been such a preoccupation with my name? Don't throw that bit about identity at me. I mean the name itself. I've often said it over and over. I make jokes about it. I tell stories about it. I mean it; I'm hung up on a name. Oh, well, as old ma says, "It's a pretty name."

I once read in a comic book that it means "A brave and agile warrior." For some reason or other, probably it has more to do with the contents of the comic book, the source of reference as it were; it seems to me that I remember feeling that the definition was descriptive of a German soldier. I think it was during the second war that I read that bit of info. It was inside the comic book in those sections where the authors gave

you all sorts of wonderful FACTS. Usually on the reverse side
of *Ripley's Believe It or Not.*

That was the extent of my extracurricular intellectual
endeavors: Comic Books. They're in vogue now—1966. This is
the year of the Batman craze and the rest of the Pop art scene.
I feel a bit offended, which is, I suppose the essence and purpose of that stuff. But when I was a kid, comic books were all I
ever read. Except for the Sea Bees Manual, which my father
brought back from the war and was absolutely convinced that
if we committed it to memory we would someday be appointed
to the Naval Academy—how very little he knew of the real
world—or at least gain a ticket to heaven, except for that
thick blue book, the only books I remember being around the
house were loads of comic books. You'd think that by looking
at those of my generation—I'm nearly thirty-one—these modern innovators of Pop art would be put on notice of the sickness that it produces. I mean, we are the precursors of the
comic book mentality and all you have to do is look at us to see
what it did to us. Maybe, in a way at least, this book is dedicated to the proposition that whosoever is raised on comic
books, a comic book life will he have.

To get back to what I started to say, my name is Oscar
Acosta. The reason I say it is an incongruous name is that one
would think that with a name like Acosta one would be given
the honest-to-god Christian name of Juan, or Tomás, or even
Pedro. I'm glad, though, that she at least had the good sense
not to give a name like Pedro or Mateo or something like that.
Can you imagine what sort of life I would have had with a
name like that? I'm convinced that names mean something.
What exactly I don't know. Maybe I shouldn't say I'm *convinced*, because that presupposes some rational thought precedent to the conclusion; but at least I *feel* that names mean
something. Have you, for instance, ever heard of anyone of
any worth named *Pete*? I mean, Pete is the sort of name that
goes with a "Hey, Pete!" or an "What's say, Pete?" and can you
imagine a broad saying, "Oh, Pete, darling..." Christ, the
more I think of it, maybe Oscar *is* a pretty name.

⁓

So the brave and agile warrior was born in the midst of
the depression. What is the first thing that happened to me,

you ask? Just like you, buddy, I got a swat on the butt. They cut me off the lifeline, unhooked me, made me mix my own blood around and suck in my own air and slapped my rump. I *guess* birth is a trauma! And of course one remembers it. Maybe not the way one remembers his name or the color of his true love's hair, but remember it he does. If memory is the product of both conscious and unconscious awareness and perception, then certainly the birth experience is remembered by all. The simple analogy is the memory of dreams. Your conscious mind is at rest. You are dead to the world. Sawing logs and making meemees and you see things and feel things and the next day you *know*, don't you? The first dream that I remember remembering is one where I was a cowboy. We crept silently over the hard, smooth rock to attack the Indians. When we reached the top I could see the feathers sticking out over the crest of the mountain. I took my Jim Bowie knife and clipped the feathers off! That did it! They were dead, man! I killed them dead with one fell swoop of my Bowie.

I was five years old when I had that one. I lived with my father and mother in a two-room shack in Riverbank, California, Pop. 5,280, Stanislaus County, San Joaquín Valley. We had been in California less than a year and my father had a job for the first time where he could bring home enough to buy the flour and beans in *hundred*-pound sacks that my ma used to make dish dryers with. Had she been smarter she could have used the burlap in which the beans came in to make curtains instead of the flimsy dime-store crap that covered the single-pane light holes.

The floor was wood in the front room where we all slept and the rear, which we used for the kitchen and dining room and bath room and just general knockabout room, it was about the size of a modern pantry and storeroom and had a dirt floor. My brother Bob and I had to get up in time to chop wood and carry in water from the well for the breakfast.

How well I remember the war songs on KTRB: *Remember Pearl Harbor* (as we go to victory, we will always remember, how they died to make us free, etc., etc., and bullshit!) And then there was the Maddox Brothers and Rose: Give us a big smile, Rose! He, he, he, he, he, he, he!! And at six o'clock: "Oh, say can you see, by the dawn's early light, etc."

The old man tries to make his voice authoritative and deeper than we knew it to be: "Come on, boys. Stand up.

Salute. Come on, Bob and Oscar. Get up now, it's time to hit the deck."

We groan. We moan. We twist and turn. I crawl up on my knees and get that last bit of sweetness. I hug the warmth of the smelly blanket and have that final snuggle of the black womb.

"Okay, boys, up and at 'em. That's the sons. You're supposed to stand up."

I remember. I'm conscious now. I know Bob is sleepier than I. I'll beat him. I'll please my dad. Show him he has a wonderful son: Me. Up I jump and to hell with that sissy stuff or sleep. Stand up straight on top of my bed.

"And the rockets screaming, the bombs bursting in air, gave proof through the night, that our flag was still there..."

I salute the soldier way and my flabby chest is bursting with pride. Not so much at being an American, for I have never been nationalistic, but bursting with a pride of confidence. You could say I felt that I belonged to something, to someone, and that is what put the bubbles in my hairless, titty chest. As I see it now, it may have been the war. Maybe the reason I felt patriotic was because I knew the enemy: Hitler, Tojo, Mussolini, the Nazis, the Japs.

But that was later. I'm getting ahead of myself.

II

Sometimes I wish I knew more about my origin, about my ancestors. I've never really tried to learn. The things I think I know are part history and part story. I have written and thought so much about it that I can no longer, if I ever could, distinguish fact from fiction. The little old lady who taught me used to tell us stories about herself usually late at night before bedtime. They were also part fact and part story. There was usually a plot involved and it ended up being something of a ghost story. So if you chose not to believe me, that's okay, because I'm not certain I believe it either. At this point we could get into a long-winded discussion about the philosophical differences between fact and fiction. But when all is said I suspect it's a difference without a distinction. I've read too many cases where different people testify to the same event in such different terms that one can only suspect that either

numerous things happened all at once or else that each person
has his own bird's-eye view of things and tells it as he sees it.
You might say that I'm really a relativist at heart. All I know
is that it no longer bothers me that there are no absolutes,
including that one.

It wasn't always like this...

The kid was born in El Paso. I don't add the state name
because that city isn't really a part of Texas no matter what
the maps say. Not that I'm an authority on Texas history or
on El Paso, but believe me, I wasn't born in Texas!

The kid's father used to hang around with the motorcycle
gang. You'd never know it now by looking at him, but from the
stories I've heard and the pictures I've seen, Manuel used to
be quite a swinger in his young days. He used to wear a little
thin mustache black over his smirking lips. I see him now as
the stolid Indian that he is, but as I remember him he was a
Mexican in the new country, not his.

Manuel is the son of a woman who never quite got over
the fact that her husband left her. Though they tell me that he
died, I choose to believe that he upped and left. She was born
with a corncob up her ass and it's still stuck in the same place.
I will say that she has guts. She brought a son and a daughter
across the border all by herself, which isn't an easy thing to do
since the oldest, my father, was only twelve-years old at the
time.

That bunch came from Durango, Mexico. The revolution
had ended and nothing had changed. Instead of being in
bondage to the landowners, they were now enslaved to the
generals. The man who stole the strongest stallion, who shot
the straightest steel balls, the man who fucked the hardest
and cursed the loudest, this was the man who got to be a general.

In the beginning an idealism burned all their hearts.
They were the same men that had forever rebelled. There is
no difference between men bred of a revolutionary spirit
whether they be Russian, English or Mexican. They were tired
of having nothing. They were bored with life. When a man
cannot show off, when he cannot show his woman that he
really is a man, that is, that he is not the same sort of being,
the same sort of animal as she is, this is the man who will
prove it to her by banding together with other men in a like
situation and start a rebellion. So long as men are fat and

have gifts to give to their women, these are men who will not
rebel against anything for they are being men in their fatness.

Unfortunately, my grandfather was not a general. He was
too romantic. He *believed*! What few possessions he had when
the rebellion started he lost. And he could never fuck the
women in the villages that refused to co-operate with the ban-
didos. He would stand aside while the others plundered and
dream of his little wench back on the farm slapping the cornmeal into tortilla shapes.

Perhaps I do the old man an injustice. But what difference does it make? He is long ago dead now and the law is
clear: The deed cannot be defamed. I didn't study law for nothing. I know what I'm doing.

I would like to contribute gobs of words to the story of my
paternal grandfather and to the life of my own father prior to
my birth, but the fact is I know nothing of them. So if there is
anyone to blame, push it off on my grandmother who told me
nothing of his memory. The only thing she ever said to me was
to wipe my shoes before I came into her house. One can't write
a history of toilet-training problems, can one?

In any event, I know little enough about my father and
my mother and will have to make up a whole lot as it is. There
will be plenty of time for fiction as this labor of love progress-
es.

My grandmother brought my father and my Aunt Mary to
live in El Paso. I am told that she married again. But I'm not
even sure of that. It's another one of the ghosts in the closet
that has been shut up all these years. Not long ago, when I
was home visiting, my mother, while in one of her bitchy
moods, said, "You know that your Uncle Hector is only your
dad's half brother, don't you?"

I nodded as if I knew. Hell, it was the first time I'd heard
the rumor. But I wasn't about to encourage gossip. If they
chose not to tell me about my ancestors, I guess it's their business; probably not a hell of a lot to say anyway.

So my father went to work to support the family and
received his entire formal education while still a child. He can
read and write, but the things they teach one in the third
grade isn't quite enough to get one a very decent job in later
life. So, as it turned out, my father's best job was that of a janitor for a school. He's still hard at it with the brooms and the
little kids' bubble gum under the desks.

III

When I was fifteen years old I was a part-time bartender for my uncle and my father's bar in Riverbank. One night an old man drunk in his beer told me the story of a man he had known years before in Mexico.

"Christ, but you should have known the bastard, kid. He was one of the best. He had so much money that every holiday, you know, the days of the saints, he would line up the people of the village and give them food and clothes. He had so much land that if he rode all day he could not see the opposite borders of his estate."

The town drunk who was telling me this story was called Chihuahua. He died not so long ago and they say it was quite some funeral, the old guy had so many friends.

He went on to tell me that this other man, who was my maternal grandfather, was the first man in Mexico to own an automobile and that after the revolution he was able to bring enough of the money into El Paso so that by the time of his death in '38 or '39, he still owned several bars and a couple of theatres.

From that account one would think that I was at least the grandson of a rich man. But the rest of the story is one of the really closed chapters of my life. I have it on pure hearsay that several years before his death my grandfather had left my grandmother, Martina Fierro, and gone to live with his mistress. He was purportedly shot by a thief or a gangster, and my grandmother was so proud that she would not claim one cent of his estate because the mistress was still living in the house where the old man's belongings were.

Instead she chose to raise six or seven kids on the strength of her female vanity. God, when I think of how different it could have been for all of us if that story is true I get sick. Instead of having a decent home and education, all the Fierros grew up on the bread lines along with the rest of poverty-stricken depression kids.

I was three or four years old when the old man died, and I still remember two of my aunts taking me to the hospital to see the old man dying. I remember being raised up to his bed to kiss him and knowing that he was very sick. He died not long after that.

That is all I know of my two grandfathers. That is all I will write of them. Perhaps I would have been a different person if they had lived. The first real character I created is an old man who analytically is the grandfather I never had. I'm convinced that children need grandparents as much as, and possibly more so, than parents. The parent lives too close to the child. Their egos are pitted one against the other, and of course there's the thing of competition for the mother's love between young boys and their fathers. The father nags, begs, cajoles the kid into *being* something, or out of jealousy prevents him from being what he's capable of, inhibits him. On the other hand, a grandfather is more the teacher, the kindly philosopher. His love of the child is much more purely platonic. Usually he is so much older than the kid that there is no time left to be in competition. The old man's race is over. He's either made it or he's too old to give a damn. It is not so much the race that the grandpa is concerned with as he is with the runners.

Anyway, I always have wanted a grandfather. Since I didn't have one, I created one. Actually, he came into being long before I started writing. When I was twelve-years old, I was such an old grouch that my cousin Delia used to call my grandpa. Later you will come to see how I dominated my family, how I became the one who was really the center of things. One example should do: My sisters are small girls. They want to go to the movies. They ask ma, she says ask pa, he says he doesn't know. They ask me, I say okay but be careful, so they go. I am no more than fourteen-years old at the time.

IV

The first five years I lived in El Paso. My father worked at odd jobs in grocery stores and garages. He used to give us our *domingo*, or what you'd call an allowance. On Sundays, Bob, my brother who was two years older, and I would go to the movie called El Calsetin, which is to say The Sock, or, The Stocking. I'm not certain if that was the real name, but it is the name I remember calling it. We'd have around ten or fifteen cents each with which we'd get into the movie and buy an ice cream or an ice cone, popcorn and a small soda pop that came in little bottles the shape and size of a hot sauce bottle.

The theatre was like all theatres for kids, noisy and dirty. The entrance into the actual theatre was under the stage, so that whenever one entered, the light would diffuse the movie and there'd be yells and catcalls to hurry and close the door.

Bob and I were at that time very close. We grew up together almost as twins, since he is only two years my elder. We look and talk and act very much the same and have always been mistaken one for the other. Now that we are in our thirties, we are only physically alike. Our goals are dissimilar, and our problems akin only insofar as most men have basically the same problems. Since our early childhood traumas were not too dissimilar, it is no wonder that our emotional conflicts are somewhat the same.

I remember three of the apartments we lived in between the ages of three and five, or at least I have memories of experiences. It is a rather strange experience to sit here now in the early hours of the morning before the sun has come up and think upon these things. I must stop and on a separate sheet list the things I remember, the actual visions I have. I'm not sure whether I can trust myself. Is it possible that my memory still contains these things? I have pictures in my mind of about two dozen experiences and yet, historically at least, some of them must have occurred when I was between two and three years old. Can a man at the age of thirty-one sit in a quiet apartment on Leavenworth Street in San Francisco and truly recall these things? And for what purpose? What does it avail him or what does he give to the world by writing of the things that happened to him at the age of three? Surely not to instruct, not to change the world. Is it a therapeutic exercise? Perhaps it is all and possibly none of these things. But the question is as puzzling as the answer one presupposes exists. Why do men ask questions of things eternal? What is it about our species that it has the capacity to pose problems? Is this the one distinguishing characteristic of the homo sapien, that he does in fact ask questions? Curiosity did a hell of a lot more than kill a cat; it killed all animals and made the one animal, man, superior to all else. I suppose that is why at this point in the history of homo sapien that the western world is in power and the virtues of science and technology are the supreme guide to a good life according to our philosophical and religious teachers; that is, because at some point in the history of man he stopped and asked questions like: what is this thing that burns my hand? Should I use this rock to kill rather than my hand which is smaller than the claw of that beast? Because man has asked questions and because the scientist and the advertising man are still in the business of posing problems to be solved and because the Western world is the best in this business, I say that is why the Western world and those nations which are in effect western by adopting our system of values, they and we are in power and will remain so as long as we continue to ask questions and strive to solve the problems. Now it is enough for me that I at least ask the question, Why do I sit here and tell of the things that possibly happened to me? It is for the reader to determine for himself, what, if any there be, the answer, or answers, is, or are.

The kids went to the store in their ragamuffin outfits and got the goods of Mexican sausage, that is, chorizo, red and hot and greasy, and milk, always milk; milk, like water, must be a universal drink and magic. Only until recently with the new reports of cholesterol and fat hearts has milk been considered by all to have some magic potency. We drank it by the gallons with the cream on top and easily curdled. I never could stand the thick cheese-like bits in milk any more than I could stomach the hardened bumps in hot cereal. I have never tasted buttermilk and I'm positive that I shall die without that experience. I much prefer skim milk and yogurt in these days of the diet. But then we ate mostly Mexican food. That is, we had tortillas every morning with scrambled eggs and chorizo and usually a side of refried beans. For holidays or special occasions, the women would on the night before grind the corn for the dough and paste the cornmeal in the corn leaves filled with bits of beef or pork and chili sauce for the tamales. They'd always make sweet ones for the kids with brown sugar and raisins. The kitchen was always hot and steam-filled and welcome.

Every day we'd go through the same ritual with the store clerk:

"Got any samples today?"

"Samples? What'd you think this is, a church?"

"Ain't you got our samples?"

"We *sell* here, kid! This is a store!"

We'd stand there in our bare feet and tattered clothes looking sad as hell. We knew better than to demand what we knew was a matter of right. Pick up the sack slowly, eyes downcast and look every inch the beggar boys that we were. Beaten, bowed, burdened, starving and poor, that's what we were in those days.

"Hey, where you going?" He enjoyed the act as much as we. "Don't you guys want your samples today?"

We'd grab up the gumballs or candy kisses and run out without a word of thanks. He'd get this big sadistic laugh and we'd get our grubby hands on the loot and scat for home as if we'd just pulled a caper. I was six-years old and living in another state before I found out that not all stores provided samples for us. In those early days the sample was as much a part of the sale as the change from a dollar bill is today. Some sophisticated sucker might say it was the store's good will or advertising and mark it off on the tax return. But to us it was simply a part of the bargain. We had a choice of several stores to patronize. Our mothers didn't tell us which store to go to, so it wasn't exactly a one-way street or a gift of charity; as I've said, it was part of the bargain.

V

I guess I was four-years old when I suffered my first real injury. My father had a good job as I remember. He worked for an old lady rich as hell. He was her gardener and chauffeur. The old lady lived in a big house on one of the few hills in El Paso. She saved bottles and paper sacks. There was a whole garage full of them. It was the Fourth of July and Bob and I were given a whole bag full of firecrackers and sparklers and bombs. In those days the Fourth of July was just as noisy as the Chinese New Years are in San Francisco. Every kid had firecrackers and there was no fear of the police. It may be that this made it less exciting because we weren't breaking any laws, but I doubt it. Even today people get the same kick from watching fireworks during a policed and permitted fireworks display. Wars which are perfectly legal are productive of the same excitement as rebellions without sanction of law. I'm convinced that we enjoyed the firecrackers the same as the Chinese boys do in Chinatown in 1966.

I had lit a giant red cracker. The fuse burned short and fizzled. I carefully backtracked. I relit it, slowly and with caution. It wouldn't take. I stuffed a piece of paper around the fuse and lit it again. I ran, but not fast enough cause when I tripped I was only a few feet away. The thing gave its giant blast and my leg burned. Since we wore short pants in those days the burn went directly into the skin. The screams brought my parents out and I was gallantly carried into the medical tent to receive treatment for the wound.

Commotion within. Mother is nervous, father is so scared he's anxious. He yells at her. She bites him with a lash of the tongue.

"Lard! Put lard on it, for Christ's sake!" he hollers.

She merely cuts him down with a flare of an eyelash or two. She rubbed the greasy stuff into the burn and I was laid up for a whole hour before my father took me back to the battlefield and sent the rockets screaming into the air while I sat and watched in awe.

I never had a broken bone and I've only been cut really bad once, but that was when I was twelve-years old. Fires have been my menace. The only real injuries, the only times I've come close to death have been with fires. One would think I should be afraid of fire, the flames, the dancing tongues of red-orange. I'm not. I have no fear of fire or water. Knives and fish scare the hell out of me, flying objects give me the willies. I would rather fight a lion than be put in a room full of bats. I'm a good swimmer. If it weren't for being out of shape I could stay underwater for an hour. But if I see so much as a goldfish in the womb with me, I panic. But fire, it's nothing. Not long after the firecracker thing I was in the toilet with Bob. We had a community toilet for all the people of the apartment building and it was late one dark night when Bob and I went there. We always burned newspaper to keep the ghosts and spooks away. I sit on the stool while Bob burns the papers. It is cold and dark and the flames die down and the darkness creeps in again. Before the poops finish falling, my pants catch on fire. I jump up and both of us are thrown outside by the force of my startled jump. I'm kicking away at my pants and Bob is trying to pull them off and the dirt is cold on my ass. My father comes out and my mother quietly gets the lard. There were no scars from this one. We continued to burn funnies in toilets until I was twelve-years old when we first got an indoor toilet with lights. To this day toilets are strange, dark places for me and not places of comfort and relaxation as they rightly should be.

We were living on Durango Street when I burned my pants. It was the toughest neighborhood I ever lived in. There were gangs and wars and all the problems of growing up that we are all familiar with. I really have nothing to add; we've all read the Chicago stories, the Harlem scenes, and we've all seen the spectacular musicals. There will be time for that when I come to the grammar school days and the high school parts, but in these first five I lived amongst the toughest and meanest bunch I ever did. I remember them only as wearing black clothes and swearing dirty words constantly. I was only four or five but I was old enough to know they were really evil guys. I tried to join them once. The Durango gang was on the street and I walked up to them. They didn't pay any attention to me. They were discussing strategy. They were going to rob a freight-train load of bananas. The tracks were not far from the neighborhood. Teen-agers in black clothes and black long hair and those who could sporting mustaches, smoking fags and every word a fuck, crap, shit, same old preoccupation with the genitals on a sunny Saturday. I close in on them. They can't even see me. The appointments are made and the assignments given. I leave with one of the groups that heads for the tracks. We walk and run and they keep puffing on their fags. I'm thrilled because I've been accepted by not having been kicked out. I run with them and we come to the tracks where the loot is. We walk slowly along the deserted line, kicking the rocks and walking on the rails with precision balance. When we come to the car that we were told contained the goods we look around to see if the lookout will give us the signal. He has positioned himself where he can see the round-house where the railroad people are in small shacks. He waves the go-ahead signal. The lock is easily broken with a hammer and chisel. I'm in there unloading the bananas with the big guys. I stop to eat one and I get a swat on the head by one of the leaders. We're not to eat until we've completed the haul! We get all we can carry and start running. The signal is running toward us. We've been spotted and the railroad dick is coming down fast. The lookout is about a block ahead of him. Most of the gang drop their loot and we run and run until the lungs burst with the dick chasing after us and screaming for the cops. He never had a chance with guys twenty years younger. We have reached the hiding place where the others are and everyone is excited and gasping for

air and trying to talk all at once. The leader is angry at those
who dropped the loot. I'm a minor hero for a minute because I
held on to mine. I'm an example of coolness according to the
leader. Someone must have tipped the dick off. The leader is
certain that one of the punks on the street told the railroad
people. The punks are not a gang. They are the non-members
of the Durangos, which includes everyone else on the block.
There will have to be a war. Someone must go to give the declaration. I am chosen because I'm too young and innocent to
be held as a hostage. Now I am truly a member of the gang.

I went to find a leader whose position was not clear. I was
told to tell them. Either it didn't matter who "them" was or
else I was supposed to know. Of course I'd tell them. I wasn't
stupid and I wasn't a punk kid, so I went to find a titular
leader. I knew a boy about my age who had several brothers
the age of the Durangos and who unlike the rest of us lived in
a house. It was a natural meeting place because it was a
three-story house with a huge yard and big, green trees for
climbing surrounded by a wooden, walled fence. I found them
and told them the story. The kid didn't believe me. He thought
I had made it up to make myself look big because they had
accepted me. The older brother believed me and accepted the
challenge. The war would take place in the rear of the house
where a vacant lot and two shacks made it a perfect battle-
ground. The brothers told me to go tell them. Matters had
become serious. The others started collecting sticks and rocks
for weapons and garbage can lids for shields. Branches were
cut from the willow tree for lances and for whips in case of
close combat. I was too afraid to return to the Durangos. I
could not admit it, of course. One learns at a very early age
the invincibility of man, that man means strength and fear is
reserved for women and sissys. But one also learns to hide it;
that is the cunning of man, that he learns the myths and the
lies all at once. I told them that since I wanted to fight on the
side of the good guys I couldn't return to the Durangos. They
believed me and instead sent the young brother to tell them
where the battle would take place. I gave the brothers some of
the bananas I had brought with me. Now I was a member of
both gangs. Truly I was a bright kid.

The battle raged for over an hour. We fought from the
tops of the shacks. Rocks and bottles were our missiles. Nose-
bleeds and broken heads were our injuries. The war ended at

the same time that all wars end. When the excitement wore off and when the supplies for battle were expended, when it was time to go home and eat and when the parents could be heard throughout the neighborhood calling their young to run the errands for the evening, this is when my first war came to its halt. My pants were torn and my face was scratched by a flying rock. It was my first reason for my latter-day pacifism.

VI

We lived in the poor sections of the poor town. But of course poverty was unknown to me at that time because I was too young to understand it. To attribute poverty to children is like attributing feeling to animals. Children have no feeling one way or the other about poverty; to them its a question of possessions, and, although it may at first glance sound like the same thing, it is not. I am speaking of young children, say, between the ages of one and five. But I can hear all the arguments already. Perhaps I should withdraw that statement. Or I should limit it to include only myself. Maybe I mean that I as a young child did not know the meaning of poverty in spite of the fact that by all definitions I lived in it. I don't particularly wish to quarrel with you on such an observation. Let me then say that in my opinion children do not know the meaning of poverty. Why is it that when we qualify a statement by the phrase "in my opinion" or "it seems to me," in other words, when a man is not too cocksure he does not draw the same quality of objections as when he makes a flat generalization? Is it not clear that all statements of one's belief are but opinions? Although we purport to speak from observation, from our own perceptions, although we think we are recreating a factual experience, in truth we are merely giving our impression, our opinion. It would be too tedious to qualify each statement with an "in my opinion," albeit it is impliedly included in each statement. So let us remember that the very least I am aware of the simple truth that no man knows for certain whether he is speaking from experience or from opinion. At the very least I presuppose a hypothetical has been put to me and I am testifying as an expert not necessarily from direct observation but from knowledge acquired by training and experience.

When I was four-years old I lost my mother's wedding
band. The analyst would have a field day with that, wouldn't
he? I had been left under the care of my brother while my parents went to the store. Bob had the propensity to judge in
those days. He was skinny and except for his adrenaline I
could have beat him on any given occasion. He was prone to
nag me and to boss me around. This was especially true when
my mother unwittingly gave the order, "I'm going now. Bob,
you watch out for Oscar. And you behave yourself, Oscar. Do
what your big brother tells you." Christ, that's all he needed to
get him to act as if he were King Kong! They tell the baby
story of Bob that when he was two or three he was taken to
see the movie of the giant gorilla and how thereafter he would
stand on top of his bed and pound his chest and proclaim, "Me
King Kong, me King Kong!"

So it was all my mother's fault that I lost those rings. I
don't remember exactly what started it. Bob ordered me to do
something. I refused and instead walked into my parent's
room. I was looking at the rings which she'd left on top of the
dresser. Bob followed me into the room and kept nagging at
me. "Put those rings away. Leave them alone. I'm going to tell
mom if you don't." Nag, nag! I grabbed them up and he lunged
at me. I ran out of the house. I ran across the front lawn. He
chased after me yelling for me to stop. "You better come back.
You're gonna get it!"

I am running across the neighbor's lawn and hearing the
commands and the threats. I know that he will tell and that I
will get a walloping. Why does he always nag me? He reminds
me of my dad's mother. They are cut from the same cloth with
their thin lips and split tongues. I know he will catch me for I
am fat and slow. He is skinny and fast and in another second
he will be upon me and beat me. Okay, so he wants the rings!
"Here, here they are!" I shout, and without looking back, I
fling them over my head without looking at him. He doesn't
hear me nor does he see where they fall. He catches up with
me and throws me to the ground. We wrestle and scramble
around a bit. He pins my arms to the ground and straddles me
like a horse, sitting on my stomach. I tell him I don't have
them. He refuses to believe me until he opens my palms.

We went back and searched for them. There is a frog in
my throat and my insides are mush. The butterflies fly at random within my belly. The die is cast. I have insured for myself

a good, hard wallop from my mother. Bob is ecstatic with joy.
He too knows that I will get it. We were still searching for the
rings in the lawn when my parents returned. Of course, Bob
ran up to them to tell them the good news that Christ had
died for all sin but mine. My eyes are blankets of blood and
tears. Hell, even at the age of four I understood the symbolic
implications of losing the parents' wedding rings. They didn't
say a word to me. We all searched for the little cheap things
for a couple of hours. We never found them. Perhaps because
they too understood the unconscious motives for the destruction of evidence they didn't spank me that day. Twenty-five
years later my dad got my mother another set of rings. At the
risk of sounding pompous, that little episode was the beginning of my rule over the family. I had in some dramatic way
come between my parents. I never had to compete for my
mother's love with my father, only with Bob. Since the old
man didn't wallop me or even bawl me out, we all knew that I
had won the first round. I was just four and was it my fault
that she left them on the dresser and that she told Bob to boss
me and that Bob in fact did prod me to do something so dramatic as that?

Consciously, I do not find fault with myself. I do not
regret anything I have done. My therapist disagrees with me.
He accuses me of constantly putting myself down. He says I
find fault with everything I do. But I can not see it. Even such
a trite example as the above. Even in that, I do not find that I
was the cause of the lost rings. I chose to believe that I was
but the occasion for their loss, but not the cause; that is, in
some deterministic way they were bound to be lost, almost as
if God had willed it; if one accepts the inevitable, if one
believes that all things that happen happen for either the
good or the bad but not at our will, not because we cause them
to happen, not because it is our will that they happen, but
simply because before the beginning of time it was ordained
that on such and such a date a certain thing should come to
pass, namely that my mother's wedding rings should be lost. I
say if one accepts that scheme of things then it follows that
the fact that they were lost was no more through my fault
than as a result of my mother's telling Bob to boss me.

The question is really one of proximate cause. Every time
a thing happens we ask ourselves, What caused it? Who is
responsible for that thing? If we try to pin the blame on one

specific event we get into trouble because no one thing exists alone. If for example we say that Oscar is to blame for the rings being lost, I would argue that the grass is just as much to blame for the loss as I am, since if there were a smooth ground the rings could easily be seen. The counterargument is that the grass came before I did, that I must take things as I find them in their natural state. I would then say that if Bob had not threatened me, if my parents had not ordered him to boss me, if they had not left the rings on the dresser, if I were not four-years old, all these sine qua non factors lead to the conclusion that I alone am not to blame. I am not alone responsible for the loss of the rings. And if it should be found that I am responsible, then at least I have put up a good argument. And isn't that all that matters? I would rather be a worthy competitor than an easy victor. Do you not see how I really am what my name means: the brave and agile warrior.

Of course I joke a lot. I'm not always entirely serious. But the name of the game is to find out when I'm serious. If ever. It is the game I have played all my adult life. I play it even with myself. When all is done it may be that I was nothing but a big fraud. Time will find me out. It is too early to judge now. Let's wait and see.

VII

Not long after that I had my first screw. We were living in this apartment where we all shared the community toilets. There were three toilets for about twenty families. Directly across the street and running parallel to the block was a single spur off the main railroad line. Every day some man in a model A would drive his car on the tracks. I mean that the way it sounds. The tires fit perfectly and he would drive on the tracks and blow his horn when he passed our neighborhood. As ridiculous as it sounds, that is the memory I have. Even now I can see the stupid black car driving down the tracks and blowing the horn as we sit out on the sidewalk and play marbles.

On that particular morning I was passing one of the apartments and I heard talking. It was the apartment of my uncles Hilario and Pete. They were both young men in the C.O. Camp. They wore military-looking uniforms and they went around with loose women. I knocked on the door and they lay in their beds with a hangover. I was on the way to the store and my mother had asked me to stop and ask them if they needed anything. They said no and not to bother them because they were sick. I apologized and told them that it was only on my mother's orders that I had opened the door. They sensed my embarrassment and Hilario said to me, "Here, take this for your troubles. Buy yourself some campanitas." He gave me a nickel and told me to buy myself some Hershey kisses or, as we called them, little bells. If I have not made it clear before, let me say it now. As a child I spoke in my tongue; my native tongue was Spanish. Of course, all that changed when I started school, but when I was growing up I spoke more Spanish than English.

I bought myself the candy kisses, and after I had delivered the groceries I went in the back of the house to eat them. The boy whose father owned the corner store had seen me buy them. He and his older sister came to me and asked me for some. I saw no reason why I should share with them, especially since their father owned a whole room full of candy. The two of us were five and the girl was probably eight. I refused to share with them. They started telling me all the favors they had done for me in the past, all the times they had shared with me, but I had no memory of their stories. I steadfastly refused to give them even one little Hershey kiss.

"If you give me one I'll give you a kiss for it," the girl said.

There was not the double entendre in Spanish because, as I've said, we called them little bells.

"Kiss? Who wants a kiss from you, stupid?" I said matter-of-factly. Those were the days when kisses came free. Little did I know that some men killed for those little things and all men did stupid things for them. It seems the older men get the more foolish they become with respect to kisses. But in those days my sloberings were reserved for mom and dad, sometimes for grandma, or as we called her, Guelita, which is the way little kids pronounce abuelita, that is to say grandmother.

"You just don't know how to kiss, that's why you're afraid," the temptress egged me on. "If you weren't so little I'd show you."

"I know how, dumb one. You just do this." I puckered my lips.

They laughed at me. The boy because I looked foolish and the girl because she was speaking of other things. "If you give me just one campanita I'll show you how the big people kiss."

I slowly peeled the tinfoil off my first chocolate bell. "Oh, heck, I've seen that. They do it the same. They just take longer."

Again she laughed at me and then I began to doubt myself. Even then my ears were tuned to a put-on. I could sense mockery and was sensitive to any attempt. This same sensitivity was to get me in many a fight in later years.

"Listen, stupid, I'm not talking about kissing with the mouth. I mean the way they kiss when they're in bed at night. I bet you don't know that, do you?" She was determined to have her candy kiss.

I hesitated for a moment but then the curiosity made my eyes squint and my forehead wrinkle, and I knew that I had just lost at least one of the Hershey bells. "Well, okay, but just one."

"One for me and one for him," she demanded.

I cannot do it now and I could not do it then; when it comes to bartering I am the weakest person in the world. I have no strength of character, no backbone; I am a mushy at bargaining. I say it is because I have no real love for money or possessions, that it doesn't really matter whether I pay ten or twenty for something I want, but that is all after-the-fact rationalization, for when the time arrived to drive a bargain I begin at the disadvantaged position of being basically a mushy.

I consented and wondered what this unknown way meant. If I were to say now that I sensed sex, you would not believe me. But I know that I did. For if sex is at least something mysterious, something that is primarily reserved for adults, a thing that involves a physical contact, a thing that requires two persons of the opposite gender, at least partly forbidden, if sex is all these things, then I sensed it. I knew as we walked into the community toilets that it was sex that we were going after. The three of us went in and I refused to give her her candy until she showed me how to kiss the way adults do. At least I had the sense to make that much of a bargain that would be to my advantage. She made me promise that I would not tell anyone, and she told her brother that is he told their parents she would tell them that he had lifted up her

dress. Hurry up, I told her not from passion but from my distaste for toilets in the dark. She lifted up her dress and pulled
her panties down. She told me that I'd have to do the same
thing. I refused. She said that it couldn't be done any other
way. It was in the semi-darkness and that is why I was able to
do it. I'm sure that if it had been in daylight I wouldn't have
had the guts to do it. But being dark, I complied with her
order and pulled my pants down.

"Now put it close to mine," she told me.

I did as she asked and waited for the next order.

"Well, kiss me, stupid," she told me.

"Kiss you?" I was already getting bored with the new way.
It did nothing for me. It was even uncomfortable standing
there so close to this little whore with smelly clothes and bad
breath from eating so much candy. I did as she asked. I kissed
her on the cheek very fast.

"No, no, not like that, dummy. Kiss me down there, with
your thing you touch my thing. Put it up against me."

It was then I first realized how strange and how very
ridiculous the act of fornication is. Of course, it was then not
necessary and thus I did not have to go through with it to any
climax. But still, it is not really much different as an adult.
Still, you have to go into a dark toilet and there is always
someone else present whether it be literally or in spirit. Still,
it involves uncomfortable positions and bad breath.

I guess I rubbed my penis against her thigh since she was
taller than I and when she said to get it high, laughed because
I had to stand on my toes to comply. By then the three of us
were giggling when we heard the voice of doom. It was my
Aunt Elisa.

Elisa is the oldest child of the Fierro family. The family
has five sisters and two brothers. The father is dead and so
Elisa was the boss, even over my Guelita. She is a boisterous,
booming woman with a sense of humor to boot. She won't take
any nonsense from you, but at the same time there's a twinkle
in her eye. In a word, she's a delightful fraud. A major-domo-
type woman who really wants to be a lady and a friend, but
upon whom life has cast the burden of being the straw boss of
the whole crew and thus doesn't have too much time for fool-
ing around.

"Who's in there? Come on, boys, quit the playing. Who is
it?" she rapped on the door. My heart sank as low as my

pants. We all froze. The girl motioned for us not to say anything.

"It's me, Elisa, I'm in here," the girl volunteered.

"Oh, I thought I heard more than one. Well, hurry up, the
other toilets are full, too. I have to go in real bad."

"I can't hurry. I just came in. And I have a stomach ache.
You better go to another one." The little whore was a smart
one. My heart was still eating away at my chest. I had pulled
my pants up and could not breathe.

I heard the old aunt cuss a word or two and go to the
building next door. Each building contained four apartments
and had an outside toilet for the four families. There were at
least four buildings, so she had her choice.

When we heard her walk away, the girl again made us
promise not to tell anyone or else we'd all be in trouble. "You
know we're not supposed to do this. My cousin, Johnny, who
showed me how to do this, is twelve-years old and he says if
my mother knows she'll cut my hair like a boy's, so you better
not tell anyone. Okay, I'll go out first and then if no one is
looking, I'll tell you." She started to open the door but quickly
shut it. "Oh, I forgot. Give me my candy bell." After I gave her
her payment she walked out and gave us the signal. I wonder
what ever happened to her? Do you think she became a real
whore as an adult? What would happen if I were suddenly to
meet her? Would she remember? Probably not. Maybe it never
even happened. Who knows? All I know is that I have a memory of it. And that's the way it was when I had my first screw.

VIII

Guelita was my grandmother, my grandfather and my
part-time mother. She's a little woman who has lived to see
her great-grandchildren. She is now a third-generation
babysitter and housekeeper. She has at one time or another
helped us all to grow up. Though I think of her as *my* Guelita,
she is truly *our* Guelita for she has had the good sense never
to pick a favorite, or if she has she's never let us know it. She
is at once the most cunning and the most kind person I have
ever known. She has the wisdom of the ages etched in her
brown, wrinkled, leathery skin. She wears clothes the way
children wear adults' clothes when they play house. She wears

things by the doubles: Two skirts, two pairs of stockings and little black shoes with short, fat heels. I doubt if she was ever of a pretty face or a handsome figure, her beauty being all in the soul. Except for my son, she is the only other person I have ever known for whom I have no regrets for ever having known. If there is a rude memory of her, it is buried beneath all the delightful ones.

The cousins would sit on the doorsteps and listen to her stories of her youth in the evenings after we had tired from our games. It was best when one was fortunate enough to get her all to one's self for a ghost story or two. I remember one night when my mother had not returned from work and Guelita stayed with Bob and I to wait for my parents. We sat outside on the doorsteps and listened to the stories. She had a totally serious way of talking, there was absolutely no hint that the story was anything but a factual recreation of facts. She never for a moment suggested that there was any fiction involved. She spoke softly and matter of factly, whispering at the right moments and using slow gestures for emphasis only when absolutely necessary. She used a method that is unbeatable for ghost stories in that she began her story with a true event, usually something that we were all familiar with, and then it turned into a fiction, but where the demarcation point was we could never tell. This is not simply because we were children, for I have as an adult spoken to her and I still cannot tell when she is lost in a dream of fiction or telling something that really happened.

On that one night she told us the story of her own mother, but she began by speaking of our mother, who was somewhere on the loose in Juárez dancing in some cantina because she had fought with my father the night before:

"Where can she be? How I wish that she would return. It is not proper for a woman with children to be out in the streets dancing with other men. God will surely punish her. Believe me, when the Lord sees a mother in a cantina with other men, He will find some way to punish her for her misdeeds. *Ay, ay, ay,* where can your mother be?" She would give great sighs as if she had but one breath left, slowly nodding her head wistfully.

"People think they can hide their evil ways from the Lord. They think that the things they do that displease God are done in secret. They do not know the ways of the Lord. They

don't understand the manner of his presence in all places at
one and the same time. I remember my own mother telling me
how God punished her for trying to hide from Him. It was during the revolution and your great-grandfather was away at
war. He fought with the rebels to free us from the evil government that made slaves of all the people. My parents had not
yet married, for my father said in case something happened to
him he did not want to leave a young girl as a widow to live
out her life dressed in black. He was a man who liked ponchos
and serapes of many colors, and the color black seemed to him
as being only for the dead. His father had left him a small plot
of land where he planted corn and grew tomatoes and green
squash, beans and, of course, *chile verde*. When he went away
he told my mother, who was then a young girl, to take care of
his land. The corn had already been planted so she only had to
water it and see that the weeds did not choke the tiny green
shoots. There is little to do while the plants are coming up, the
God of harvest sees to all that. The summer sun and the careful moons watch over the food for the poor people who keep
the faith. It is simply a question of turning the water loose on
the earth. But to this young girl it seemed a heavy burden.
She felt tied to the land. Because she had to rise early and
make the tortillas for her old father and two uncles, because
she had to see that the children were fed, her mother had died
giving birth to the youngest boy, my favorite uncle, because on
top of all this she had to watch out after the field of corn, she
felt strapped to the work. She was not like the others. She had
a sharp tongue and even spoke back to her uncles when they
bothered her with their tales of the war and of their injuries.
Though she was Indian like the rest of us, she had a fine
Spanish nose. Her father often told her in jest that she was
not his daughter with a nose like that; that she must have
been the child of one of the traveling Spanish priests that
came to the village. She would reprimand him for desecrating
the memory of her mother. He would prod her on even as he
had often done with her mother."

   Guelita would stop talking and gaze into the darkness as
if she could see my mother in the blackness of the early
evening. Again she would nod her head and murmur a short
supplication for her safe return. We would remind her that
she had promised us a ghost story. "What do you want those

bad stories for? Do you want the *coco* to come and get you?"
We shuddered at the thought of *that One.*

"Well, as you can see my mother was tired from the work.
She had nothing but men to care for. She had to wash them
and clothe them and feed them. And now with her *novio* in the
war she had his land to look after. And she longed for female
friends. She had no time to go and visit those she had known
as a little girl. They were all married now. They had children
of their own and at the very least a hut they could say their
own man had built from the adobe in the nearby riverbed. So
it is not surprising that the poor girl often got evil thoughts of
running into the village. While she picked the pebbles out of
the beans or while she patted dough for the tortillas, she
thought of what it would be like to go into the village just for
one day. As the summer continued and she saw the corn grow
to her height, and as the moon grew larger each night, and as
the coyotes bayed in the distant hills, she longed more and
more to talk to someone her own age. She of course heard no
word from her *novio*, for in those days they had no post office
and even if they had one it would have been to no avail since
the man could neither read nor write.

"One day while out in the corn field, a stranger with a
bandaged head came out from the hills and asked for some
water and for directions into the village. Under his torn
clothes and muddied shoes she could see that he was a young
man despite the face covered with whiskers and blood. He carried a rifle and told her that he was in the rebellion. He asked
her if the village was on the side of the rebels or on the side of
the government. The girl told him she knew nothing of politics. Do the men of this town fight with the soldiers or with
the rebels? he asked her. What does it matter? she said curtly.
They just fight, she said. The young man told her he had to
know so that he might know how to approach the people. As
you can see, he said, I am without food and, of course, I have
no money. If I go to beg and they ask me who I fought with, I
had better be prepared to give them the right answer. As you
can see I can no longer fight. I don't want to anyway even if I
could. I am tired; I am weary from all this blood. I just want to
eat so that I can be on my way. She asked him where his des-
tination was. He told her in a wavering voice that he did not
know. I just want to leave this country. I am tired of this life. I
can no longer kill my own countrymen even if they are sol-

diers. She caught his word and interrupted, Does that mean you are a rebel? He smiled at her ability to grasp things. He only laughed. I am not going to tell you what I am. I'll only tell you who I am. My name is Juan Tomás and I have killed too many men. Both with this rifle in my hands and with my hands themselves. Is it such a crime not to want to kill anymore? Haven't you ever come to a point in your life where you are weary? Where you want to leave it all for something new, different? He smiled again and said, No, I guess not, you are too young to have experienced bitterness. Her eyes widened in instant anger, I am not young and I have experienced these very things. Do you think I am one of those silly little girls you have probably seen throughout the countryside who are just sitting home sewing and waiting for their man to return from this silly war, who spend their entire day just making gossip with the neighbor?"

"They talked for a long time and he drank more of her water. Soon she offered him some of the corn she was picking. He ate it quickly and uncooked after cutting away the ends with the worms. Then he helped her to pick the corn and they continued to talk. It was the day for the irrigation and so together they watered the corn. This required merely a waiting and watching that the water did not seep over the furrows. They were able to talk and laugh while they waited. She shared the tacos she had brought with her and soon they were talking and laughing even as old friends or lonely people do."

When the irrigation was coming to an end, the young man started talking more rapidly, knowing that soon she would have to return to the family she had told him all about to cook their supper. He said to her that it was too bad that she was tied to such chores. It was a shame that such a young and beautiful person should have to feed so many hungry men. You are wasting your life here, he said to her. You should be dancing and singing with people your own age. This is no life for people like you and me, he tempted her. Now is the time of our youth, now is the day of song, you should have more than corn and tortillas to look forward to when you awake each morning. Because she had thought these same things herself, she could not resist his arguments. How could she deny that what he said was true when she herself had been in misery even that same morning before she met him. He continued to talk to her, to tempt her, to tease her, to make her miserable in her inextricable position. And then when he saw that she was truly weak from his argument, he said to her, why don't you come with me? No, don't answer yet, let me finish what I have to say. If you come with me your life will be just as hard as it is now. But you will be working for yourself. Or should I say we would be working together for both of us, for each of us. Yes, that is the way it would be. Not as it is now for you. Today you are a slave to your family, and what if tomorrow you marry, what then will all this work have been for? Surely not for yourself. It is work for others that makes one a slave. Don't be misled into thinking that only those in bondage, those in chains, are slaves. We are all slaves that work for others and cannot leave. If you were to come with me I would promise you but one thing... A full life."

The old woman would stop her stories and look at us to see if we had fallen asleep. Sometimes we would close our eyes only to rest them and then feel ourselves being lifted up into the arms of the old woman or into the arms of my father who would come out on the doorstep and catch the last part of the stories. On this particular night the story was never finished because my father returned empty-handed from his search for my mother who would not return until the early hours of the morning, chewing gum rapidly and popping it with great dexterity. There followed the usual fighting, the screaming, the shouting, cursing, throwing of things, running, hitting, castigation, insults against the family names, the never ending battle of the strong-willed woman who refused to accept the husband as the head of the family, the somewhat silent and angry Indian whose pride forbade him from telling her how things should be, for as a woman she should have known her place in the family. To this day I do not know if that story was true or not; it appears that it could have been the story of my Guelita herself, but I guess I'll never know, for she is too old now to remember, and when I ask my parents or my brother about things that happened so long ago they do not believe that I can remember that far back, they accuse me of making the stories up myself. I suppose there's the possibility that they're right, but I do have these pictures in my mind.

These first five years were filled with moments of happiness and very few moments of sadness. The great conflicts that would result in traumas did not really begin until I was in a different land, in a different state. As a young child I had

so many people to love me and look after me that there was
never any need to seek out love in the blind ways that I did
later in life. Then my grandmother and my aunts, my father
and my mother, my cousins and my brother all were people
watching over me. I did not lack caretakers, that is for sure. I
remember warm houses and good food, hot Mexican chocolate
that was better to eat as candy rather than as a drink. I
remember in kindergarten when I pulled the chair out from
under a boy while we all stood to give the pledge of allegiance.
The boy fell when he sat to eat his milk and crackers and hurt
his head. I was sent home for being such a bad boy. If I was
spanked I don't remember it, in fact I can't ever remember
being hit prior to coming to California. I guess we were poor,
but I don't have memories of poverty, but rather of a full and
good life. I remember that my brother was skinny and that my
parents forced him to take cod liver oil and would buy special
meat for him. My father was determined to fatten his first
born by feeding him steaks. Bob stayed skinny until he went
in the Coast Guard at the age of eighteen when he started to
drink and eat like most young men do. If I had to make an
evaluation of those first five, I would say that they were as
good of formative years as anyone could expect. I don't think it
would have mattered too much if we had been rich or white or
living in another country, for as it turned out those were the
best years of my life and I have no regrets and make no apologies for them.

IX

I was five-years old when we moved to California. My
father had an aunt living in Riverbank and his mother and
two brothers and a sister had already gone ahead. The reasons were purely economic. I don't believe there was any great
dissatisfaction with El Paso, but then again, like so many
other things, I really don't know, for my parents have never
found it necessary to tell me very much of their early days of
marriage. Now they talk quite a bit, but the past is forgotten
and not likely to be revived. I can only make guesses at the
reasons for the moves. I do know that Manuel was only earn-
ing about five dollars a week as a mechanic. The idea of being
paid according to one's ability excited him. He was fully confi-

dent that given the opportunity he could do as well as any other man. I think he settled that with himself years ago. His only problem was that he never put himself in any position where the really big opportunities could reach him. He has never had a good job and has never made any money. But he has been successful if one takes into account what he had to begin with. It isn't easy for a first generation to make a fortune. He has the obvious disadvantage of a language problem, no education and the entire cultural differences which make it difficult if not impossible to be terribly successful.

Writing this crap makes me feel like some sort of jackass sociologist, which is the last thing I want to be. There is nothing very subtle about my bland generalizations, so I should be content in telling you what it is that happened.

He took a Greyhound across the deserts of the Southwest and promised to send for us as soon as he had earned enough for our passage. I remember the excitement about his departure. He was so confident that he was going to the wild west where gold nuggets still could be found just waiting for someone like him to pick them up. I've often wondered what he dreamt on those nights on his way out here. Surely he must have had some real dramatic dreams about his future. He had two sons at that time who would be starting school in the fall. He was penniless and had for a wife a woman who would not be content with the same things that the relatives had. I do not say that my mother was a grubber, but on the other hand she was not to be so easily satisfied as the average Mexican woman, whatever the hell that is.

Average. What a funny word. We use it as an excuse or by way of explanation of our limited knowledge. Since it means a certain numerical quantity obtained by dividing the sum by the number of objects, one would think that we were speaking with some approximate precision. When the sum is something like a million, one would think that at least a fair size had been added in order to speculate. In my case, for example, in order for me to say what the average Mexican woman wants presupposes that I know what, at the very least, two of them want. Hell, I don't even know what one (1) wants let alone a larger number. So then how can I say what the average is? How can anyone? The simple answer is that one can't. And further, the word is not used in its mathematical definition. It means that one's observations have led one to conclude that so and so is different than the others of the same kind. Thus, at best I can only say that it seems to me that my mother is a bit different than other Mexican women I've known. The next question is obvious, no? How many Mexican woman have you known, Osc? Answer: None! I've know a few girls as a boy, mainly my cousins and aunts, but to say that I've known Mexican women, no. Not even in the biblical sense! Thus I am reduced to this proposition: My mother wanted more. Period. I cannot make comparisons. If I am to be held to such a scrutiny then the results would be more dull than this diarrheal diary already has become.

Perhaps it would have turned out differently if I hadn't seen so many movies. I've read of many great men who were influenced in early life by books, some by great music, and then there are those whose lives turned because they met a great person. I even know a piano player who quit playing football because after a concert he went backstage and shook hands with Stan Kenton; he keeps the autographed program stuck to his dresser mirror with Scotch tape. People who Scotch tape anyone's picture at the age of twenty-five are ill. I can say, and I do say with a sense of great accomplishment, that I've never had a hero who was a living person. I think I'm the only person that I've ever known who can make such a statement. I'm sure everyone I've ever known has at one time or another felt desirous of being like some other person they know or know of. I'm not talking about kids who want to be a policeman or Superman. I mean people like my friend Sig who would rather be Stan Kenton than the Harry Sigurdson he is. Or people like Ramon who bows every time he's introduced to someone because he read where Pablo Picasso is very polite to his guests; he even wears a scarf in the summertime and wraps it around and around his neck when he paints his flamboyant crucifixes in blacks and reds. I know a lot of people like this and it wouldn't surprise me if it turned out You are the same. I might as well get it straight now: I'll capitalize Your name until I finish this letter of resignation, but after that I'll only think of You as I do of any other person who is now dead and gone forever. But for the little while I'll try and restrain myself and show the proper respect; it's the least I can do in memory of the three years we've spent together.

Like I said, I was too influenced by movies. It could be that I ate them up when I first came to San Francisco because back in Modesto I seldom went to them I was so busy drinking and chasing after the little Okie girls. It was a special thing, a treat, a big date to go to the theatres in Modesto. I didn't live in the big city. I lived out in the sticks in Riverbank and went to school in Oakdale, so it was a big deal to go to the movies in Modesto. In case You haven't been out there lately, Riverbank is still famous for having had the largest Tomato Paste Cannery in the world; for a town with a population of five thousand or so that's not bad. Oakdale is noted for its clover seed. I knew a kid in high school whose father died when we were freshman and left him about fifty acres. He planted clover seed because it requires very little care; just irrigate it once or twice a month and then mow it down and sell it when it grows. By the time we graduated he had over a hundred-thousand bucks in the bank. He was the most popular kid in school not because he had so much money of his own but because he was known to go to the whorehouses in Jackson up on the Columbia River every week. He was the horniest guy I ever knew. I'll bet he was born with a hard-on. I remember the first time I introduced him to my girlfriend, Nita, he said, "Man, I'd eat her box right now." I thought that was funny as hell his saying that to her boyfriend. It made me feel big. As You can see I wasn't exactly what one would call sophisticated or what Sig would call hip. I mean, what poor taste it is to say a thing like that to the lover. Sure it makes the guy feel big cause he's got something the other fellow wants, but it's still no class. The dumb thing is that the jerk of a lover takes it as a compliment. How strange that that was the beginning of my downfall. You might say that was our introduction. You and me, we met when Chet first saw my girl, Nita, and made that rude remark.

It isn't easy for me to sit here now and write this letter to You about all the things that led up to our real first meeting, but I think it's important that we find out why I got involved with You in the first place. It wasn't a natural relationship, You'll have to admit to that. I could easily have gone all through life and never have been saved. And surely it wasn't written in The Book that I should have been a preacher. I wasn't cut out to be one, You can see that, can't You? But I'm getting ahead of myself. I'll make the apologies and the arguments later on. Now it's important that You understand how it is that I came to know You.

Like I said, I was influenced by the movies I saw. I came up here to be a jazz trumpet player. I really thought I'd make it. I'd bought every album of Chet Baker, Dizzy, Ferguson and all the others. I bet I can whistle every solo they've ever recorded. And if you can whistle it you can play it. The funny thing is that I might have made it but for You. I'd worked hard enough. Eight years of constant study is enough to tell whether a guy's got it or hasn't. The few auditions I made, the few really good guys I blew with, told me I had it. No, they don't come out and say it—hell, it's not like playing football where the coach slaps your rump and says You're My Boy. At least jazz is a bit more subtle than that. You get into a session and you start moving your fingers and blowing the wind into the horn. It's a question of feeling it and working with the others in the same groove. When you start thinking alike then you know you've made it. But it doesn't just come to you. Some people think all they have to do is snap their fingers and stomp their feet and then they're with it. Man, it ain't like that at all. The snapping of the fingers and the stomping of the feet have never played one single note. And music is notes, chords and scales and wind and fingers moving in tandem.

When I moved to the city I came up with the expectation of finding a group to work with within a matter of a week or two. It had been that way in Oakdale High School, so why not in San Francisco? In Oakdale I was the hottest musician they'd ever had; they all gathered around the stage when I started playing one of my hot solos and commenced to clap their hands in rhythm to egg me on to blow louder. I could see their flushed faces staring up at me with smacking lips and half-closed eyes for the mood. Come on, come on, yeah, yeah! The more they yelled, the louder I played. Blow, man, blow! Yeah, man, blow it all out!

Christ, to even write it down now makes me want to puke. How could I have been so blind? What in the world ever possessed me to think that that was music? God, I'll never forget the first time I played in the city. To even think of it now, that great moment of embarrassment is a bit masochistic. I know, but I have to explain it to You. I had enrolled at S.F. State as a music major. It was the first day of band rehearsal. I had already auditioned for the dance band and had passed the exams mainly because of my ability to sight-read everything the conductor's assistant put up. Christ, was I eager! I just knew that nothing would stop me. I had been watching the little girls in their black stockings lingering around with black-stained eyes and sheet music to try out for the singers' role. I ran up and down all the scales, blowing louder than necessary to warm up the horn. High notes held clear and steady, no waiver of the lips, then slowly letting the vibrato take hold. Oh, yeah, man, was I the hot stuff. Loud, brassy tones of whole milk and thick, brown cork. Beautiful, baby, simply beautiful!

The conductor walked in, an older man with balding, graying hair, thin lips and just a hint of blue eyes. A quick smile and down to business. Okay, men, let's get to it. Let's fill in the seats, he said.

No one had taken any of the lead chairs; some had sat in the back rows, but no one was willing to commit themselves to the solo chairs. I had always played solo so I gracefully and without much ado sat in the lead trumpet's chair. No one looked at me; no one said anything. I sat there as of right. Soon all the chairs were filled. He motioned for my b-flat and the band tuned to me. Soon we were playing a full arrangement in the Kenton tradition. Sig played the piano solo, but I didn't know him until after the rehearsal. He played it just as simply as it's done on the original. Ernie Turduci wailed away at the Muso solo with the fat wail of the dirty saxophone. Then it was my turn. The first note, the very first note of the Ferguson trumpet solo was about seventeen notes higher than I could reach. I squeezed my lips and grit my gut but it wouldn't come. Richard Harris, the conductor, stopped the band. Try it again he motioned me. I tried, but it was simply too high. Forget the high note, try it an octave lower. I did, but all I saw was black notes sixteenths juxtaposed with sixty-fourths and a million black dots all over an otherwise white sheet of paper. I froze up. Nothing worth mentioning came up. The room was motionless and silent. All that could be heard was the echo of my attempt. I couldn't look at anything but the sheet covered with black notes. I was afraid to look up for fear that one of the girls in the black stockings would be staring at my disaster. I thought silently that no one but Maynard Ferguson could play anything as difficult as that. I could read, I could play, but that was simply asking too much. It would require weeks of studied concentration, but don't ask someone to do it on sight. It just couldn't be done.

He asked if anyone else wanted to try it. No one answered. He pointed at one of the guys and said, how about
you? Try it, will you? I picked up the sheet and handed it to
him. He was a negro with a thin mustache and a fat lip hardened by blowing the trumpet. Harris took it from the start and
when he came to the trumpet solo, Don Officer played it as if
he had written it himself. He was flawless in its execution.
Short, high, squealing brass, staccatoed perfectly like bits of
steel tacks. Up and down and around the sheet of braying
sounds, he didn't make a single mistake. He played it perfectly and beautifully.

When he finished, the room was silent. Then the girls
waiting their opportunities became an audience and aban-
doned themselves to clapping for the performance they'd just
witnessed.

That was the first of many things I was to learn those
four years at that school in this big city. As it turned out, Don
Officer and many of the others were professional musicians
who had gone back to school rather than go to Korea where
only Taps are played for the dead. The following day I took the
last chair because I had learned that although I was the
hottest thing Oakdale had ever seen, I was now with the big
fellows where the snapping of the fingers only means that
you're nervous, but has nothing to do with the execution of
music.

[Circa 1971]

ASSORTED POEMS

POEMS FOR SPRING DAYS

I

Some guys think Baldwin's got it bad.
Hell, no one even knows me, let alone my name.
I can cry loud as hell
You think that'll bring 'em out?

Have you ever counted the days I've sat here
Waiting for you to come and feed me,
Or have you ever stopped to think
How many times I've cried
For Moctezuma's dead son?
Hell, no, you've never even learned
To count,
Let alone my miseries.

Angry is as angry does.
Cute, no?

If it's true
dead men tell no tales
then let's kill 'em all
to stop their wails.

A missy named Gail
Was kept in the jail
for raising her dress
Instead of her bail.

[March 1966]

II

That little old lady with green hair tried to tell me that I
was a'gone.
Christ, can you imagine? Someone with tennies
never even been on a tennis court and
doesn't even know who Pancho is,
or is it "was"?

That little old lady with green hair tried to tell me that I
was a'gone.
Christ, can you imagine? Someone with a smear
of apple pie over red rouge not even knowing that
Temple is Black and not any longer Shirley?

That little old lady with green hair tried to tell me that I
was a'gone.
Christ, can you imagine? Someone with a flag
of an ass waving in the wind not even knowing
of the destructibility of contingent remainders?

[November 1967]

III

How slowly it turns
the clock hand
and, like a cricket caught in the whirlpool
of a sewer, it seems that it shall never find the top.
Even the tiny ant who walks in darkness,
it, too, must circle the green-yellow phlegm left on
the sidewalk by the tramp with the bottle hanging
from his pocket.
Why did you leave it there, the ant asks?
Did you want me to swallow it?
No. But why leave it in my way?
The tramp with shoes that shadow like a tree
steps and kills the ant because the ant stuck its
tongue out at him.

Did you have to slit his throat?
What is it to you? He raped your mother, didn't he?
Yes. Yes. But did you notice the way the blood poured?
For ten years the turtle waited on the island for
the man with the tattoo of a wasp on his ear lobe.
The chairs brown and engraved with lacquer sat waiting
for the woman in the bed to die. The Madonna above
the head saw the spider as it unfolded its flurry.
The blinds were shut with thin ashes of yellow sneaking
in through the corners...but they did not reach her in time.

If it must be said, let it be said now: she died of heartburn.
The old woman, fat with grease and wine, saw all these things
as she waited for her son to bring home the bacon.

They're going to hang him.
Who?
The skinny guy with the beard.
Why?
Because he's got a big mouth.

The white belly palpitates.
Every ten seconds the sound pierces...
But it's too late...the gun has been fired.

[Undated]

IV

How many echoes of the sublime
would inform us of reality's line.
To see the shape take all the
poets' lines and super-impose upon
the words of the Christ.

Hear is here—

The one surfaced two surfaced living
symbol
wartime, love time, wait time—
a present from time in
form of Present time
pictures saved from eons
reprojected ions—for
pleasure—for pain—
for meaning—for
change
small change—social change
and do you know anyone
who makes a loaf of good bread?

[November 1967]

V

Big bellied
beer and fear bellied
the dear old janitor
missionary
cleaning the spots
from the awful lawful
cloth.

he puts his desecrated time
down
and down in static tangible
types to hype his Looker
into easy virtuous pointing
at the spots
the awful ol' spot in the
cloth.

'tween times he speaks
of insanity to his neighbor
of secret things to his son
of reality to his friend
'tween the changing times
'tween times of weariness
'tween times of wisdom elevated
and if we two would reach for
the surety of our instincts
we would laugh as children
at the cloth—which only
reflects—and is not—
the reeling of scenes of Real.

Once the fabric is recognized,
studied reproduction is possible.
The lawful system and the prison's place,
recognized,
reveals to the daring, freedom's face.

[November 1967]

VI

Like the man said, "Nowadays I ain't paying too much
        attention
to poets and presidents...", etc.
Like I said, I'm paying too goddamn much attention to myself!
Knowing full well that a man can't write verse
on a belly full of beer
no more than fish can swim
in oil or lard
nevertheless I sit and swivel sandlike particles
and molecules with Bud Shank
from Azusa,
California... Hoping that you will join me
in the desecration of this temple.

I once read lots of things
that went to my head,
e.g.,
The Beatles is Bob Dylan
in drag,
&
God ain't dead
he just doesn't want to get
involved.
Which kind of pissed me off
because that same guy told
me that not one bird falls
without him knowing, etc.

Well, hell, let's get these
things straight!

The reason most experts'
opinions aren't taken
as given
is because they're
too
cocksure.

So...
Here's a wishy-
washie
for you:
Where is Andy-
W?　　(For that matter, where is W?)

[November 1967]

SELECTED LETTERS

BETTY DAVES

[24 October 1957]

Betty,

I am a rotten son-of-a-bitch. Now what shall I do? I'm miserable, but, what shall I do? How could I try when I didn't know what to try or work at?

Please believe me. I will try to be serious. I know that you are the best woman that I have ever known. You are, above all, loyal, and you are what the Mexicans call "buena persona," that is a good, kind, considerate person.

There have been certain things which you have exhibited that displease me, but, holy smoke, not enough to make me do and act the way in which I did. Basically, the problem or the reason for the conflict lies within me. But so help me, I don't know what to do!

Please forgive me for being a sick bastard. Maybe I'll go to a neurotic psychiatrist. Maybe?

Your husband,

*

[December 1957]

I love you, Betty, I love you now in Dec. 1957 and I'll love you until the Dec. of the year of my death, be assured of that. I see your face, so lovely and so true on this paper that I'm writing. I want to touch it, gently and tenderly. I want to feel your beautiful mouth around mine, tightly and passionately.

We have so much, we two, we have love and youth and a great life filled with sorrow and success, happiness and cruelty, misery and joy to live, but we'll live it together and we'll help each other and try to make the burden lighter. We'll laugh, my love, we'll dance and we'll walk and sometimes we'll drink and maybe gamble, but no matter what we do we'll do it together, with our hands tightly grasped so that the fire that burns within us shall keep us warm from the cold world of people and things.

Together, my only wife, together, just you and I and our Mark and Lisa, we'll live a long and happy, useful, productive life.

Your loyal husband,

⌐⌐⌐

[April, 1959, Tuesday PM]

Dearest Betty,

I have thought all day how I should answer your letter. The only thing that kept ringing in my mind every minute of the day was the word MAY, the month of May, not even this one but next one. The spring would pass and the long summer and the fall then the winter and the holiday seasons and then the cold winter again and still the spring... God, my love, do you not realize that I love you and that I love my son? I promise I will not bug you with my pleas, that I swear, but I must in all honesty ask you this one question: Could *you* live apart from our son for a year and a half? I wrote once that words are cheap, by which I meant that they had no real meaning; they are but symbols that can be manipulated, misunderstood, spoken by all, read by all, kicked around and just nothing. It is feelings that are important; what a man feels within himself, his blood, his nerves, these are the things that count... And yet, how can I show you my feelings when we are so far apart? I must depend upon the very things that for me are so meaningless in terms of my real self. Betty, when I tell you that I suffer every minute of every day that I am apart from you *and* my son, do you know how I mean it? That is why I say, ask yourself how you would *feel* if you, for whatever reason, had to be separated from your son.

No one knows that whatever is happening is the result of my own doing. No one is punishing themselves any more than I for being the ass that I have been for so long. But if there is to be any help it must be apart from self-condemnation. How long will I last if I remind myself every day that I suffer because I am without you and Marco? And that I am apart from you because of my own immaturity, my own neurosis, my own history, my own foolish ambitions, my own selfish desires, my own petty gripes. The thing that I ask myself is, how long shall I suffer?

I have tried to tell you in my past letters that I know now that I can be a man if I have something to live for, something to work for, some hope, some goal, some person. I tell you again, my wife, that if I am to be a man it must be because there is some reason for it. No one, nothing, can be a reason other than you or my son. That is why I have been asking you to give me some hope. A smattering of it, just a pinch, so that I can work and grow and look forward to being with both of you. But in your letter you tell me that you *might* return in fourteen months, maybe, and nothing about returning to me, your husband and the father of your child.

I hesitate in sending you this letter for fear that you shall have the same picture of me that I have been in the past. If ever you believed in me, Betty, please believe in me now. I am not pleading with you as a child or as a lost human. I am pleading with you as a man that loves his wife and his child. I am merely asking you to give me hope.

I suppose today has been a bad one all around. First the letter, then I found out I was not eligible for unemployment because: (1) I left my job voluntarily, (2) I left it for personal and domestic reasons, (3) I have no proof that there was any real reason for going to see you and Marco, and (4) I was not the major wage earner in the family. Secondly, I did not get the cook job. Now, isn't that enough reason for paranoia?

Honey, about all the stuff. As I told you in my previous letter, they have left, Bob and Phyl, and if I send you all that stuff, well, what shall I do? I wish you could at least let me keep it until you get your own place.

It should be fairly obvious why I must vehemently deny materialism. After all, I preached vehemently against it for three years. Hell, you know damn good and well I love things as well as the next materialist...but I must not admit it, at least not quite as honestly as you. I believe in art, etc., but I want to be successful for the simple reason that I want to make loot: el, o, o, tee. And why do I want to make loot? To acquire goods, things, stuff, junk, crap, whatever it's called.

By naturalist I mean a believer in man as a product of his environment and that beauty exists only in nature. I'm sure that it's the wrong term, but as I told you, I never went to school. Furthermore, that if there is to be any form of salvation (did you know that if you inserted an 'I' in that word, it would be closer to its real meaning? sal*i*vation) for man it must be in his relation to his environment. That is why at the end of the book, the boy tells his father that he, the father, is wrong. The father gave him the willow tree as an example, the bending of it, etc., and he said that the boy must look to himself, his own being, for his salvation. The kid said no, it is only in his relation to his environment that he could possibly have found it. This I firmly believe is the basic difference between religion and psychology; the religionist says, trust in god, look to god, forget the world, abandon it; the psychiatrist says, trust neither god nor man, but learn to live with both of them even though neither of them exist.

I got the couch from Dick and Ruth. It's nice. Old fashioned but comfortable, clean and in almost perfect condition. Martha is clearing out the trash in the bedroom and is going to get the whole house straightened out. I'm going to scrub and mop and clean and completely fumigate the house this weekend. Martha had put away the good things, the dishes, the silverware, the set from Bob and Virginia, etc., so nothing has been harmed. If it were not for the money part, I would even ask Martha to get her own place, but I guess I'll let her stay until she gets hitched or until you return. I haven't seen Mr. Reverso yet, but when I do I'm going to start hinting about buying the place. I'd like to get a one-year lease with an option to buy at the end of a year. I doubt very much if he'd go for it, but there's no harm in asking. I'm fixing the tax forms this week, so in about six weeks we should get the money.

I got a letter from GET today and they sent a check for $47 to Crocker Anglo for money that we had left as a down payment that they had forgotten to include. Which means, I guess, that I won't have to make a payment to them for the next two months. I'm going to call and make sure tomorrow.

About the snow...wow! Tell pop that although he can't be on an island sipping on a mint julep looking at the snow on the mountaintops, that he can at least be glad that he doesn't have to get out and dig ditches in that weather. Betty, please take care of Charco, I'm so worried, he's had two colds since he's been there already. And yourself, honey, for god's sake, don't be working overtime if you're sick. In fact, I wish you wouldn't work overtime anyway. The weather here is, as usual, sunny and pleasantly warm. I guess I missed the rainy season here; looks like spring has come to stay.

How many ways are there to say it? How many ways shall I bore you? ILOVEYOUILOVEYOUILOVEYOUILOVE YOUILOVEYOUILOVELYOUILOVEYOUILOVEYOU.

[12 November 1959]

Dearest Betty,

I received your most welcome letter today; ol' paranoid me, I thought you were not going to write. The days seem so terribly long and lonely, but today after your letter (the day, though it was cold and gray like steel), I was able to feel confident of my existence and even able to laugh at my neurotic behavior. I hope you will write more than once a week; every man should have more than one day a week in which he can feel some sort of comfort. As I sit here and type I feel not exactly good, but I feel your presence, and that, because I have your letter before me. I know we agreed not to send letters that would indicate our loneliness (I said not to get mushy?) yet I just want you to know that I miss you and my son in a way that, thank God, is unlike the way I have missed you before. I am not rushing about trying to find something to fill your place, unless spending money can be said to be that "doing." I have drank with some seriousness only once. Tuesday night I went to the Mantilla and met Larry. We drank till two and then we came over to my house (our) and played cards and listened to records until six. Then we returned to Haight Street and met Norman in a bar. Norm and I drank until noon and then went to Bob's house where the three (Band, Phyl and Cap) were making lunch. We ate and then went to playland where we rode the cars and all that jazz. I finally got home at ten last night and, boy, was I beat. It is when I am terribly tired that for some reason I miss you so much. I guess like a child needing his mommy, the conflict arises when (now, as opposed to other separations) I miss my son. On the one hand I miss you because I need you and on the other I miss my son because I want to play with him and give him the help I can. Take care of my boy, dear.

I hope this letter reaches you in time. Find out when the Roberto Iglesias dance company is going to be in town and if you have to move heaven and earth to see it, for my sake do. I think that I am an average theater goer. Certainly I am more than average in movie going and in musical deals. Last Saturday I treated myself to a box seat at the Opera house and saw this Spanish Flamenco group. Betty, I have never in all my life been so close to beauty and art. I felt throughout the show that I had at long last found myself. I felt pangs of identification; pride and passion boiled within my soul as I saw the modern and the old blended into one act. The dancing was exciting, it was superb! The men's waists were thinner than the girls' who were so beautiful that I think I fell in love with them all. They did not hide a thing. They were not ashamed to yell and whistle and love there on stage. But enough! Go see it, if you can, I think they will be in St. Louis.

After the show I went to a Flamenco club in North Beach: El Patio Andaluz. I went there thinking like a little boy: they will be there at the club and I shall meet these people and talk to them. Unlike a child, my dreams were realized. Half the group was there and they danced and sang, etc. I talked to some of them after the show closed. I sat next to them and could not take my eyes away from them. At the opera, like at the club, there were nine Spanish people for every non-Spanish. I liked it, although I am not really a full-blooded Latin, my one great wish is to become one. I think that has been one of my great troubles. Not to overdo it, but I believe that because I have not had a country or a people with which I can fully identify myself, I have been so lost. More than anything else in the world, I think that I want to live in Spain, or at least try it and see if it is the place where I can find my peace with society. To find peace with myself I know it has nothing to do with the environment. I am not speaking of that; I am not so psychologically naive that I do not see the fallacy in that. I am speaking of my peace with the people around me. I want to see people on the street corners that I can talk to without any reservations, without having to think (both consciously and unconsciously) what they think of me or etc. I doubt very much if I'll find that in any city or town in the U.S.

For even in places like North Beach where one is judged not by what he looks like, even in these places I cannot feel at home. I will wait and be patient until my book is published and then maybe we can talk about it. But be assured of this, for the satisfaction of my life, I must at least try it. I must at least go to Spain and see if that is the promised land. I hope you will understand this and of course, because it means so much to me, so very much, I hope (pray) that you will feel the same way. That you will feel this so that you and Marco can go, too.

After much trouble, Martha finally got her car yesterday. Not the one that she was going to get here in San Francisco, she got this one in Modesto. The guy here in town was a crook. At the last offer, he wanted nine hundred more than what he had originally asked for. It was such a crooked deal that I went to see the manager of the *Examiner*. The guy told me that it was a racket and the only trouble was that unless I was prepared to get a lawyer, etc., I would not be able to do anything. He was very polite and truthful. I am still in good graces there, so I can get a job there when the PO lays me off in February. I'll send you a picture of it.

After trying to sleep downstairs for a week I finally moved upstairs. I'm sleeping in the bed in the study room. It's much nicer and comfortable. We didn't get a housemaid. Instead we cleaned it ourselves. The house is in good shape. I hung the large mirror in the hall entrance, next to the telephone table, so that it is full length now instead of parallel to the floor. I bought another suit at the same place and three ties and three shorts and a belt and another white shirt.

I sent your things, the suitcase and the sewing machine. Thirteen dollars! Tell me when you want me to send your other stuff (junk?). The hot weather has left. It is foggy and cold and the weather is propitious for loneliness. Be that as it may, I have occupied myself so that I won't have time to think about it, but not so much that I'll have another breakdown. I am, I think, slowly learning to relax. The doctor told me last week (when I woke up today I forgot that it was Thurs. because of the holiday, I think, and I didn't get to see the head shrinker today) that I had to learn how to loaf. I told him that as the plane took off I had very mixed feelings. I felt so strange that I believed if I could just shrug real hard or yell loud enough that my catharsis would be produced. He said,

"Oh, you felt like taking a laxative?" When I told him about
the kid that I met in Modesto (the one who also had the
absurd dreams that I've been having for the past eight years:
about the girl) he started laughing. At first I was taken aback,
then I joined him. It was terribly funny, in a satirical sort of
way. But really, he and I agreed, that it was a most fortunate
thing for the therapeutic value that will ensue. Doug is just
about finished with my manuscript. He's been doing a terrific
job of editing. The grammar and the punctuation and a few
words have been added. I felt a little guilty about it at first,
but then after talking to him and reading it (he hasn't
changed anything that I do not approve of), I realized that I
had no grounds for my favorite feeling: guilt. When I left the
doctor's office last Thurs., I told him, "Well, see you next week.
I'll see if I can find something new to worry about during the
week." He answered, "Say, you know, you ought to go into this
professionally. You're so good at it, you ought to see if you can
make a living at it." He's quite a card, that doctor of mine.

I haven't seen Virginia. I called them last Friday and they
were going out and Bob asked me to call him again. I, for some
reason, do not want to. I don't want to feel that I'm going to
their house for help or something like that. I know that if I go
they will not return the visit, and you know I do not like that.
Maybe later on, but right now, I have enough to do and,
besides, one doctor at a time is enough for me.

I hope you will not mind my typing this letter. The typer
has become a very useful instrument for me. It is even more
personal than my handwriting now. I guess it should be, since
I've typed nearly a hundred-thousand words on this machine
in the past nine months. But still, I make mistakes. I am in
too much of a rush when I type.

Darling, I will close for now. Don't wait for an answer
before you write. I miss you very much and I miss Marco; tell
him that I love him and that I miss him. If he wrinkles his
face when you do, don't spank him. He can't help it; he's just a
kid, a crazy mixed-up kid.

By, my love, and take care of yourself.

P.S.: Tell your folks hello and tell your dad not to become too
attached to his grandson since he won't be there forever. Tell
them again that I am very thankful for all the help that
they've given us, especially now when we need it so much.

⌐⌐

[December 1959, Wednesday PM]

Dearest Wife of Mine,

I must have caught your cold from talking to you on the phone last Saturday. I've had a miserable one for the past two days and am full to the gills of bromo-quinine and super anti-hist. The weather has been hotter than the dickens and it's made me more miserable when I'm knocking on door bells. I've sold two deals this week, but one was turned down because of bad credit. Also I have two promised for this Saturday. Of course, they'll probably change their minds by then.

Tonight we finished early—eight p.m.—and so I went to a Mexican movie. It was pretty interesting, but I had to leave before it was over because I almost started crying, the tears were in my throat. Halfway through the movie, the hero, who is deaf, adopts a baby boy. Five minutes later he is, the boy, a year old and he looked so much like our son, Marco, that I just got up and walked out. I've had two dreams about him this week, and yesterday when we were talking to one of our customers in his home, he was holding a little five-month-old baby boy; although he was a negro child he started cooing like Marco does and I got so upset I had to let Ray do the rest of the talking. Betty, my son's ghost is haunting me and I cannot possibly explain to you in my meager words how much I miss him and how much I love him. I have never felt about anyone the way I feel about him; I suppose there is nothing to compare with parental love. With a woman there are memories of unpleasant scenes and I suppose deep-rooted differences, but with your own flesh and blood there can be nothing but pure love, inexplicable and untarnished.

I am not so egotistical that I believe that my son cannot live without me; I know that I am not the best man in the world. In fact, there exists the strong possibility that I may be the worst scoundrel that ever lived. However, it is certain that I cannot live without my son; he is too much within me even in the few weeks that I have lived with him, the few diapers that I changed and the few hours that I played with him. Betty, my beloved wife, I ask of you something in a way that I have never asked anything of anyone in my life: do not take

my son away from me. Keep him from me, if you must, for a
month or a year, as you see fit, but for my sake—since I suppose in the last analysis it boils down to that—do not take him
from me and place yourself in a position where he or you
would take another name other than my name.

No one knows better than I how these last few letters,
and possibly every one that I have written to you since I left,
have been so filled with the whimperings of a man in fear; but
no matter, for me, my life is at stake. I consider you and our
child more important than my own life. Foolish thing that it
may be, and it being so precious and wonderful—your life—I
will whimper and kneel if necessary to the end that you might
not separate your life and my son's life from me. You are in a
position where you can separate yourself from me completely
and you have every moral and legal right to do so, I know;
therefore for me it is in the form of a goal, to work, to beg, to
write, to change my foolish life of the past, to become a man
capable of giving the security of a man, to do whatever is necessary to have you give me one more chance.

There is one great difference between this separation and
all others, Betty. I am not even speaking of Marco, but of my
own attitude toward the hopes of reconciliation: I have never
said to you during previous separations that I was willing to
change my childish notions and useless ways for the sake of
your welfare. In fact, the first time you were pregnant...you
remember it, I cannot bear to write about it lest it sear my
conscience more than it has for so many months. Betty, I had
never been repentant, never. Even when we got together
again in Sausalito, I told you that I could not change, etc. The
fact is that I have changed already and am changing each day.
There is no way for me to prove it to you, I know. I can only
wait until I see you and that will be as I have told you within
a few months; just for a weekend, but nevertheless, it will be
stronger than my words on a piece of paper. In many ways it
is becoming more obvious to me that you no longer can possibly believe me, or trust me, or even love me, and that is all my
fault, I know. You have written a total of three letters in six
weeks and have even refrained from saying that you or my
son or my father-in-law misses me or loves me. As I said, I
acknowledge the fault as being entirely mine and I am suffering the wages of it. I have no right to ask for clemency. I have
no right to ask for even a scant bit of your attention. In fact, I

forfeited all my rights when I moved out from Shenandoah Street. But even a murderer is given a last meal, Betty, even a mad dog with rabies is not slaughtered.

I have sat before this wall and above this typewriter for the past ten minutes thinking and thinking, "What can I say to her? What can I do? What can I say to her?" But there is nothing for me to say, is there? There is nothing I can do, is there? God, Betty, even a Christian before the lions had more possibilities than I for hope. At least he could pray! I have tried that, over and over again, since I saw you last. I have literally prayed, audibly and verbally, many times to something that I do not believe in since I have been back.

I am not surprised or shocked—as you asked me in your last letter—that you are not willing to rush back into the same relationship. *I am not either*, I have told you that, I think, in every letter. I want nothing of the old relationship except you. I do not necessarily want a "square" home or a "bourgeois" home. I want a decent home, a home strong in its structure, secure in its existence, and reasonable in its intents. I tell you, Betty, that my fights with the beats or the moralists has ended. If I fight henceforth with them it will be done on paper; no longer shall it be within me. No longer am I afraid of the existence of love and beauty in human relationships, in objects d'arte—be they a Mixmaster or a Japanese print—and in the mind. They may be transcendental, but then I still prefer green or light-blue toilet paper as opposed to ordinary white. Betty, my love, I do not fear one iota of words, one cell of any living being, even the enigmatical things like sex, I do not fear. I am as capable as any man and certainly more intelligent and sensitive than most; the only thing I fear, the only thing that makes me fall into reveries at the oddest moments, is the fear that I may lose you and my son. If I do, I shall live, certainly, but I shall live like the ants: the sum total of a niggardly existence, paltry and vacuous. And that because I am too far in my therapy to be psychologically naive. I will not be able to rationalize, to feel sorry for myself, to blame you, etc. Before, I could lose myself in a bottle, try to cram into its meaningless depths, or seek the futilities of nothingness. Yes *before*, I could do that, but now I cannot because I want to live a well-examined life. To paraphrase an old friend of the people, I want to recapture the security of my dreams and turn them into realities. I can do this with what I have, if I

still have it or if I can get it back: Betty and Marco Federico
Manuel (Eddy) Acosta.

Before I close, tell your dad that I have given our son one
more name because I felt that he didn't have enough to choose
from when he comes of age: his. I have missed your father
more than I thought I would. I have talked about him with
everyone that I have spoken to since I returned. I have as
much respect for him as I do for my own father, which is saying quite a mouthful, as you well know. I know that someday
when you and I have settled to a normal life, your mother and
I shall also find common ground for respect. I do not want to
write to them until you and I are on more settled terms
because I do not want to involve them anymore than they
already have been, for I know that if I were to write to them
now I would either consciously or unconsciously try to have
them "talk" to you in my stead.

Betty, tell my son that I love him, and each time you see
yourself in his eyes remember that though we are miles apart
I am there also.

~

[January 1960, Tuesday PM]

Dearest Betty,

It would be out of the question for me to ask the old
cliche, "What have I done to deserve this?" I know only too
well what I have done; it is seared in my memory forever. I
will always know that I failed you, failed my child, failed
myself...in other words, I've failed!

But how long, my love, must I live under this burden?
How, I ask you, can I quit punishing myself when I have the
bald evidence striking me in the face each time I enter my
room? On my desk are three letters. In seven weeks I have
received three letters from you. If I cared not for you or for our
son it would make no difference how many letters I had
received, if I did not love you as I do, as passionately and as
deeply as I do.

I beg of you, Betty, forgive me for my failures, forgive me
that I did not give you what you wanted and needed and

deserved...forgive me. Give me, I pray you, give me one more chance because I know that I do not want to live without you and my son.

Has the love that you once had for me dwindled to so little? Can you not at least understand that my son is my blood, that you have my name, that you are my wife? Dearest, most precious Betty, my love will be sufficient for both of us, for the three of us; I swear to you that no man has ever had as great a love for another human as I do for you and my son who, to me, are one now. Even if you cannot love me anymore, can you at least tolerate me to the extent that you would let me be the father of my child?

And all this is the terrible thing about therapy! The saner I get the more I realize that I really made a mess of my life and that there is the possibility that it can never be repaired. At least before I could say, "Oh, well, this is the life that every artist must go through to stain that..." That bullshit! My own voice and the voice of the doctor goad me like a harness...and at the same time I must realize my own worth! At the same time I must quit thinking that I am a no-good, etc.

Darling, not out of pity for my mind—it doesn't amount to much—but out of pity for my heart, I ask you once again to give me the opportunity to show you that I am capable of bringing happiness into your life and that of my son; for though my mind grows stronger each day, my heart is breaking from the heavy weight of loneliness even at this moment.

Betty, I love you.

[Easter Sunday, 1960]

My Darling Wife,

I just arrived from Riverbank and thought I should answer your beautiful letter right away, since I haven't written in so long. I had not written because I was waiting to hear you say that you still love me and want me for your husband and the father of our baby.

You said, "I hope you really mean all that you say." Betty, I am not a prophet, nor am I God, but as a man who is secure in himself, a man with a certain amount of self-esteem, not afraid of the big, bad wolf or the world of pettiness in which we live, I can say in complete honesty that I have finally, after so many years of confusion, found myself. The wonderful thing about it so far as you are concerned is that having found myself, I actually like myself; I am content with what I picked up along the sick path that I travelled. Goodness knows that I would not suggest to anyone who is as sick as I was to go into what I did, but since I did and things have turned out as they did, I am very grateful and joyful that I am what I am and I have what I have.

I do not want to become fat and complacent in my comfort; I have no intention of becoming one of the mass simply because I am no longer sick, for to do so would be to go back into a world that I am not suited for; but whether I like it or not, I suppose—excepting my moments of snobbery—that I am not really too much unlike others. That is, I too want a decent and happy life with my family, I too want to eventually be financially satisfied, I too want to make some contribution to those around me.

The whole thing was like awaking from a dream, very slowly, over a period of several weeks, and even now I am still rubbing the sleep from my eyes. When I stop to realize the foolishness, the sickness, that I went through for so many years, I almost feel like kissing Freud's—because he started it—feet. Drink, religion, and debauchery failed for me; neither did they bring peace of mind or completion of integration. Through some mysterious way (mysterious to me because I know so little of it), therapy has helped me to acquire a certain strength, a certain comfort, a certain joy and a certain integration of my intellect with my emotion. For this I am grateful not only to Dr. Serbin and Mt. Zion, but above all I am grateful to you, my wife, for having put up with it all, for having seen me through the vow which we took, "In sickness and in health."

Betty, dearest Betty, trust in me! Let me show you the beauty of life which I have not shown you and which, since I am the only man you have been married to, you have never seen. I will not promise to feed you in bed every day or to wash the dishes every day, but I do promise to take the trash out every week; now that's not a bad bargain, is it? Where else could you find a man that is willing to sign a contract promising to take the trash out every single week, till death do us part? Eh?

As I told you over the phone today, I will not send you money unless you really need it, at least not this month, because I am being quite tight with it. I plan to pay about thirteen-hundred bucks of debts between now and November. I'm trying to find a part-time job working one night a week and on Saturdays so that I can eat a donut with my coffee and not feel the guilters. And then I have bought you your birthday gift which will take several weeks to pay off, so please try and live with what you make until next month at least. But, please, please, please, if you need something, please write and let me know.

Aren't you even a little concerned about what it is that I'm giving you for your birthday? I'll give you a hint: It is about something in one of your favorite stories.

Delia and Pete stopped at the house today. Their little boy, year and a half, is so cute. He started pulling my hair and we got along just fine. I told them to tell Elisa that we might stop by her place when I go to bring you back. She says that Baby is still upset because he hasn't had a boy yet. Elisa and Manuel came to visit my grandma a couple of weeks ago and she told my mom that she told Henry that he better not marry a gringa. My mom said, after certain arguments, well, how about Betty? To which our favorite aunt replied, "Oh, Juana, but that's different. Betty is one in a million; she's even better than a Mexicana." So, my little-one-in-a-million-gringa, don't get the high hat.

I, of course, think she has her mathematics a little off. There are two and a half billion people on this earth, so I told mom that you are one-in-a-billion-and-a-half.

My love, I hope you will understand what I have to say now. I know that our plans are for you and Cho Cho to return sometime in the early winter or late fall of this year, but I want you to know that I am ready, desirous and able to have you return tonight or tomorrow or the next day. If your job or your life—or, do I dare think it, your missing me—for any reason becomes unhappy, I tell you that there is no reason in the world why you shouldn't come back to me sooner, and in fact every reason in the world why you should return sooner. I told you when I left that I would not see you again until I felt that I was capable of being a man, a husband and a father; well, I

am ready tonight. I say this because I do not really know how
you are. I know you tell me that you are fine, the baby is fine,
etc., however I must also recognize the fact that you are certainly not in a normal situation. Now that I have found a job
that I know I will be happy in, even though it is not a whole
lot of money, I know that I am capable of giving you and our
son the things that you need to be comfortable and happy. I
say this in the hope that you will always know that your home
is ready for you at a moment's notice or without any notice at
all.

There are many other things to say, but I'd better hit the
sack now. It is eleven and my bedtime has been about ten for
the past month. And, too, I am now a quarter of a century old
and must have my sleep.

I love you, my darling. Kiss my son and tell him that I
love him.

⌒

[Undated]

Hi Honey,

I've been in bed all afternoon with the flu again and I'm
tired of doing nothing so I'll write until I get too weak. It's
unfair, this flu, I just had it two weeks ago and here it is
again. The weather is beautiful outside, the sun in its splen-
dor and the sky is an ocean of blue, the wind lightly is ruffling
the Venetian blinds and me...I have a cold and the flu at
once!

I went to the doctor this morning, the head shrinker, and
had a lively session with him. I told him that I wasn't sure if
this work of mine, selling, was at all consistent with my writing and art, et cetera. I told him that I had a hunch that art,
when it interferes with the practical necessities of life, such as
making money, might possibly be a bunch of horseshit...he
agreed with me. We discussed some of my recent dreams and
both arrived at eh conclusion that even in my dreams I am
accomplishing a certain amount of self-fulfillment. All told,
therapy is really progressing, which is to say, I am progressing. I've not had such a level-headed mind as I have in the

past two weeks since I was a child. It's a nice feeling to know that the world is not flat after all.

He said not to worry about my loneliness for Marco; in fact, he said, that my recognizing the loneliness for him, my son, is a good sign in itself. He said that this job, meeting people, etc., is one of the best signs I have yet shown in my recovery from my insecurities, etc. I agreed with him.

Sunday PM: I didn't finish this letter so I'll start again. I'm over the flu now and feel much better. Talking to you those two times this week was like a big chunk of heaven. I wish I could do that more often, which I will as soon as I start making some money. I figure, since I'm not spending my money on drinks anymore, I can spend it on phone calls. I went to the show this morning at ten a.m., saw three goodies, all for sixty cents. They were so good I can't remember the names of them. When I got out, the St. Patrick's Day Parade was in session. New cars, soldiers, bands, new cars, negro girls drill teams, soldiers, new cars, that's all it was. I left before it was over. Besides, I thought that in all that crowd somebody might pick my pocket. I'm waiting for a call from Ray. I think we'll go make some calls tonight; he was lucky yesterday, he sold two deals; 300 bucks. Not bad for one day's work, eh? I hope to heck I can start hitting it lucky pretty soon!

Concerning Ibsen's *A Doll's House*, I'm not sure whether I should even comment. Betty, my darling wife, if it's one thing I have never been it's shallow. I've been a fool and a bastard, etc., but I have never been so light-minded and selfish that I was a puny, shallow, flighty creature like Helmer. And, honey, I have abused you, I know, but I have never *used* you. Darling, I pray that you do not think so little of me that you should compare me to that oaf. As for Nora, I pity her that she should have remained with that simpleton for eight years. What she desired, and almost let herself hope for at the end—a real wedlock—is what I desire and can do with you and my son. For me, my darling Betty, at moments like this, the universe does not extend beyond the circumference of your open arms. I have it within me, to the very marrow of my bones, to love you as no man has ever loved, to protect you and shelter you, to make life such a wonderful thing for you that even the cruelty of people or the bitterness of nature will be but mere apparitions of things unknown to you. My one desire, my one hope, the big thing in my life, is my family, you and Marco and Lisa, to love eternally. Dearest one, listen to me! Let me show you how great my love is for you, give me the opportunity to pour upon you all this that is within me, let me undo all the foolish and evil things that have happened to us in the past. You do not even have to love me, just let me love you and prove to you that I am a man with great tenderness and passion for you.

Later at night: Ray came by and we went on a couple of pitches...no luck as yet, but the people said they would call us tomorrow. We talked our heads off and really put the pressure on, but they got too confused and said to let them sleep on it. God, God, God! How my son's ghost haunts me! The people were from Nicaragua and the man held a seven-month-old little boy in his lap all the time we were there; he has the same complexion as our little boy and he was cute like Chooch. Betty, my darling, can you realize how much I miss my boy? Really, this is not a romantic notion, I mean it...do you know how I yearn to see him and hold him and hear him and talk to him? My love, if I thought that I could never see him again, I think I would lose all my zest for life. Betty, have pity for me if nothing else. I do not even ask for understanding, just for pity. Please know that I want you two so badly even at this moment that my insides are bursting with love for you. Grant me another chance to show you my love, please. I have suffered for so long, tell me that you will not take away from me the two people that mean my life to me. Write to me and do not condemn me any longer. Heaven knows how much I do that to myself as it is. Tell me, I beg of you, that you will give me another chance!!

Oh, I know that when I feel as I do I probably should not write to you, but since I cannot talk to you or to anyone else I must write. I have not even seen Douglas Empringham, our Doug, in three weeks, nor anyone else that I can talk to; but I know you won't believe it, I'm not lonely for company or for friends, I am perfectly content to know that each door that I knock on, each bell that I ring, I am doing it for us. I want only to work and work for us. Try and believe that.

Don't forget that in case anything happens the phone number upstairs is Ju. 5-0799.

Honey, please write to me. It's been seven weeks and I've received a total of three letters from you.

Betty, please answer this question!! Do you tire of my letters? Are they too maudlin for you? Would you rather that I quit writing so often? I wonder if that is not what you want, because you write so little I sometimes think that maybe that's the "message" you're trying to send. I realize that I am overtly passionate and emotional; I do not expect you or anyone else to be that way. I feel things very deeply, I always have. If my heart cries out for you and for my son, I can no more intellectualize it than I can fly faster than the speed of light, nor can I close it, stop it, any more than I can stop the cold war. You have in the past called me an animal, and I agree with you. In many ways I am an animal. I can at once be as angry as a bull and as tender as a baby chick. How or why I do not know, but I have seen myself that way many times.

I guess I'd better go to bed. Betty, my most lovely and only wife, even if you don't think of me, remind my son about his father. Tell him every day that he does have one who loves him more than any man has ever loved any one thing or person; even if you have to whisper it to him. But please, kiss him for me and whisper to him that I want him more than I want my own life, that I love him and his mother each minute of each day. Good night, my love.

~

[Undated]
Amarillo, Tex.

Dearest Betty,

At last I am comfortable! 8 hundred miles behind me and I'm ready to turn back because there is some 12 hundred left. I was so tired and dirty and sleepy that I stopped at this plush YMCA in Amarillo—two-fifty a night—to rest before starting out again tomorrow morning. The shower alone was worth the stop. I haven't tried the bed yet. I had a T-bone steak and went to see the *Gazebo*. And now after this letter I'll hit the

sack and start catching up on all the dreams I've missed in
the past two days.

I have never read Elliot's *The Wasteland*, but the title certainly fits my conception of Arkansas, Oklahoma, and Texas. I
have the feeling that at one time people lived around here, but
now they've packed up and left, leaving dust and trash. The
weeds blowing across the paved roads and the Burma Shave
signs, the complete absence of humans, 50 miles to the next
Shell Station, You are now entering Miami, Oklahoma. Welcome; gods, I can see a great sequel to *The Grapes of Wrath*.

Betty, are you okay? I hope so. I feel so guilty for all the
crap that I've given you in the past three years. Really, the
only thing I can say is that I'm sorry, I'm terribly sorry, I'm
terribly sorry and if rending myself in sack cloth and ashes
would do the job I would not hesitate.

The whole St. Louis stay has taught me one thing, something that I should have realized long ago...I cannot act as a
man simply because I am not one yet. And I am not trying to
punish myself either! I do know that for some reasons I have
not yet learned to be a man. And now, that is my job. Before I
offer myself to you or to my son, I must learn how to be a man.
I do not know how I will learn that, but I will not rest until I
do. If it means going to a hospital or to a doctor, I will. Whatever it includes, if it is within my power, I shall do it. Even if
it means not seeing either of you for a long time or ever, but I
know that I will learn that or not offer myself to you or to any
other woman again.

Betty, tell your parents what you think is best for them.
My feelings are too mixed at the moment to know what to say.
I never did thank them for letting us stay there nor for letting
them take you back after all the fuss. I will write to your dad
and I hope you can understand why, at least at the present, I
cannot write to your mother. Please try to understand this,
Betty, in the light of my own damn neurotic emotions.

I disobeyed your orders and picked up a hitchhiker. Needless to say, it was not e.t. He was a dirty, dirty Okie from
Monterey. He was broke, flat broke, and had not eaten for several days. He ate a whole bottle of peanut butter and smoked
half my ciggies. I couldn't stand it any longer, so when we got
to Amarillo I told him I would have to let him out. I felt sorry
for the poor bastard, but then I'm not as rich as the Good

Samaritan. I won't pick up any others unless, of course, I happen to see e.t. on the road.

If they do charge me to cross Arizona and New Mexico, I guess I'll have to wire home for loot cause I just have enough to make it for gas and eats. But I don't mind; I'm not so despondent now and I won't mind waiting in some hick town for the money.

Betty, I forgot to get the address of the company where I worked. Look it up and mail this letter I'm sending you to them. It's the U.S. Paint Lacquer and Chemical on Singleton Road or Avenue. I think 2100. They may have sent me my bye-bye papers already. They have the Shenandoah address. So look in the mail box and sign the check if it is there.

Honey, do me a favor. No matter what happens to us, please tell Charco every day, every singe day, that I love him very much. Take care of him, Betty, don't spoil him and give him the O.C.

Say hello to Florence and tell her that I'll write to her as soon as I get settled in San Francisco or Riverbank.

Bye, for now, darling.

[Undated]

Darling Betty,

I have not written to you for so long it seems strange to talk to you this way again; but I must stop phoning so much. I'm tired of working on my book and the Giants are losing to the Reds right now, so since it's only nine I have plenty of time.

First of all, don't forget to write right away and tell me if you received the material and the check. I hope you like it, cause I certainly do and I think it will look very beautiful on you; you wear those dark colors so well, like your purple dress, that I'm sure you will like it. But if you don't, tell me, cause they'll exchange it. I thought it would be better to take that money now while we had it and get it out now because you never know what will come up. I hope you can manage with the two-fifty.

While I'm on he subject of loot, I'd better tell you what my plans are. Unless something goes wrong I should have the State Employees bill just about finished by the time you return and the doctor bill and most of the Household Finance one. We'll just have the furniture bill—which will drop to 14 bucks a month next February—and what's left of the HFC, 13 bucks per month. In March, I can refinance the loan at the *Examiner* and pay off all the debts. It's the best deal cause I don't need cosigners and they just take five bucks a week out of my check. Also, I'm getting insurance for you and the baby next week with the *Examiner*, so I'll send you the details on that later. They pay all of the hospital bill for pregnancies and part of the doctor bill, so it's pretty good. I haven't gotten a part-time job cause I want to finish the manuscript first; I should finish the final draft within a couple of weeks or a month, then I'll start looking. Honey, I'm paying the bills at the rate of forty bucks a week and as it is, unless I get a part-time job, I won't be able to save too much; I'm saving about ten a month at the *Examiner*, but that won't be enough for the trip. If you can, and please don't let this change any of your plans, *I repeat*, if you can, try and save a few bucks for when I go back. I figure we'll need at least two hundred for the whole trip. One hundred for my plane ticket and another hundred for our trip back.

My lovely wife, I am so thrilled at the way things are beginning to work out for us. I have never in my whole life been as content as I have this past month, since you told me that you would be willing to come back to me. I have been feeling very good and maybe I'll be through with therapy by next month. I wish you could believe me when I say that I am a very different person from the one you had known; and one that I think you'll be able to love.

Betty, I love you so very much. I think of you and our son every single day; you are constantly on my mind and I so long for November to come around.

I have been working about two hours extra—without pay, of course—every day. I hope that within the next two weeks we will finally be caught up. I get up at six every day and get to work by seven thirty; I'm not supposed to be there until eight-thirty but I want to get caught up. The work is going fine and everything is still the same at that fruity joint; I want you to meet my boss when you get back and some of the other married guys—and their wives—because we talk about you and Marco quite a bit; especially Chooch. I still have a bet with Amo, the guy whose wife had her baby by Dr. Miller, that Chooch can whip Alexander when he gets back...damn but I long to see him. I wish you could come out for Martha's wedding.

Honey, why don't you write more often? I'll tell you why I don't. Because every time I sit down to write to you I miss you too much; I almost feel like crying when I start writing to you.

I stopped by to see Dick and Ruth last Sunday morning; I walked up to their house. Their cat had more kittens and I'm taking one to Stella for her birthday next week. I'm going to call it Lolita. It has white feet like mittens and is black and white. She said she wanted one, so Martha and I are going down there next Sunday.

Is Florence still there? Tell her I said hello and that I still plan to write to her; tell her that if she would write first I'd probably answer right away. I sure would like to get a card from your folks; but I understand if they don't write.

Dearest Betty, why do I love you so much? I have never loved anyone so much as I do you; I have never been so willing to give myself, to adjust myself, for anyone as I do for you...know it, my love, know that I love you.

JUDGE BUSH

[17 December 1964]

Dear Judge Bush,

I am taking the liberty to write this letter because of certain information that may be pertinent in the rendering of a judgement with respect to a criminal defendant appearing before you in the near future. I am not certain what the specific charge is nor when he will appear for sentence, but since it may be within the week I thought it important enough to reach you personally at this address.

Roberto Acosta of Modesto has been in trouble with the law for the past ten years, the violations ranging from common drunk to narcotics. If one were to merely consider the offenses and their repetition, no one would question the necessary repercussion of a long jail sentence. It is in fact the position the entire family had taken following his most recent crime. After ten years of giving and trying without a single sign of rehabilitation, the family concluded that "Maybe jail is the best thing." Were it not for your having sent him to Vacaville, I would not be writing this letter.

Prior to his voluntary withdrawal from Hastings, Roberto's most criminal act was a weekend drunk. We never knew why he quit; until then he had been a model student and a responsible human being with a wonderful future ahead of him. We were not really aware of his truly broken condition. But in the months that followed, beginning in that summer of 1957, he ran from drunkenness to a Mexico marriage and the inevitable divorce. He neither worked nor studied for any length. His friends from school and even his family finally, after several years, tired of his behavior and his new associates in crime. I saw him before he was sent to San Bruno for narcotics violation and it was then I concluded he was in need of psychiatric therapy. He was not yet, in 1961, so addicted that immediate treatment would have at the very least con-

fronted him with his dilemma. I wrote to the judge and asked
that he commit him to a hospital. He was, instead, sent to a
place where both the temptation and the means of narcotics
are more readily available than anywhere else. I know this
not only from the statements of prisoners but also from statements from friends who work in the institutions.

When Roberto was released from San Bruno he was much
sicker than when he entered. He was less of a human being
and more of a criminal as a direct result of his incarceration
without medical treatment.

I spoke to him last month. I cannot impress you enough
with the simple fact that he has changed. He has, at long last,
been confronted with himself. He knows for the first time that
he is sick. He has admitted to himself that he alone cannot
find the solution to his illness and has at last sought the help
of others who can. Most important, he has not embraced therapy as a panacea. He knows that it is but a useless deviation
unless he, himself, is willing to work at it.

For the first time in ten years I am able to look upon him
with something other than sympathy. He is no longer the
pathetic little Mexican boy who turned to narcotics when the
going got tough. I know, because I have known him all my life,
that he still has it in him to be the man that is within him.

I was going to say this is not a plea for mercy. I wanted to
appeal to your sense of justice based on reason. But having
studied the law for four years has led me to believe that the
law is what a judge will do with certain facts. And the fact is
that Roberto is my brother and I want to help him. I cannot if
he is once again sent to a place where he will only be punished
for his crimes. Without a sense of humanity, without mercy,
he will in all probability continue the life he has lived the past
ten years. This may be our last opportunity and his last
chance.

Please be assured I am not merely asking you to dismiss
him. I ask you to put him on probation with an order he continue therapy. I have a friend who is a therapist at San Quentin
who is willing to give him treatment, and until he is able I can
give him room and board. There are many judgments you can
make that would be for the good of all, but the one I beg you do
not make is to send him to a prison where he will not get the
therapeutic treatment he is at last responsive to.

Thank you very much for the concern you have shown.

DOCTOR'S HOSPITAL

[10 September 65]

Doctor's Hospital
Modesto, California

Sirs:

Notice is hereby given of denial of any and all alleged obligations whether express or implied purportedly made by myself, Oscar Acosta, or by any agent or representative, including Manuel M. Acosta or Juana F. Acosta.

Notice and demand is made upon you, Doctor's Hospital, and against your representatives and agents including your Ambulance Company, your admitting physician, your nurses and hospital staff who knowingly and wilfully confined me in the boundaries of your hospital premises against my will with the specific intent to deprive me of the freedom of bodily movement which I made known to you and your agents and representatives; such demand is made for compensation in the sum of $500.00 for the injury suffered by me as the proximate result of your intentionally depriving me of the above mentioned freedom.

Notice is made upon you and demand for compensation is directed at you and your agents in the sum of $300.00 for the injury proximately caused me by your negligent conduct while attempting to treat me as a patient in your hospital on the dates of 24 and 25 May, 1965, in that you failed to give me the proper care and treatment as recognized by the average standards of hospitals in the area and as you held yourself to by your representations to me; as a direct and proximate result of your negligent conduct I was forced to leave before I had recovered from the illness for which I was brought to your hospital without my consent and as a direct and proximate result of this forced leaving I thereupon suffered injuries to the extent mentioned above.

I am considering including a count for slander but at this
time will consider negotiations for a settlement without such
inclusion. This notice, of course, is not intended as binding
with respect to the amount of compensation to be demanded
in the future, but is merely a beginning point for settlement
purposes. Nor am I waiving any other causes of action I
presently have against you or your agents and representatives. Finally, this demand and notice in no way limits nor is a
statement of any liability you may have as to Manuel M. Acosta or Juana F. Acosta for the intentional infliction of emotional distress or other tort liability.

Frankly, I would welcome the opportunity to expose the
method of your treatment of patients. It seems that you are
operating under a system whose standards of ethics are best
suited for the marketplace, rather than as the honorable profession the medical people are known for. I honestly believe
that I would be doing a service to the community to make
known the conditions which you set before any hospital-
patient relationship can be entered into. One is accustomed to
bargaining with butchers and pawnbrokers, but to be forced to
wait an hour while is one under great pain until the patient
can produce security for expenses is intolerable. Your refusal
to honor my insurance company (Kaiser) and your insistence
that I produce an exorbitant amount of cash—at 11 o'clock at
night!—and then your coercing my father to sign a paper in
the face of my insistence that I and only I was responsible for
my actions is beyond the limits of even the lowest standards.
The humiliation you caused my father and myself for not
being able to come up with $125.00 at 11 o'clock at night in
front of third parties is really too much. What in the world do
you think people buy insurance for? Why you would not accept
the assignment of my insurance benefits when I offered them
to you as security is beyond me. Instead, you insulted and
humiliated us and then the following morning kept it right up
until I was in such a nervous condition that staying there simply meant aggravation of my injuries. You didn't even allow
me to eat my breakfast by your insistence that I produce cash!
And then when I demanded that I be allowed to leave! That
was it! What sort of people are you? Don't you know that when
a man says he wants to leave, assuming he's sane, he has a
right to leave? Instead you forced me to stay. When I was
finally able to secure my release I had to walk two miles—

since my car had been, as you well knew, wrecked. If you do not think it is painful to walk with an injured neck and back the morning following an accident, try it some time.

I shall await your reply before filing suit.

~

[23 September 65]

Doctor's Hospital
Modesto, California

Sirs:

This is to notify you of receipt of your telegram of 22 September 1965.

It seems you misunderstood the effect of my letter of 10 September, 1965. I attempted to tell you that I deny any and all liability, contractual (either express or implied in fact) or otherwise.

To make it more specific, I am forthwith denying by this letter that I am now indebted to you. I do hereby deny that I ever have been indebted to you. Any further attempt on your part to notify me of the alleged liability will be treated as most redundant, and cumulative material representing false statements are: In the garbage can!

Notice and demand is made upon you, Doctor's Hospital and your agents for compensation for the injuries suffered by my minor son, Marco F. Acosta, as a direct and proximate result of your negligent treatment of him on or about 1 August 1965, in the sum of $500.00.

Marco F. Acosta had been taken to your hospital for treatment of a mouth injury incurred by a fall. Your admitting personnel refused to treat him, though he was bleeding and in great pain as they well knew. You insisted that I pay cash for the treatment. You refused to accept his own insurance benefits as security or in full satisfaction. Not until I absolutely demanded that you immediately give him emergency treatment did you consent.

The reason I could not promise to pay cash for the treatment was that it was obvious to me that he would need X-rays to determine the extent of the mouth injuries. Since this would result in a greater sum of cash than I had with me, I could not in good faith promise to pay cash immediately.

While I, Oscar Acosta, was being harassed for the payment of the alleged balance due on the supposed contract, one of your doctors and his attendant, in the most cursory and slipshod of methods, merely looked at his mouth and negligently concluded that all that was required was an *ice pack*!

I asked the doctor if X-rays would be necessary. He replied that I should not worry about it, that in a couple of days the swelling would go down and all would be okay.

Last week, approximately six weeks after your treatment, the child complained of earaches, headaches and toothaches. I immediately took him to a specialist and an immediate operation was performed.

The examining doctor and the specialist both concluded—and they have agreed to give me a statement to that effect—that the operation was necessitated by the injury suffered by him in August. It seems that—I do not pretend to know the medical facts—the teeth were pushed into the gums and since no immediate treatment—other than an ice pack—was prescribed, inflammation and pus formed in the upper front teeth. X-rays *were* taken to show the necessity for the operation.

It is obvious that proper examination would have revealed the extent of the injury. It is further obvious that proper treatment would have prevented the pain and suffering of the six-year-old boy. The amount of compensation I have requested is not meant as an admission, but is merely a given sum to begin a satisfactory settlement.

To keep down the costs I am perfectly willing to negotiate the settlement myself with one of your attorneys.

It is clear that there is a bona fide dispute between the two of us. I am not making specious allegations. I did truly suffer both physically and mentally as a result of our dealings. I am not an unusually sensitive person. I am quite familiar with hospital routines, having worked in them for several years. I further recognize the necessity for prompt payment of bills. It is obvious that hospitals cannot be operated without funds. But our dealings were not the usual. I specifically told you and those who had brought me to the hospital that if you would not accept my insurance benefits as a deposit, to transfer me to the County Hospital. I was so specific about this that one witness asked me to calm down. But in spite of my protest you nevertheless continued to harass me and my parents, and then when I went unconscious you X-rayed me and placed me on one of your beds. You coerced my father into signing a paper after I had made it clear to you that I absolutely forbade anyone from signing anything for me. You embarrassed me and my family in front of others. The following day your behavior was not merely negligent, but it was in fact intentionally disregardful of my rights. I have in my previous letter explained how your nurses and attendants refused to let me leave when I made my many demands. How they on the one hand demanded I come up with cash—when I told them I had none since I was unemployed and that in any event they should accept my insurance benefits which they refused—and on the other told me I could not leave without seeing the doctor. Isn't it clear that seeing the doctor meant increasing the demand your attendants and clerks were making upon me? If I didn't have the cash deposit for the X-rays, how could I have it to see more doctors? It is the most stupid bit of logic I have ever seen in a hospital.

Finally, I never consciously spoke to any doctor. I never saw any X-rays. I was given absolutely no medical advice or treatment. I was not even washed or fed. I do admit to sleeping in your bed for six hours!

I have taken all this trouble to make it plain to you that there is a dispute between us. If you would only take the trouble to consult an attorney, you would realize that the matter involves much more than a paltry $93.50. I myself have consulted an attorney. The only reason I am writing this letter rather than those I've spoken to is that I need the practice, since I expect to begin the practice of law myself by the first of next year.

Again, I would like to remind you that the entire contents of this letter are for the specific purpose, and solely for negotiation, of a just settlement between us. I am writing this solely from memory and without legal advice other than the fact that I have spoken to an attorney about the matter in a very general way. I do not bind myself to any statements of fact or opinion contained herein. The amounts of compensation I have demanded are, of course, subject to revision and intended as purely a negotiation figure.

HUNTER S. THOMPSON

[Circa 1972]

Hunter,

God works his wonders in mysterious ways, etc. I got myself a serious Miss It—she's a six-foot tall, blonde jazz-singer with a group at the Holiday Inn in the Financial Center at Jackson and Kearney... They call her Fabulous Leila. I've been with her every night for the last two weeks, since the first night I met her. It's the first talented broad I ever made it with... What shall I do?

I have gone into a new life. I met a writer-editor, Jess Ritter, the week I got back to Frisco. Through him I've met Jerry Kamstra, a writer who bought a car off you in the early sixties. They call him The Frisco Kid... and on to Leila. I've been hanging around with musicians lately.

All of which made me get back to the typewriter and take a closer look. Alan Rinzler has been destructive in his East Coast-style of dealing and hustling. Barbara absolutely refuses to discuss the manuscript. So here I am, once again, all alone in my writing... Except that this time I got the draw on them. (Like I said, I'm fucking again.) The depression comes from the stupid idea that I had that the second one would be easier than the first one...it was always that way for the peaches. I wrote *Buffalo* in no more than five weeks of actual writing time... On *Cockroach*, I've already written some ten weeks and I ain't got much to show for it in terms of completion. But I do have some hot-ass fifty pages of that scene at the Whiskey A Go Go with Little Richard...I've cut out the entire Las Vegas thing as such. I decided you wouldn't understand it and that others might accuse me of using your book as my notes, etc.... And just because you were nice, the man's name is Stonewall Jackson, professional journalist from Mofo, Georgia, and an expert on volleyball.

Alan said that David Sanchez, the Prime Minister of the Brown Berets (the one with the baby lips), called and demanded the right of censorship. He knows I know that he is, in fact, a punk. At least, on one occasion, they caught him humping one of the kids.

Perhaps after I write it all out, all of you will come to understand just exactly what you did by coming down to L.A. I think I can make a pretty good argument that it was you, or God through you, that called a halt to the bombings... Which means you'll be remembered as the Benedict Arnold of the cockroach revolt.

I'm going with Felton tomorrow night to dinner at Kay Boyle's house. Pray for me. I understand she's an intellectual. And that she marched in the strike at San Francisco State.

Maryanne hustled the shit out of me. I took her to hear Leila; she got jealous and left with tears in her eyes. She kept asking me who I really was and what had I really done... Three days later Barbara Whol called me and wanted to get together to discuss my future. She'd been offered a job of sorts with Trans Media... She hustled me. Said all she wanted was twenty-five percent. And no ass.

And here I am, still broke. Alan won't give me a cent. Says he's not even interested, remotely, in talking about a contract for a third book until we finish the second. Jesus, how did I ever get into this racket?

Would you have me live off this white woman? She's offered me her house. I'm gonna try it. But she refuses to give me any spending money. She claims it's for my own good.

What the fuck more can I say? I'm working at the right tempo; the stuff is coming out but I need some more help. If you can do it or if you can give me a connection for some fast money, I'd appreciate it from down in my ass.

I am sleeping nights at 863-8787 and by Xmas day will be there days.

PLAYBOY

[15 October 1973]

The *Playboy* Forum
Playboy Building
919 North Michigan Avenue
Chicago, Illinois 60611

Sir:

Your November issue, "On The Scene" section on Mr. Hunter S. Thompson as the creator of Gonzo Journalism, which you say he both created and named... Well, sir, I beg to take issue with you. And with anyone else who says that. In point in fact, Doctor Duke and I—the world famous Doctor Gonzo—together we both, hand in hand, sought out the teachings and curative powers of the world famous Savage Henry, the Scag Baron of Las Vegas, and in point of fact the term *and* methodology of reporting crucial events under fire and drugs, which are of course essential to any good writing in this age of confusion—all this I say came from out of the mouth of our teacher who is also known by the name of Owl. These matters I point out not as a threat of legalities or etcetera but simply to inform you and to invite serious discussion on the subject.

Yours very truly,
Oscar Zeta Acosta
Chicano Lawyer

P.S. The guacamole and XX he got from me.

WILLIE L. BROWN, JR.

[1970]

Dear Willie,

I have, after several days of consideration, decided to write to you explaining why I will no longer be a part of the campaign. The hesitancy was based primarily on the fear of being considered presumptuous. However, on reconsideration, I concluded that neither of us being the exclusive possessors of wisdom, the letter might be beneficial to both of us; for me, the writing would more clearly bring my reasoning into focus, and for you, that you might know of my position and for your own career try to understand it.

As you know, I am but a babe in political activity. I've not experienced the chagrin that undoubtedly follows unsuccessful activity, thereby creating cynicism, or the belief in political expediency as the best means to accomplish the desired goal. Being practical has never appealed to me. I have been a creature of the arts for too long. Truth and beauty have been more desirable than achievement. I do not mean to say that goals of power should be sacrificed on the altar of truth, but I have simply desired the power of truth, or better, power through truth, as opposed to the achievement of power by means of practical politics, which is, to me, a distortion of truth.

As a lawyer you will probably more readily appreciate the facts rather than an exposition of my ideals. But the facts are difficult to find. As I look back upon the past months to find exactly what it is that displeased me, that caused me to make this decision, it is not easy, the exact words elude me. As I restate them they sound petty. They are as if from the mind of a child. It seems, at times as this, that being practical is maybe a more mature position. I know I have mentioned some of these things to others and they've looked at me with that mocking eye, or what I mistook for such, and said, "Come on, man!"

Nevertheless, here are a few.

I am against discrimination... all of it. You say you are
too... Yet you speak of the white and the non-white vote.
What you really mean is the Negro and the non-Negro vote.
You are spending the majority of your time, money and labor
on the Negro vote. You will continue to do the same until
June.

How about those of us who are neither white nor non-
white? That is, who shall represent those of us who are neither Negro nor white?

There are too many people in this world who view life this
way. No one ever really thought that Lincoln or the Civil War
cleared the mess up, but those of us with sufficient intelli-
gence, awareness and sophistication hoped that these generalizations would soon dissipate themselves with the advent of
the 1960s.

I heard you tell the Negro ministers that the whole thing
depended on them... Jesus, man, how do you swallow this!
You said afterwards that this was political expediency. Do you
think they, the ministers, thought that? Isn't this merely fur-
thering the thing all intelligent people are trying to kill?

It is the same with the whole party. When you speak of
civil rights, civil liberties, etc., you think of black vs. white.
When there's talk of investigation of these rights, of federal
grants for education, of cheap housing, in other words, discrimination, you speak of Negroes. At the Chinese banquet
when all the big whigs got up to talk, they mentioned first
Negroes, and, second Chinese... And that's the way it goes.
All America is divided into three parts, white, black and yellow... How about me?

It doesn't end here, Willie. As I said, it sounds petty when
repeated. But when I heard it, when I saw it, it was not. Obviously, it was not these two examples alone that caused my
decision. The others are too personal to repeat. They are petty,
in the sense that they affected me because of my sensitivity. I
mention these only because they can be discussed without getting into personalities.

There is no doubt in anyone's mind that is worth consideration that you are the best candidate. Yet you have found it
necessary to tell this only to the non-white community, to
spend most of your time in the non-white community, and
most of your money. I am against this; practicality be damned!
Because this is discrimination and that is an evil. My life and

your life and the life of our society will not be bettered by the continuance of this method of political activity.

This letter is for you, Willie, and for you alone. I hope you will consider it in the light in which it was written.

I wish you all the best in your efforts and hope that we can still consider ourselves friends.

DOUGLAS EMPRINGHAM

Douglas,

Among other things...I became an acidhead and a Chicano full-time. And after a nine-year layoff, I started writing again. I discount the legal stuff and the propaganda. The use of a typewriter does not necessarily mean one is writing, any more than wearing a beret makes one a revolutionary.

As you'll recall, if your head is on straight, I did not write for those years because I could not find my voice. After some time in therapy and more particularly, some time in the mountains and about a hundred acid trips, I realized it had nothing to do with a voice—but with an identity. And when that came, Shazam! I work at it, the words, the revolution and the law about twelve hours a day.

In the process, I married a flamenco dancer who digs my style and became, as they say, a leader of my people.

I've often wondered whatever happened to you and others of your team...Holt, Anderson, Lovelace, Reed. But I guess not enough to seek them out. More than likely, they're still looking for their place in the son-in-law.

You, however, might just possibly have found it, despite your second-class writer status. I'd be interested in finding out if you can stand the pressure of my vast ego which, incidentally, the acid has not been able to touch.

I started working on *The Catalina Papers* last June as a showpiece for a producer, with the idea of getting a contract for a T.V. bit...within two or three weeks I should have one, probably for, ugh, *Mod Squad*.

But as I got into it, I realized I was working on something as important as the novel. I've re-written it four times, and feel that it's ready for showing to counsel prior to writing the final draft. All the guys I work with down here are either lily-livered liberals or loud-mouthed radicals, neither of whom can give me any advice on something like it. I like the thing well enough to seriously look for someone to produce it... It even has the possibility of being a moneymaker, since it has, among other things, religion, sex and violence.

You being one of the two persons I know who does not allow professional jealousy to interfere with his criticism—the other is Hunter Thompson, of *Hells Angels* fame—how about doing me the favor? No holds barred.

Also, what have *you* done with acid?

[Circa 1970]

FICTION

PERLA IS A PIG

PART I

He was an old man who peddled corn in the Mexican *barrio* and he had gone five days now without a sale because the rumor had spread that he urinated in his cornfield.

On the evening of this fifth day he slowly pushed his orange cart to the pig's pen to dispose of the freshly cut corn. Those which had become yellow, he fed to the black sow.

"It is the same, Perla," the old man whispered in his native Spanish. "Our misfortune is your joy. Or so it seems." The fat, black pig grunted as it crushed the tender corn ears. "So eat and grow fatter. We'll have you when you're ready."

He chuckled and playfully threw one of the ears at the pig. Then he rolled the cart behind the one-room adobe shack and went to the water pump. He could see no one from there, for in the spring he had planted the tiny kernels of corn in circular furrows surrounding the shack, the pig's pen and his outhouse. Now it was summer and the green stalks were higher than a man's head.

He removed his eye-patch that hid a purple socket, which he rubbed as though he were scrubbing an elbow, to clean the phlegmy, white particles that caked there during the day. He washed only his face. He did not trouble to roll up his sleeves and so his cuffs were always brown and wrinkled, as were his other garments. He dried his face with his shirt tails, then with his hands still wet, he flattened his few thin strands of yellow hair.

He went into the outhouse to complete his toiletry. He laughed to himself about the new rumor as he urinated.

He took some corn and picked green squash growing alongside the plum tree next to the shack to prepare the meal for the guest he was expecting within the hour.

The corn had not yet cooked when the old man heard his guest's whistle. "I'm in here, Nico. Come on in," he responded.

Nico, the business invitee, was about half the old man's size. He wore a Levi jacket, Levi pants, and Lama boots. His brilliant black hair was immaculate. He wore a long mustachio, as did the Mexican cowboys in Texas from whom he had learned all there was to know of manhood. This same little man had also learned from his mother that no gentleman should be out in the streets without a pencil, a pad of paper, a comb and, at the very least, fifty cents on his person.

He entered and said, "Ah, here you are, eh? I thought you might be out pissing." He giggled the shrill laugh of a dirty boy.

"Excuse my bad manners, but I'm at the stove now," the old man explained. "Sit down, Nico. Take all that weight off your feet."

Nicolás hung his nose over the boiling pots. "No meat, Huero?" he asked the old man whom they called *el Huero*, because of his light skin, green eye and yellow hair.

"Sorry, but she's not ready yet."

"Ah, what luck. When my mother told me you said it was urgent, I thought, or at least I had hoped, that you were ready to stick the knife in its throat."

"In her neck," the old man corrected.

"In its neck, in its throat, what does it matter? So long as we can get to it. I saw it when I came in. He's going to be beautiful; he'll bring in a lot."

"She is beautiful, Nico... Why don't you sit down?"

"Can I help?"

"No, just rest yourself."

"I thought you might want me to help set the table. I don't mind, Huero. Shall I get the wine glasses?"

"No, we won't need them. I thought we might drink some goat's milk. It's nice and fresh," the old man said, smiling.

"Goat's milk? Yes, it's nice. My mother serves it every night. Says it's supposed to be good for your liver."

"I know, you've told me. That's why I thought you might like it."

The little cowboy waited a moment. "I wouldn't mind trying some of your wine though, Huero," he suggested.

"Wine? But, Nico, what would your mother say? She'd smell it, you know."

"That is of no consequence, Huero!... Besides, I can stop at Lodi's and get some sweets on the way home."

The old man turned and faced Nicolás. "Well, if you want. But don't tell the old lady. She's mad at me as it is. Like all the others, she wouldn't buy my corn today because of this new rumor. It's up to you."

"Jesus, hombre! I'm fifty-five! You think I worry about her?"

"Well, I don't know, Nico. She's what? Seventy-five?"

"I don't know. I suppose."

"I don't mind, Nico. You're the one living with her."

"So what? Come on, *viejo*, don't play games with me...I have to stop at Lodi's anyway. She wants some of that Mexican chocolate."

The two men ate the meal and drank the wine. They did not speak of the business for which the cowboy had come. When they finished, they sat outside and watched the orange, purple sun silently disappear somewhere behind the brown foothills surrounding their valley of San Joaquín. They sat on huge logs smoking slowly. The mosquitoes from the cornfield picked at the little cowboy. He constantly swung at them and cursed them. Huero, the older man, made no such motions. Even if one were to rest on his eyeless socket, he did not bother it.

"Well, Nico, we'd better start on the business," the old man said suddenly, throwing the cigarette at the water pump.

"Business! What business?" Nicolás asked with surprise.

"Don't come at me with foolishness, Nico. You know it well."

"If you have some, well go ahead, but I don't know what you have in mind," the little cowboy said innocently.

"Then why are you here?" Huero said impatiently. "Are you here only to eat and drink?"

"My mother only said you wanted me for dinner as a guest."

"Guest? Ah, what a guest!... You know, Nico, sometimes you are like a pimp."

"A pimp? A pimp! Huero, you slander me."

"Quiet yourself. I say it without malice. What I mean is, you try to hide your business, your true business, I mean."

"Business? That I am a pimp? You know, Huero, sometimes I seriously believe you're losing it. Maybe what they said was true...maybe you did lose your eye from syphilis."

"Don't start, Nico."

"Well, I don't know, Huero. How should I know? How does anyone know anything?"

"Let it alone, *viejo!*" the old man of one eye warned.

"But the little cowboy would not let it alone. "God only knows, *viejo*, but I should know. I who am your friend. Your counselor. Your business agent. Of a truth, if anyone should know, if anyone should know how you lost your eye, it should be me. But you are stubborn; you don't know who your true friends are."

"Look, Nico, we haven't time for that. This new rumor is serious. I've not sold one *elote* all week."

"But it might be important to this case," Nicolás reasoned. "Perhaps the original rumor has not died down. Perhaps it is a recurrence of the same thing."

"It is not the same thing, you jackass! I tell you this is new gossip, a new rumor. Forget the others. I tell you I've not sold all week. You know corn must be sold within a day or two lest it rot."

"Huero, you are using too many vile names. I cannot concentrate when you are rude to me."

"He's gone and started another one on me, Nico. I know it is he. And you know the children need their corn."

"Who?"

"*Ay*, but look at what a mosquito you are. Who? Who else but the fat Spaniard, you runt!"

"Lodi? Lodi Ulloa?"

"And he's using the same tricks. He has no morals, that *español*! To use one's children to spread evil gossip shows poor education. To gain a business advantage one should not have to lie. He is poorly educated, that one is."

"Huero, if you have something to tell me, why do you hide it? I know nothing of any rumor. I know only of the ones I helped you with in the past."

"But why do you play the part of the cat with this mouse? If indeed you do not know, then why did you ask me if I was pissing in the cornfield when you first entered?"

"Well, that is a natural thing, Huero. Surely you know that."

"You think I don't know what you're doing? You think I am such a fool?" The old man brought out another cigarette. He lit it carefully, deliberately. He inhaled evenly and waited for the words to come to him; for now the bargaining had begun. His words came firmly: "So you know nothing of this new rumor, is that it, Nico? You have no knowledge of the pissing in the cornfield, of the condition of sales. You are here only as a guest."

"The counselor cowboy arose and stepped on the stub of his cigarette with the heel of his boot. "*Viejo*, I'm merely here sitting, smoking, and listening to the talk of a man whom it seems to me has a problem, and who is talking like a mad one... A man, I should remind you, who claims to be a *Mejicano*, though he has blond hair and one green eye."

"*Ay, dios*, save me from this imbecile! I tell you we have work to do, we have plans to make, arrangements and terms of the agreement to decide... And if my color is different from the others, of what concern is that now?"

Nicolás scratched his ear. "How should I know? I remember some years back there was talk you were a gringo."

The old man did not speak now. He saw Nicolás pull at his ear with his thumb and forefinger. He watched him as he stared at the ground and occasionally at the sky which was now black and dotted with pinpoints of white and orange.

Nicolás paced the ground before the old man. Now and then he would stop and look directly into the old man's face. Now that the counselor cowboy was at work, the old man did not interfere. "Shall I tell you the details?" Nicolás finally asked.

"You know you have charge in the matter."

"With the thing about your being a gringo... sst! Nothing. A word here, a suggestion in the right ear... nothing! A child could have thought that one... That was the first rumor, no?"

"As I recall. And this is harder?"

"A gringo! Eh, it was so simple I've forgotten how I did it."

"You made me paint the Mexican flag on the cart."

"Ah, *sí*. A flag... sst! A child could have done that one." The cowboy pulled up his slight shoulders. "But you shouldn't have taken it off. Who knows, if you had left it on, and it wasn't that bad looking, maybe you wouldn't be facing this now."

"It looked like a child's drawing," the old man said simply.

"What's that to you. It served its purpose. They thought you were a gringo, because of your color. They would not let you drink in peace at the cantina..."

"And so you had me paint a flag on my peddler's cart to prove I am a *Mejicano*."

"Yes, if that's what it took, why not? They no longer bother you at the cantina with their questions, do they? I don't know, Huero, you bring these things on yourself."

"That's of no consequence now, Nico. Let's get on with it."

"No? But that's your problem. You concern yourself only with your own ways, with the things of today. You are like a mule; each day you must learn what you were taught the day before. You do not see the continuity of things."

"Don't start again, Nico," the old man pleaded.

"No, you are stubborn! You surround yourself too much with yourself thinking that by so doing you are hiding from others. But you are only calling attention to yourself."

"How's that?"

Nicolás stopped his pacing. Looking down at the corn peddler like a judge from his bench, he said, "Like this corn. Look at it!" He pointed to the circular furrows.

"What's the matter?"

"Well, look. *Jesús y María*, what a man you are! Who ever heard of a round field?"

"It helps the land. It rotates the soil, Nico."

"What a help! Don't you come at me with this foolishness. I know why you did this. And as you can see, everyone else knows."

"What? How's that?"

"To help the land! What nonsense. Who ever saw a round field of corn? It is clear to me, Huero. You did it to hide them. Do you think we are such fools? Even to the children it is clear."

"Hide? But what have I to hide?"

"Well, what else but the pig. And perhaps your plums. There is nothing else. Unless it was to hide your laziness. So that you could piss outside your house without being detected."

"I hide nothing, you *idiota*!" Huero exclaimed.

"But look at yourself. I try to help you. I give you counsel. You do well with my instructions at the beginning, but then as soon as you are doing well then you refuse to abide by my directions. Either you forget or you are a fool. When will you learn?" The cowboy shook his head and sucked at his teeth.

"I should have left that flag painted on my cart? What for? They took that, a child's drawing, as evidence of my *raza*? Anyway, I choose not to go to the cantina anymore?"

"Yes, and now you come to me for help again."

"Yes, but I know I will not always need the counsel of a spider. God will forgive me this weakness...but as I have said, this is a different matter."

"That is where you are a fool or a child. Can you not see it? Are you really such a *pendejo*?"

The old man pondered. "You really think this is the same thing?"

"It is for the same reasons," Nicolás said, tossing an obvious rule of law to the wind.

Huero tugged at the cigarette and nodded at the sky. He inhaled the warm breeze and fixed his gaze on Venus. "And the syphilis? That came after the gringo thing. Was that also part of it?"

Now the little cowboy from Texas was in his glory. "Exactly. Look... First it was the gringo. They would not give you the drinks, right? So you painted a flag. It was a simple idea, true, but it was good, and it worked... Then you removed it. And then what happened? Then they started the rumor of the syphilis; that you lost your eye because of syphilis."

"Well, it wasn't clear. It was sin, I think."

"Sin, syphilis, they are one and the same."

The teacher continued without interest in the obvious past. "Look, dumb one. Pay attention. Sin, syphilis, what does it matter what they think. The reason behind the acceptance of a rumor hardly matters. What matters is that you cure them."

"I went to church as you suggested."

"Yes, you went to the mass... One time."

"I couldn't do it, Nico. I went the one time to show them where my religious thoughts were. I didn't mind that one time to prove to them, but to continue... Besides, the padre was a gringo, an Italian, they say."

"Sometimes I think you do have syphilis, Huero. It has spoiled your brain like a squash that has rotted from the frost... Can't you see it was not for religion that I sent you there? It was to dispel the suggestion of sin."

"You believe that, Nicholas?"

"No, of course not. I am merely a counselor giving argument."

"I can't see it," the old man said, scratching his socket.

"Sure, look, it is very simple. If you had continued to go, if you had gone but a month and waited for the padre to hear of your sins. If you would have had the padre bless you in front of all the people...sst! You think Lodi would have dared start another rumor after that? Not even an español would be so stupid!"

The old man laughed fully. He slapped the ground and nodded slowly, saying, "Ay, qué cabrón, what a bastard you are! You have such crazy notions."

"It is not a thing to laugh at. You refused to carry out my instruction; you refused to go get blessed and so now what? Now you have to wear that patch over your eye, that is what. But that is not all, and this is what you still do not see... This thing of the passing is the same thing."

"I guess I'm too old."

"Then listen... You've worn that patch for three years now. And the people have forgotten about the syphilis. But the patch was your idea, it was certainly not one of mine. I am like a surgeon. I cut away the roots. With that patch you merely delayed this new one. You merely hid the sin. Now Lodi has seen fit to start another one because you have been selling too well in the past few years...so there you have it. Listen to my counsel and you will be cured once and for all."

The crickets lessened their clicking and the frogs took up their place. Mosquitoes hummed and buzzed while the fireflies occasionally lit the night air. Now there was a suggestion of a moon, as the Mexican cowboy issued his judgment. The counselor paced before the old man. He smoked and sighed now and again. "I have it! I have found it!" Nicolás burst suddenly. "Ho, ho, there we have it, viejo!" he shouted to the old man.

"Has the wine gone to your head, Nico?" asked the old man, thinking that perhaps Nicolás was drunk.

"Si, Nico! Nicolás Bordona! Old Nico has done it again. Go and get us some wine, old man," the cowboy ordered.

"Sit down and tell me. Calm yourself before your heart falls to your feet," said the old man.

"No, give me some wine first!" Nicolás paraded before the peddler like a proud bantam rooster after the battle. "Bah! who has need of wine when his head is full like mine?"

"Have you a good plan, a big one?" asked the old man.

"Good? You say *good*? *Ay, ay, ay*! Don't use such small words."

"Well, tell me. What clown do I play this time, doctor?"

"Sst! Clown? I'm not a beginner anymore, old man. My ideas have grown with me. I remember before I used to need the quiet of my home, a certain solitude, before they came to me... Clown? No more."

"Well, hurry and say it, Nico." The old man was impatient with the cowboy's crowing.

"Yes, I'm growing big in my old age. You should see what ideas I have. Before, the thing of the flag, of the church, they were nothing. Sst! *Nada*, not a thing. A child, an idiot could have worked those up. But this one? I'm telling you, Huero, right from up there."

"You're telling me nothing, Nico."

"Nothing, I tell you," he continued without paying heed to the old man. "In those earlier years it was nothing..."

"For the love of God, Nico, say it and be done with it!"

With that the counselor returned to earth from his exaltation and began to unfold his plan before the peddler of corn who had gone five days without a sale because of the rumor in the Mexican *barrio* that said he urinated in his round cornfield. "Here you have it," began the cowboy. "This plan must dispel, once and for all, all the bad feelings of these people, these Mexicans of superstition. This plan must wipe out from their minds the idea that you are different, or that you are unclean. These are the things that tell the people that you are not one of us, and it is for these reasons that they accept the rumors about you. It is a universal occurrence that people will believe what they want to believe according to their feelings of the person in question; and these people, perhaps because they are but poor Mexicans, these people will believe any malicious gossip about you until you can show them..."

The old man interrupted, "Nico, please. I have no need for speeches."

"Just tell me what I must do, *por favor*."

"I see. Here, I will show you... You see, the people, including the children, they believe you have planted your round rows of corn to hide something. To hide what? you may ask. Well, that I do not know, but again you stand apart, again you show your difference and thus again you give them cause for suspicion. Maybe they think you have something

special, your pig, your plums, who knows? But I do know that
it is because of that that they find it so easy to accept the
accusation of this pissing."

"Nico! Jesus, hombre, speak! Say something!"

"Yes, yes. You are without learning. You have no love of
philosophy in you."

"It is not philosophy I seek from you, worm. Nor these
devious words of yours. I only want to know what I must do to
sell my corn. Now, will you counsel me or shall I seek out
another?"

The counselor sighed deeply and shook his head more in
pity than in disgust at the old man of such little knowledge,
and then he said, "You will give your plums to the children."

"Give my plums?"

"Yes. To get them, and this is why I like this plan, to get
them to spread, as it were, a rumor come from you. In a word,
to get them on your side."

The old man turned his one eye up toward the little cowboy. *Surely the wine has gone to this one's head*, the old man
thought. *For I ask him to sell my corn and he tells me to give
away my plums.*

The gnarled, black-trunked tree blossomed violet each
spring and when the sun assaulted the hot fields in July the
boys from the *barrio* crept through the tall green, yellow
stalks and stole away the old man's plums. He knew of their
entrance; he saw them run through the field, their pockets
laden with the purple fruit. He heard them giggle their fear
away, but he never once in all those years prevented their taking, without asking, the gorgeous, tender fruit, sweet to the
dry mouths of brown-baked Mexican boys.

"Give them my plums, eh? To get them on my side?"

"Yes, that is the first part. I will go and tell them that you
have decided to give away your plums. Then, and this is
where the plan intrigues me, then I will go and see Lodi and
compliment him on his good meat."

"His meat?"

"Yes, his meat. I will tell him he has the best meat in the
entire valley... And then, and then, ho, ho, ho...and then I
will tell him that others have said the same thing."

The old man scratched at his eyeless socket. "That he has
good meat, the best in the valley."

"Yes, and then...but this is good! Then I will, ever so slowly, suggest to him that if I were he I'd raise the price. *It is worth it, Lodi,* I shall say. *Not only is it the best, but it saves us a trip to Riverbank; and above all, we do not have to deal with the gringos.* I can do such a thing, you know, Huero. You know I have a way with words. Si, Lodi, were it not for you we would have to buy from those fucking gringos. And then, Huero, as you shall see, and then he will in fact raise the price of his meat. And it would not surprise me if he raises all his prices, for I will blow up his head 'til it is like a pumpkin, you'll see."

The old man nodded in amazement. He could barely speak. "I see, he'll raise the price of his meat, that's it?"

"Sure. And then all you have to do is sell yours for about ten cents cheaper."

The old man shook his face and scratched at his head. He spoke quietly. "Nico, I am not selling meat! I'm trying to sell my corn."

"Well, sell meat, dumb one."

"But it is you who are the dumb one. I have no meat to sell."

"And the pig?"

"Perla? She is not ready yet."

"Ready? Why not? The animal looks good and ready to me."

Huero looked toward the pig's pen. "Then I am not ready, frog!"

"We must truly come from different countries, Huero. I cannot understand how it is your head works. Here I've arrived at a solution, what appears to me to be the ultimate solution to your problem. A plan that will not only help you sell your pig and your corn but most important it will endear you to these people. For as even you can see, when the women learn from their sons that you are a generous man given to kindness, they will think well of you. When you tell the children that you planted the round field to keep away the dust from the roads to protect your beautiful animal so that she would be clean, how can they not think well of you?... And then when these same women learn that the *español,* that fat one who is not a *Mejicano,* when they hear that he has raised all his prices... Can't you see it? There you are, a kind man selling clean pork at bargain prices on Sunday afternoon in front of the church...Jesus, hombre, it is a beauty!"

"What? What's this of the church? And this thing about the dust not getting on Perla, what is that? So again you would have me play the clown and tell more lies. Again you would have me fight one lie with another one."

"So what? What is that to you? Look, you fool, you'll sell cheaper, true, but you'll sell it all in one day, or in two at the most while the story circulates. It'll mean less work and then next week you can go back to your corn. By then that story will be dead... It is simple. You kill the pig tomorrow. You give the boys the plums and tell them the story. Sunday you take the pig to the church at twelve noon. I'll leave as they're saying the last prayers and when the women start coming out I'll tell them you're selling Perla for much less than what Lodi sells for. You watch, you'll sell all the pig before the sun has set."

The old man sat quietly. He looked to the moon. He nodded his head slowly as the blood rose to his head. He clenched his fists and shouted at the little Texan, "Jesus Christ! I must be as dumb as my pig. Why do I ask you to counsel me? Why must I always turn to the spiders and the mosquitoes for assistance?... All I want to do is sell my corn and be left in peace. If I don't sell it, the worms will have it. It is too late to have it dried for cornmeal; I've given it too much water for that. And even if the worms don't get to it, the sun will take up the sweetness... And you will have me slaughter Perla when she is not ready...God, but I am surely a fool!"

The old man was explaining these things for himself, because he knew now that he had already committed himself to the plan by simply having asked the little man to counsel him. But he wanted, for a later time, to have this seeming rebellion as a comfort. He knew this would be his only outburst. Now he was but a soldier offering his distaste for war, knowing all along he would concede to his general.

He arose and went into his shack. He soon returned with two glasses full of wine. They drank slowly while the old man finished the examination of his conscience.

When he spoke again his voice was soft and without emotion. "I'll fix the pig and be at the church at noon. Take some corn on your way out. It is still fresh; I cut it only yesterday."

Nicolás had seen the old man like this before, so he did not speak further on the matter. He took only an armful of the green *elotes*. His fee was all the corn he desired throughout the season.

PART II

The old man had begun the fires under two large tin tubs filled with water. He honed at a long knife with a stone he had found at the river, while his pig snorted and grunted unaware and oblivious.

The line of boys came noisily through the dense field of green, yellow, brown stalks of seven, eight, nine feet. They walked single file, all barefooted and in short-sleeved shirts or in none at all. They wore patched pants or swimming trunks. All were brown like earth, all had black eyes or brown hair too long or too short. Fifteen Mexican boys coming for their plums. They ceased their hornet's nest buzzing as they carefully approached the old man.

One came forward. "Well, here we are..." He hesitated. "Uh, Huero?"

The old man continued to sharpen the knife. "*¿Sí muchachos? ¿Qué es?*"

The brown boy looked at his own mud-caked feet. "Well, Nico, Nicolás Bordona, he said... He said we could have the, some plums."

"Oh, *sí, muchachos.*" The old man hesitated, for he was unaccustomed to dealing with the children. "Take them. There they are."

"They have asked me to speak for them," the boy said.

"No, we didn't!" One of the boys standing in file broke away. "You said we should let you talk, but I want to say it for myself."

"Well, speak," the old man said.

"Senor Huero. We, I want to thank you for the plums... And I am sorry I told those lies about you. But I had to. My father says it is for my own good. He made me."

"You're one of the Ulloa boys?"

"Sí, senor. But I didn't believe the story."

"It's all right. One has to obey his father. It is that way."

"I know. My mother said so, too. But aren't you mad at me?"

"No, son. I am not angry with you. If a father tells his son to lie, then he must lie. Sometimes one must lie of necessity."

The boys murmured. "See?" one reminded the others.

"I said it, too," the shortest one called in.

"Huero," another said, "Huero, I'm sorry I called you a...*el ciego*. I was just kidding."

"Eh, what does it matter? I wish I were blind. For all the good my one eye does me, I might as well be blind."

"You can see, can't you?"

"Some things. But if I were totally blind then the government would pay me. They give you money if you cannot see anything."

"Huero?" Another one called in. "Huero, I stole a piece of sugar cane once when you weren't looking."

"Ah, what's a piece of sugar cane?"

"Me, too, 'ere," the shortest one squealed. "Oh, no, it was a tomato, I think."

The others laughed at him and the old man smiled.

"One time you gave me too much change," another said, "and I kept it. I'm sorry."

Each one in his turn confessed his sin before the old man. He laughed or smiled and tried to offer consolation. But he was running out of absolutions. Although he had been amongst these children for seven years, this was the first time they had come to him. The plan, the counselor's scheme, kept twisting within him. He looked at his sow and he saw the water giving up the steam. He ran his finger along the knife's edge. He used his eyeless socket to advantage. When he did not want others to see him he turned that void toward the speaker. When people told stories, or made attempts at a laughing matter he wished not to hear, he would turn away from them. No one truly expected a man with one eye to have all his wits or to be completely competent in his perception, and therefore no one called this rudeness to his attention.

So now as the boys looked upon him without their accustomed rudeness, the scheme raced through him. He turned away from them because he did not like to look upon people when they could measure his emotion. He looked at his plum tree and at his pig. He exhaled deeply, resignedly and decisively. "Look, *muchachos*, did not Nico tell you you could have the plums? Have I not said, take them? Well, take them, they are yours... Not just now, but whenever you want them. This year and the next. They are yours. It will be your tree."

"Always?" one asked.

"Yes. It is yours...but there is just one condition. You must do me just one favor in exchange... You must not tell anyone about this... You must keep this a secret between us. Not even the girls. Because, well...the more people know, the fewer plums it will be for you." He smiled and saw it was not so difficult to speak to them. He saw clearly that they were but little boys with dirty bare feet and that all he wanted was to peddle his corn.

"Huero, you say *always*? With your permission, may I ask, are you going away?"

"Don't you like the plums, Huero?" another asked. "Do they make you sick? My mother says if you eat too many you'll get sick."

"No, I'm not going away. Not now, at least."

"But you are going away? You say not now?"

"Well, everyone goes away someday, you know."

The short one chirped in, "You mean to die? My dog died. My father said he was going away. I know he just died." This shortest one, a little bit of a boy, he was not the age of the others. He had merely come with his older brother to the feast.

"Boys, why don't you just take the plums."

"Are you very sick?"

"No, not very sick," the old man answered.

"My dog had a sickness. His eye was all red, and white, too. It was ugly. He had blood in it. Is that what you have, 'ero?" the little one asked.

The other boys turned to him and with their eyes and their faces they tried to warn him, to silence him. Their embarrassment compelled them to turn away from the old man with one eye.

"Well, in a way it is my eye, *hijo*."

"Oh, I am sorry, 'ero. I'm very sorry you have the leprosy."

"Shut up, Paquito," his brother yelled.

"Why? I am sorry. And I know about it. The sisters told me about leprosy in catechism. It's like what Teto, my dog, that's what he had. He had it, too. Isn't that what you have, 'ero?"

The old man chuckled. "I don't know, Paquito. Maybe I'll die of that, like your dog. His name was Teto, eh?"

"Sí. I called him that for my Uncle Hector. And the sister said he just went away, too. But I know he just died of the leprosy."

"I see. Well, look, boys, you've thanked me for the plums. I say you are welcome. Now take them, they are yours. They are ripe now."

The boys did not wait. They leaped to the tree and pulled at the branches. The purple tender balls came off with a touch. They ate as they picked more to stuff in their pockets. They yelled and pushed and buzzed and filled their mouths with the fruit. It was not a big tree. Shortly it was clean of the fruit. With their mouths purple and their pockets wet, they left down the path through which they had entered.

The old man stirred the flames more. "*Bueno*, Perla it is your time. I would have waited...but you have eaten well, have you not?"

What a pearl! he thought to himself as he drove the knife into her neck. He drained her blood, he sliced her skin, he burnt and scraped the bristles. He pulled the intestines. He preserved the brain and eyes. He cut cleanly the meat from the fat.

Huero worked late into the night under a lamp beside the now thinned plum tree.

PART III

It was Sunday morning in the *barrio*. The old, wrinkled burnt-skinned Mexican women, covered with black shawls, gathered at the entrance to the wooden building. The church steeple was crowned with a bleeding Christ and housed a hornet's nest.

The children in stiff bright clothes held back their laughter. They carried black or red or white missals. The men in tight, white starched collars and pin-striped black or brown suits smoked quickly before the mass began.

"Have you heard about the old man?" a woman asked several others.

The others came closer. "*Sí, que lástima*, what a pity."

"El Huero, you mean?"

"My boy told me. It is sad."

"I wonder if we shouldn't send the men to inquire."

"I don't know, we might be intruding. I don't want to be a *metich*."

"Yes, but, Rosa, when it is a thing like this..."

"But with him? It is different. He does not join us."

"Well, it is a shame. But I could not buy his corn after what was said. My man would have thrown it in the trash."

"I know. It is the same with me. Mine would have cracked a plate over my head... Still, he does have a heart. Like my boy said—he's a little sick this morning; I guess he ate too many..."

"Isn't that a coincidence? Manuelito is sick, too. You say yours ate too many? What's that?"

"The plums. You know, Paquito said the old man gave them some plums."

"Your boys are sick? You say Huero gave them..."

"*Sí*, Paquito said all the boys went there..."

"All the boys. Elisa, what are you saying? Don't you know; didn't your boy tell you? My boy, Oscar, he told me that Huero had some bad illness. He's sick, too. He's got stomach trouble."

"Wait a minute. Paquito...but he's just a baby. He said the old man had what his dog died of. He said the old man told him he was dying of leprosy. But surely, that is just a baby talking."

"Leprosy!"

"Now wait, just wait. My boy, Oscar, he never lies. He is a good honest boy; now he said, and he is no baby..."

"Well, what is it, Rosa?"

"He did say the old man was sick, of a disease... You say leprosy? But he said it might just be a rumor..."

"*Jesús y María*! If they all went there, as you say...and he has leprosy...and now they are sick... *Dios mío*!"

Several of them crossed themselves. Two of them, without another word, turned and ran home. The others talked faster and louder and gathered momentum in their gesticulations. They called the men into their discussions.

The men laughed at them and called them *chirinoleras*. The men told their women to leave the old man alone. The men in their tight clothes returned to finish their cigarettes, for the priest had arrived.

The women continued in their anxiety. They quoted scripture to one another. One suggested it was not communicable. Another said it was the mark of Cain. They carried their grief into the church and prayed with the priest for all the sick.

But it was all too late. For the rumor had spread during the mass. During the collection, the rumor went round from one to the other, from pew to pew, that the old man had leprosy. The evidence was overwhelming, beyond a reasonable doubt. The Huero had leprosy as was proven by the illness of all the children who had eaten too many plums.

While the congregation recited their *Hail Marys*, the little cowboy slipped out to meet the old man who had rolled his cart near the entrance to the church.

"What's this about your illness?" The counselor wore a black suit and a green tie four inches wide.

"My illness? I am well."

"I don't get it all. I got here a little late. Mother wanted some fresh milk before I left. Look, here they come!" He spun around and hurried to the door to meet the women. But they would not stop to talk as was their custom. They only touched the priest's hand. They hurried away holding tightly to their children. They wanted to find a doctor. Some wanted to go to the older women; the very old and wiser women would counsel them in times of distress, the *viejitas* who found wild mint and red spinach among the peach trees for the illnesses of the children.

The women had no time for the politeness of the counselor who bid them seek out the old man's pork at bargain prices. Nicolás went from one to another pleading with them to look at the meat. They paid him no heed.

One of the women walked up to the old man standing by his cart, and the old man said, "*Ah, buenos días, señoras*. I have nice fresh meat, thirty cents to the pound. The skins are crisp and the blood is red."

"Huero, I don't come here to buy. I must know; this is a serious thing. Did my son, Paquito, did he go to your house yesterday?"

The old man arranged the meat in the cart of two unnecessarily large wheels, one painted black and the other white. The cart itself was painted orange. "Paquito? Well, what did he tell you?"

"That doesn't matter, Huero. He is just a boy. But I must know for certain. Did he?"

"Don't ask me. I know nothing of your son."

Nicolás came to his defense. "Ladies, perhaps what you should do is buy some of these *chicharrones* for your children. You know how they like them."

"You stay out of this, Nicolás Bordona. This is very serious. We have to know. Huero, we know you are sick and we know some of the boys went to your house yesterday. We have to know which ones."

"I am sick? What is this of my being sick?" he asked the excited women who eyed the pork meat with the eye of the bargain hunter.

"*Sí, viejo*, we know of it. It is out and we've got to know which boys were exposed. Now tell us!"

"Señor Huero, please, this is a serious thing. Even though the *padrecito* just told me it is not catching, still we should know. I'm sorry if she is rude, but we are all concerned," a younger one apologized.

"I'm not being rude, Carmen. But leprosy is a bad thing, don't you know?"

"Leprosy?" the old man asked. "I have leprosy?"

They all fixed their gaze upon him. "Well, do you deny it?"

The old man touched his eye patch. "Where did you hear that one?"

"From the...the boys told us. I think it was Rosa's boy, Paquito, and Elisa's boy, Oscar. He said you told them."

The old man smiled and remembered. He looked at the meat in the cart and he remembered the confessions he had heard the previous day. He saw again the boys scampering through the plum tree and he chuckled when he thought of Paquito's dog, Teto. With a twinkle in his eye he said, "I don't know, ladies. How would I know what I have. I have not talked to a doctor since I was but a child. How should I know for certain if I have leprosy...for that matter who can say he does not have it."

The women stared at him and looked with nervous eyes at one another. They tightened their shawls about them and some clutched at the missal or rosary they held in their hands.

"Well, we know, at least the father told Carmen that it is not catching... But you are right, who knows."

"Maybe it's just a coincidence that they're all sick," Carmen said.

"Or a warning," Rosa said as she hurried away.

Nicolás said, "But ladies, how about this beautiful meat?"

"The meat?... No, I think I'll wait."

"But it's fresh, and it is much less than at Lodi's," he wailed.

"No, Nico... I don't think my man would want me to buy just now. Maybe we'd better wait until tomorrow, after we see a doctor or talk to the *viejitas*. They should know."

Nicolás tried the last remaining worshippers. But their decision was the same. They would wait until the following day. If their sons were only sick from too many plums... perhaps they would reconsider.

So now I am a leper, the old man chuckled to himself as he covered the meat in the cart with a white cloth.

"How do you do it, Huero? Of all my clients, how is it that you bring me the most hardships?"

"It is over with, Nico."

"But you can bring me some problems, can't you? You cannot keep my counsel. You must always play the part of the clown."

"Leave it be, Nico. It is done."

"No, wait, *viejo*. This was a business matter. You were to take my advice for a price."

"You can have your corn, hyena. You can have all that enormous belly of yours will hold. But away with you and your advice!"

"I don't know, Huero. First a gringo, then syphilis, then the pissing... Now leprosy... But why did you not deny it? Why did you let them know that is what it is? Are you such a *pendejo*?"

"What are you saying, frog face?"

"Ah, well, never you mind, old man. I'll come up with another plan. You'll see. We'll sell your pig yet."

"Pig? But it is you who are the *pendejo*. This is not a pig. This is but pork meat, can't you see that?... Perla is a pig!"

For the first time the counselor took notice of the old man's seriousness. The little cowboy's eyes fluttered and he bit at his mustachio. "Huero, you are disappointed because the plan did not work. But then you should not have said anything about this leprosy. You should have denied it. You

should not have let them know you have it, or whatever it is...
So that is what it is. I thought, for years I had known you'd
lost that eye from something strange and mysterious."

Huero pushed his cart away. The counselor followed after
him and tried to stop him. The old man pushed his hand away
angrily. He mumbled curses at the cowboy. Nico placed himself in front of the cart.

"Jesus, hombre, but you are *loco*. *Cabrón*, but you are
weak in the head," Nico shouted.

"*Loco*? Yes, Nico, that I am. I am weak in the head. But as
it goes, *He who has no head had better have good feet*. So get
away from me before I run over you!"

Nicolás stepped away from the cart. "Jesus, but now you
are like a wild one caged too long without water."

The old man advanced toward the little cowboy from
Texas. "Nico, you know they say if a leper rubs his sore on
sweet skin it will harden and fall off like cold wax. Want me to
try it on you?"

Nicolás jumped back. "God, but now you've really gone
off."

Huero laughed fully. His whole body trembled with
delight as he watched the frightened little man scampering
away with short steps like a busy field mouse.

~~~

The old man returned to his hut surrounded by circular
furrows of tall corn stalks. He had planted it that way because
he had read in a magazine that it did the soil good.

The Mexican peddler of corn hummed an old song as he
dug a grave behind the plum tree. The grave was large
enough for the coffin, which was the cart, stuffed with the
meat of the pig that had once been his Perla.

He knew then, that he too, like Paquito's dog, would have
to leave the Mexican *barrio* of Riverbank.

Con Safos 2, no. 5 (1970): 5-14; reprinted in *Voices of Aztlán:
Chicano Literature Today*, edited by Dorothy E. Harth and Lewis M.
Baldwin (New York: Mentor, 1974): 28-48.

DRAFT:
THE AUTOBIOGRAPHY OF
A BROWN BUFFALO

I stand naked before the mirror. Every morning of my life I have seen my beastly belly from all angles. It has not changed that I can remember. It has always been brown and fat. Yet when I suck it in and hold my breath I can still have hope, even after thirty-three years, for I do have a nice profile...one big indio from Aztlán of black hair, white teeth and perfect ears.

I lower my head over the toilet bowl...I struggle, but only rancid, hot air blows. The dry heaves! My heart burns with acid dripping into that stomach burnt from an excess of *chiles*, sawdusted-hamburgers, wars and rumors of wars.

"Puke, you sonofabitch!" I command. But nothing comes. Not even my body obeys me. "Jesus, maybe I am sick. Perhaps it is a physical thing," I console myself, and note it for my psychiatrist. "But from what? I get twelve hours of sleep, day in, day out. Hardly drink anymore."

When I am satisfied I return to my mirror and concentrate on my rather insignificant eyes. I double my fist and strike my belly. "Could it be the fifteen-cent pineapple pie? Tin poisoning in the Campbell soup? The Pepsi, the candy bars? No? Yes, it's the etcetera-diet of a kid with ulcers!"

I grab the rolls of yellow lard around my waist. I sigh. I puff my chest, I suck in the belly and I recall that once I lifted iron bars and drank nothing but powdered protein, and, I did earn three stripes for varsity football...but that was long ago, when you were but a brown Mexican boy in the cornfields of Riverbank. Now you are a lawyer, an attorney at law, a counselor of old women who presently sit quietly watching with their tragic tales in that dingy, musty hallway of the Legal Aid Society.

I enter the shower and burn myself with pure hot steam. I am never out of soap. I always, in all weather, in any home I may happen to be in, I always clean myself, every morning of my life... And suddenly, without my attention, I turn on the cold water. I turn off the hot. And I smile serenely, with a mocking grin.

"If they ever catch me! Shit, I can take anything! They'd never make me talk." I fight the good fight of the spy, the soldier, the hero under freezing water or whatever torture man might devise. My face shows no pain. I am resigned, stoical, the existential man.

Only the previous week, the psychiatrist had said to me, "Did you ever stop to consider that it might simply be a form of self-love?"

"Christ, you make better excuses than I do," I replied, because I knew that wasn't the reason for the dirty things I did in the shower. But I offered no defense.

I finish my toiletry. I punctually take my pills. A blue and two yellows. The green drops are for the evening.

I drive carefully across the San Francisco-Oakland Bay Bridge unaware of the impeccable beauty of land, sea and sky. Cars, concrete and cables, these are the things that matter! I cannot distinguish the *Beatles* from the horns, from the jangled nerves, from the gas-laden belly and the voices of old, unkempt women with bloody noses from the weekend drunk crying for a divorce who are even now, before my arrival, sitting in hard chairs with tattered copies of a *Life* or a *Time* which they pretend to read.

I time it perfectly. I am never late to anything. I never miss an appointment. I who am the son of Manuel from the mountains of Durango, I did not miss one day of school in all the twelve years of my childhood education.

I enter the drab building at the corner of 14th & Fruitvale Streets in the heart of the slums of East Oakland which the President called a "target area" and which the Poverty Program swept in to overkill. I see them from a distance. Just as I described: Five fat women, their hair still matted, their tits still hanging and their children laughing and sliding on the waxed linoleum floors. I cannot enter the waiting room. They would see me and their expectations would increase. Today, I must give no hope.

I duck into the toilet. I lock the door. I lower my head for the third time that morning. This time it comes...and the designs of milk and eggs with ketchup are a sight! I ponder the fluid patterns of my rejections and consider the potentials of art.

"Good God! I didn't use any ketchup!"

I strain to puke more. I want to be certain. Sure enough, there it is again. I think of taking a specimen. But why bother? I know as sure as I know that I am sick that it is not ketchup!

"It is blood, god damn it! Blood, do you hear?"

I rush through the waiting room without a word, without so much as my usual greeting of teeth and smiles. The women eye me, without expression. I slam the door to my office and sit at my desk. I do not breathe. I stare and wait for the dizziness to calm. The telephone rings. I let it harass me while my heart pounds madly. It stops. The walls begin to spin. The light is fading.

I have sat here for twelve months now. Twelve months of divorces and welfare recipients; of poor people, tired, dirty and mostly lonely for attention. Twelve months of my pills and the angry voices of piggish creditors screaming about my clients. For twelve months now I have pleaded with vicious landlords to fix broken toilets, windows and gas heaters. I have begged snotty, arrogant, finely combed social workers to overlook the rules and give them a buck, a carton of milk; anything to stop the pain in my stomach. They have taken my sincerity for weakness and laughed.

The machine rings again and I detest it; I stare at it, daring for it to continue. She gives up on me. And now, quickly whirl the cobwebs of my past in the carnival of my head.

On my paneled wall hangs my biggest trophy of them all: my license from the State Bar. Charlie, my artist friend from Trader JJ's, framed it for me without charge. A work of art. One year ago, the week after I passed the bar, I hung it on this wall. When my head burned with the fever of an impotent missionary, when I entered the jungle in white suit and black book of the law in my hand to fight for the poor, the black, the Mexican, that is when I proudly hung my professionally framed license and decided to take them on. But now the time draws near, for I have lost the bottle.

I open my drawer and take out the bottle with the orange pills for the day's work. I pour out the regular two, and I stop to think. "Today, I need four."

My stomach burns. It hurts. My body is in pain; I ache, I'm tired, sleepy, my head is splitting. I close my eyes.

My eyes open. I lift myself from my swivel-back chair and walk to the wall. I take the frame down. I drop it into the trashcan beside the bookshelf. I never think of it again. I pick up the telephone.

"Morning, Rita," I speak softly to the secretary.

"Oh, Mr. Acosta? I've been…"

"I know…I'd like you to call Tom and tell him I've left."

"Left?… For the day?"

Silence. And then, "Tell him I'll send a letter."

She weakens. "What'll I do with the people who are waiting?"

"Tell them I'm…sick. If anyone asks for me, you just tell them I'm sick." And it is done. My escape begins.

I go out the back door. This time, I race back across the bridge. I play the radio at full blast. I sing and whistle as loud as I can to drown out the noise. It is the first time in 12 months that I have crossed the bridge before 5:00 p.m. I had always returned to my small apartment, across the bay, in the Polk District where all the fags hid from the crowd in dark, nasty bars. I had always burnt my hamburgers in five minutes flat. I always gobbled them down with Pepsis. (A habit I'd picked up from my former wife, Betty, a midwesterner with roots still in the south, but ultimately the mother of my eight-year-old son.) For twelve months, all I had done was eat, puke, take pills, stare at the idiot-box, coddle myself and watch the snakes get larger inside my head while waiting for the clock hand to turn. Time had been but a circle for this man. Only clear-headed mathematicians saw it as a straight line. And normal people did not even concern themselves with such trivia. My only conscious concern had been the pain of my body and the schedules of the television shows. I knew them all by heart. I was a living T.V. Guide; that's what I was for twelve, spaced-out months.

I drive without concern for traffic to the office of Dr. Serbin, my shrink of ten years: a quietly intelligent, Jewish psychiatrist who'd listened to my sad stories ever since he interned at Mt. Zion. He is super cool. Not once in ten years have I shaken him. Not even when I cracked up. Three times in mental wards, three days each. He didn't bat an eye. But this time, I am not thinking of his reaction. I am merely burning my bridges for my escape. He has no receptionist. I know he has another patient with him. But still I bang on the door. He opens the door slightly, his thin face still a sphinx.

"I've stopped to tell you I'm leaving town."

"If you want to talk about it," he begins.

"Fuck no. I just want to tell you I'm going to quit."

"I can see you in a few minutes," he continues.

"Look, it's cold turkey from now on!"

"I'm with another patient now. Why don't you sit," he kept on.

"I don't want to talk. See you later."

Quickly I raced to my apartment. I packed my books, my clothes, my paintings and records. I took the books to the bar where I had practically lived before the crackup of the year before, 1966. All through law school, I had prepared myself at a bar that had survived the earthquake; an old hideout for rumrunners of the 1800's. I asked Sal, the owner, if I could store them in the basement where they used to lock up the drunken sailors.

"Why, you think you're going someplace?" He always talked with a sneer, a whine and a nag.

"Never mind. Just yes or no."

Sal was the only bartender I ever knew who would prefer you didn't bring him your business; a salty, fifty-year-old Italian who pretended to be super-horny with every chick that hit him up for drinks.

I borrowed a hundred bucks from him. As he handed them to me his eyes twinkled and he laughed with a dirty, long, obnoxious sneer. "Shit, you'll be back. You can't leave here."

I borrowed another hundred from Si, who was watching Sal get at me. He was the lawyer who got me into Legal Aid in the first place. "You owe it to me, you bastard!"

Si's laugh was even worse than Sal's. "Yes, Oscar. Sure... Have fun, and I'll see you in a couple of weeks." They laughed together as I slammed the door behind me. But never mind.

And so with a head full of speed, a beer in my hand, a soft penis and two-hundred bucks in my pocket, I said good-bye to Frisco and burned rubber across the mountains and into the desert, a madman on the loose, a wild Indian gone amok.

I had nowhere to go, no map to follow... Although I had known Leary when he was still on wine, when I was still on my way out of my Jesus trip (a Baptist missionary in Panama, 1954-1956), it wasn't until that wild summer of '67 that I took his message to heart and dropped out of my own personal hell-hole. With each turn of the wheel, with each empty Budweiser can thrown at signs on the road, with every hour of the constant hum-hum-hum of hot tires on burning road, I felt an easing, a lifting, a cessation of the baying of the hounds in my head.

I drove for two days straight with my head filled with bennies. When I saw a sign that said Ketchum, Idaho, it sounded as good as any other. I stopped for a cold one in some small bar and a lady told me that Ernest Hemingway used to drink there. She told me of his grave and so I went out to pay my last respects. He and Steinbeck were the only two writers I'd ever paid much attention to, and so I shed a tear. I returned to the bar for more drinks and thought of my unpublished novel which several editors had told me was "beautiful" but unsellable in those years before the world had heard of Chicanos except from Steinbeck and the sociologists.

It did not take much to get me drunk. The bartender told me of a monument to "the old man" at the edge of town. I drove out to the river, pulled out my sleeping bag and slept beside the slab of stone in the midst of cottonwoods giving up their summer snows. I could hear explosions and I saw fireworks lighting the moonlit skies, for it was July the Fourth, 1967. I dreamed of elephants, women and the books I would presently write, now that I was no longer a lawyer.

Two days later I drove into Aspen, Colorado. Just another name on a sign to me. I drove around the small, western town until I found a cheap motel because I'd not slept in a bed for a week. When I awoke it was dark. I went out to find a bar. My head still throbbed from the roll of the tires and the amphetamines.

Only a bartender with a goatee sat in The Daisy Duck, which was at the foot of a gigantic mountain that entered the back door. He merely nodded as he served me. Soon a young, lovely girl walked in. She was wearing hardly any clothes; she had long legs and sensible breasts. I pretended not to stare.

Without warning she came up to me, introduced herself as Gerri and asked if I felt like dancing. I was astounded. I am not the sort of fellow one ever speaks to first unless it is absolutely necessary. Perhaps it is my bearing. They say I scowl, that I'm overbearing, threatening in appearance. But when I speak, my voice is soft, medium in tone and, unless I'm pissed, pleasant to hear. But girls and women almost never, ever speak to me first.

When we danced to *White Rabbit*, I had never tried rock. But it didn't matter, I had never learned any dance steps to anything, and yet I had been dancing all my life. I seemed to be but an excuse for her dancing, an escort for the lady. In any event, I was merely warming up, waiting for my chance to score. By the time it was over, several persons had entered. She pulled my hand and took me to where two men were sitting talking to the bartender.

She introduced me to Phil, the perch-faced bartender, to a short kid with fat boots named Fuller and a tall, balding one by the name of Hunter Thompson. They each seemed pleasant enough during introduction, but I was more concerned with Gerri, the plastic witch of a swinging ass. The tall one ordered a round.

"You're from San Francisco?" Fuller asked.

"Just got in this afternoon," I replied.

"Passing through?" the tall one asked.

"I'll sleep a couple of days first."

"You wouldn't by any chance know a Turk Tibeau?" Gerri said.

I thought for a second. "Tibeau? I know a guy, sort of... His name is John and I think..."

"Yeh, that's him! John Tibeau. A writer?" Fuller seemed excited.

My chest tightened because I did not care for John. He used to come into Trader JJ's, read a lousy poem or two he'd just written, bum a drink off whoever happened to be there and then split.

"What's the freak up to now?" Thompson asked. "Is he still wearing a cast?"

Fuller laughed. "Is he still going to sue you, Hunter?"

And then I connected the tall one's name. Several months before, John had driven his motorcycle into the bar while still wearing a cast on his leg. He had shown me a copy of a new book very excitedly and told me that the writer, Hunter Thompson, was a friend of his. He just had time to mention that he and Thompson had been riding on his bike when they crashed. I never got the details because Sal walked in about that time and 86'd him for bringing the bike into the bar.

"So you're the guy that broke John's leg?" I said. "As a matter of fact, John spoke to me about the possibility of a suit."

Thompson's eyes widened. "Is he serious about it?"

"Well, he *did* come to my office."

"Are *you* a lawyer?" Gerri asked in disbelief.

"Yeh," I nodded, feeling proud.

Thompson grinned. "Do you know Pierce? The lawyer?"

"I just met him once. He was with John in this bar we hang out at," I answered. "Maybe he'll defend me after he returns from Tibet."

"You been disbarred?" Thompson asked.

"Well...I don't have my license anymore."

Fuller asked, "You're not pulling a Pierce?"

I felt offended. To follow another's example showed a lack of breeding, a denial of one's manhood. "I hardly know him," I said coldly, with a straight face.

"He freaked out, closed his office and is studying to be a monk," Thompson said.

"A monk?" I asked. "Not me. I went through that a long time ago."

Fuller and Gerri went to the dance floor. While Thompson and I drank, I tried to recall what John had told me about him. I only remembered that he had lived and ridden with the motorcycle outlaws while getting material for the book and that they had nearly stomped him to death—or so John said—when he refused to share in the profits of the book. John had insisted I read the book, but I had refused. I had not read any fiction written after *The Old Man and the Sea*, which an editor for Doubleday had accused me of plagiarizing in my then unpublished short novel, *Perla Is a Pig*. That accusation, that trauma has to this day still dictated my reading habits.

"Didn't John say you were a Hell's Angel?" I took measure of his reactions.

"He might of." He grinned his thin lipped smile, looking straight ahead.

"He says a lot of crazy things," I continued.

"What can you expect from a drunken Irishman?"

"And a bum," I added, painting the portrait of his friend, not mine.

"He claims to be a poet, too," I continued.

"Every freak from San Francisco is a poet—or something. He sends me the same stuff he probably shows you."

"Not me. I read one short thing of his and that was enough for me."

"You're lucky. He cons me into reading everything he shits."

"What for? No sense in insulting someone you know."

"Yes, well, I guess I feel obligated, or some fucking thing."

I threw it at him evenly. "Why's that? Do *you* write?"

"It's not that. It was my fault he got his leg busted."

He didn't take the bait. Gerri and Fuller returned and we talked and drank faster because the hour was approaching.

"Were you guys with the rest of the gang when John busted his leg?" I asked Thompson in front of the other two.

"They were on a rumble," Fuller mocked.

"Did you guys really carry chains and bullwhips?" I needled.

Gerri asked seriously, unaware of the put-on, "What were you two doing when it happened? You've never told us."

"Oh, Ger, you know what Thompson does with young men," Fuller said.

Thompson looked me straight in the face and said, "We were out looking for greasers."

We all laughed the nervous spasms of strangers.

"I take it you didn't find them," I returned.

Fuller added, "Hunter wouldn't know what to do if he had. He'd probably interview them while they cut him up."

"Yeh, I probably would." He smiled. "If I had an interpreter."

"Are you a reporter?" I asked.

"Sort of," he smiled.

"He's a hack," Fuller said.

"Oh, come on, you guys! I think Hunter's a good writer," Gerri said, blushing.

The three of us laughed. "I thought you were an Angel?" I asked innocently. "John mentioned you rode with them."

"He did until his book came out," Fuller said.

"Go ahead and laugh, you bastards," Hunter said. "I guess I'm as much of a hack as you're a lawyer." He turned to me.

Fuller changed sides, with a smile. "Hey, man, I've heard of *shyster* lawyers, but what's a *Mexican* lawyer do?"

"They roll around in their grease," Hunter said with a straight face.

"Grease? What are you guys talking about? You three are really something else," Gerri chided us in good humor.

"That's what Mexicans use to cook gringos," I said.

By the time the bar closed we had consumed quarts of booze and smoked too many cigarettes. Every line was punctuated with laughter and boisterous camaraderie. We did not speak the language of most strangers after the initial thrusts into the things that apparently mattered to each of us. The soft spot, the tender wound, was found and attacked in tandem; if the victim showed the least bit of sensitivity the other two would join forces and mount a frontal assault, a direct series of thrusts; then, without warning, one of the two would break ranks and turn upon his partner, but only to find his new ally in conspiracy with the new victim.

It is this anarchy of socialization, this willingness to strike at all self-image masking as reality, that permitted me the freedom to open my own sores before these strangers. It is not that I had never been beaten over the head by others; for insult couched in smart talk was the permanent style of conversation at the bars I had frequented for years in San Francisco. And even prior to my arrival in San Francisco (in 1958 at the age of 23) I was accustomed to and accomplished in brutal conversations. At seventeen I had joined the Air Force Band during the Korean War and had lived four years with those jazz musicians who didn't want to get their asses shot off defending a country that, at best, was irrelevant to their interests. Jazz musicians were the hip, the perceptive and the rebellious men of that otherwise drab era. It is from those professional artists that I learned the ropes; learned to identify and to use sex, drug and music. They were the dominant themes of the fighting 573rd A. F. Band at Albrook Air Force Base in Panama between 1954 and '56. The year before, I had found Jesus and had been consumed with the Holy Ghost. When I preached instant salvation to the jazzmen, they merely told me to practice whole tones on my clarinet or invited me to a whorehouse. I discovered they would not scare as easily as did the natives I was leading by the nose in the jungles. The harder I railed at them, the more kindness and humor they threw back. Ultimately, I learned humility from a fat, Jewish oboe player, who practiced alone seven hours a day in the attic of the barracks, when he told me that he respected my commitment.

There was, however, a substantive difference between the jazzmen of the fifties, the artists and beats I knew in San Francisco as contrasted with the freaks I crashed into in

Aspen at the Daisy Duck. These latter did not wait until they knew you before they attacked your gods; introductions were intentionally omitted and descriptions of status were strictly forbidden. The assignment of value to an act or condition of one's self by one's self simply prompted a negative response; familiarity and/or friendship played no role whatsoever in the dialogue of freaks. The attack against irrelevancies was aimed at friend or foe alike. They slaughtered man, woman and child without regard to race, color or creed, these new barbarians.

It was, perhaps, this absurdist equal application of insult and attack that allowed me an escape from my usual rage whenever the issue of race entered a conversation. I cannot recall ever being referred to as a greaser or a spic by a stranger without having an automatic and violent reaction. For the first time in my life, that did not happen.

I had smoked grass several times while living in San Francisco, and I had taken L.S.D. twice, but on each occasion I was merely caught up in drunken paranoia, a trip to the gutter of fear. I saw cops behind each door, under every bed. My thoughts were of a dismal nastiness of things as they were. I had, for example, seen myself as an animal, pure and simple; a carnivorous beast of prey who could no more articulate, communicate or be aware of a world of ideas than a pig... In a word, I did not like myself under the spell of marijuana.

It was a totally different experience with Fuller and Gerri. We elevated the conversations to the seriousness of existence, the nature of man, the relationship and status of man and woman. And we did it without corn. It was not intellectualizing. It was not phony.

Throughout the entire weekend we smoked and talked of the things that mattered, that were of value to each of us. Where we had attacked one another in the bar with Hunter, now we spoke with sincerity and politeness, and at all times with a sense of humor and irony. We drove up the hill and into the mountains and experienced the thrill of seeing nature, the greenness of trees, the bigness of granite cliffs, the lightness of the cottonwoods' summer snow falling gently over the valley. We stood at the top of cliffs and tried to start miniature avalanches; we threw rocks at flying buzzards and enormous black crows. Fuller took his climbers' ropes and scaled the sides of sheer, slick rock while Gerri and I drank beer. Later I played my clarinet beside the rocky creek and read books given to me by Fuller, mainly books by Alan Watts on Zen.

The question never arose, either in conversation or in my head, of when I should leave their cabin. I had planned to stay for the weekend only, but as it turned out I lived with them for two months in the most pleasant relationship I have ever had.

There are many reasons, some known, some hidden, for making the big decisions in one's life. I am of the opinion that most of the crucial decisions in my life have been made without my conscious participation: It is through no participation on my part that I was born the son of *Mejicanos* named Manuel y Juana on April the eighth, 1935; that I enlisted in the Air Force Band at the age of seventeen at the insistence of my first love, Anita; that I became a Baptist missionary at eighteen; or that I married Betty and had Marco in my twenties... none of these crucial matters did I personally choose; they simply happened. It was the will of the gods.

And so it was in Aspen.

My first week I scored on two, older Jewish broads. Both were English teachers and friends from Miami. I had not been to bed with any woman for over a year. The reasons are perhaps better known to Dr. Serbin than they are to me. All that I can determine is that I flunked my first bar exam on the same week that a girl from Rhode Island, a cute, funny chick, told me that she didn't want to marry me; and that for the next year and a half I obeyed my psychiatrist and was unable to have an erection. Big rejections do weird things to immature men.

And so when I scored twice in one week my first few days in Aspen, I indeed believed I'd found my place; mainly on top of women. Fucking is potentially the highest form of acceptance that one being can show toward another. I believed it to be the best means devised by the gods to show both man and woman their rightful place. In those days I did not reason, I did not rationalize, I merely saw the simplistic side of my position and to hell with human kindness, and to hell with the needs and feelings of others, particularly women. I told these two, extremely straight women to drop acid, smoke dope and pull down their pants, if they wanted to be with me. And predictably, I never saw them again. But both Fuller and Gerri assured me that I'd have no trouble finding others; that a freak like me would have his bed full with Aspen's finest. Since I got on top of those two with such little effort—I bought them a beer—I fully expected my luck to continue.

But, of course, as the devil would have it, I never made it with another woman in Aspen. Throughout my sojourn in that town I would learn the meaning of sexual desire for a woman who is not of one's own race, and the relation of that lusting after white women to my predicament, my being and my future. It is not a story that comes out in action, for there was none. I cannot relate the awakening, the awareness in terms of people, for there were none to lead me. It is not a question of rejection in the active sense, for no woman ever denied me her bed. All the beautiful girls I met were that, but nothing more. There was no absence of swinging blondes, dope-smoking chicks, intelligent broads. I got loaded with the best of the bunch. We danced and played and tripped through the mountains. But they were simply friends or playmates. It never entered our minds to become sexually involved. On several occasions I kissed one or two, and each time we simply laughed at the absurdity of buddies fondling one another. It was almost as if we were of the same sex, or rather, that we were sexless, neuter and without sensuality.

But I suffered. I hurt inside and all alone. There was no love for me. There was no love object. None to seek and, unless some miracle occurred, none to be found. While all around me there were men and women falling in love, going to bed and holding hands, I had no one to wash my clothes or cook my dinner. When the men spoke of going to the bars or to the parties to look for chicks, I only hoped there would be a sufficient supply of dope and booze to keep me company. Perhaps if I'd learned the reason for the situation, I would not have suffered. If I had known, while living in Aspen, that I was simply in the wrong place, the white man's turf, perhaps I would have returned to my origins, my own people, much sooner. But as I said, I am not responsible for the big things that have happened to me. It would take six months for the gods to make their decisions about my place in the order of things.

The second week I rolled my car off a cliff and thus the decision to stay was made for me by another of those fortuitous circumstances that I have referred to. Phil, the bartender at the *Daisy Duck*, turned me on to Ouzo with a Galliano float, which he called Yellow Lightning. After the seventh one I blacked out. I continued to drink them until closing time when Phil found me in the toilet, crashed on the floor. Being drunk himself and in a hurry to get to his warm bed, he put me in my car and told me to make it. I woke up an hour later, standing in the middle of the road at the top of a fourteen-thousand-foot mountain, urinating into the moonlight over the cliff. I blacked out again and did not regain consciousness until my car, with me in it, was just going over a cliff. It was much too late to do anything, and so I said, "Well, that's that!" and closed my eyes.

Minutes later, my eyes still closed, I heard a voice, "Hey, Oscar, what the hell you doing down there?" It was some pimply-faced kid I'd met that week. I got out and in the dazzling moonlight saw my car totally smashed, having hooked on to a tree and a boulder about thirty yards down the side of the mile-long drop. By pure coincidence he was driving by when my car went over.

The next morning I went to report the accident to the sheriff because the garage mechanic said he couldn't tow it into town without a release. The sheriff wasn't there, but his wife was. She told me that he'd gone out to investigate an accident "where some drunk had run his car over a cliff, then disappeared." When I told her that I was the one with the car over the cliff, I believe if she had had a gun she would have put me in one of the cells. Seeing that she was upset, I gave her the phony story that I was a lawyer, a guest of a Mr. Thompson at his ranch outside of town, and that I was unfamiliar with Colorado law.

The following day they found me at the *Daisy Duck* and charged me with reckless driving.

Gerri pressed my suit and I went to trial the following week. I told the judge that I was an attorney from San Francisco on vacation, and then proceeded to challenge the constitutionality of the statute. Not only was he impressed, he was also afraid of me; his voice wavered, his hands shook and he was almost obsequious in his wrinkled, brown suit.

Upon cross-examination of the deputy sheriff, I found a power within me I did not know existed. (A power that would not ripen until a year later.) I made mincemeat out of him. His story was that having measured the trajectory of the skid marks, and there not being any other car involved, the slight curve could not possibly account for my driving off the cliff "unless I had been reckless, or drunk." After qualifying him as an expert on the landscape in question, and as a person who is expert on the wildlife and conditions of the area, I asked him if it weren't conceivable that a deer could have crossed in front of me, that another car could have been driving in my lane; that I could have had a seizure? "Well, yes, it's possible."

"And if the tire blew out just before rounding the curve? Would the tire skid marks have been as you saw them?" I asked quietly.

"Possible," he sneered.

Standing up, I lowered my voice to its lowest depth and asked in the most annoyed of tones, "Sir, did you check the right front tire of my automobile in the garage?"

He hesitated, then in embarrassed tones apologized, "No, Mr. Acosta. No, sir, I didn't."

The old, country judge stopped the trial right there, told the deputy he should investigate more carefully in the future and called me to his bench and shook my hand. "Sir, as you probably know, we don't often get very experienced criminal attorneys around here." I blushed for the old coot. He continued, "I want you to know it's been a pleasure seeing you at work... I take it you do a lot of federal work, the way you were reading off those Supreme Court cases."

I stood proudly in my dark, blue suit and lied through my teeth. "Well, yes, your honor. The firm has quite a few clients...income tax evasion and interstate commerce violations. You know."

Despite numerous acts of vandalism which I committed throughout the summer and fall of '67, all known to the sheriff and the deputy district attorneys, the law kept me at arm's length for the duration of my stay in Aspen.

My bread gone, friends and relatives refusing to send me any more, I decided to try my hand at dishwashing. I told a gambler, mafia-type, transplant from Las Vegas, who had a Mexican restaurant in Aspen that I was both a writer and a hard worker. He hired me at a buck and a quarter an hour, plus all I could eat. Naturally, I stole him blind. But I enjoyed the job, requiring as it did only the use of my hands. I particularly liked to wash the enchilada plates and watch the cheese melt away.

One day he gave me a fatherly talk. "Oscar, you know, I've been watching you. I like the way you work." He wore

dark, blue suits and white ties and no one doubted that he
carried a huge bankroll and a gun.

"As you might of heard, Victor is leaving soon, going back
to Mexico...and Jimmy is taking his job as head chef." He had
a hard time expressing gratitude. "Now I know you told me
you wanted to write...but you know, that's a tough racket...
Now, here, you can know where you stand."

It was my third week on the job and I felt I'd learned all
there was to learn from the enchilada plates.

He continued, very relaxed, "So what my partner and I
have decided...we'd like to promote you to assistant cook." He
waited for some reaction, but I wasn't ready. "Of course,
there'll be a raise." I bided my time, saying nothing. "In fact,
to be honest, we even talked...if it works out, of course... We
have a restaurant in Frisco and since you're from there...
Well, let's say that if things work out and you want to return
to Frisco... We might very well make you the head chef out
there."

"That's really something," I said, getting up steam. "I've
thought of going back. But you know, I haven't decided if I
really want to practice law again."

"Oh, you're thinking of going to law school? Now that
would really be something for you... You could work the job
right into your schedule."

"Not school. Been through that already."

"What do you mean?" His eyes widened.

"I'm a lawyer. I'm trying to make up my mind if I want to
practice law anymore."

"You? You're a lawyer?"

Tony never recovered from that one. He fired me three
days later for being drunk and on his booze, or so he told people. The fact is he fired me because he couldn't tolerate a Mexican dishwasher also being a lawyer and a smartass.

Sometime in August the local hippies decided to mix politics and pot. Robert McNamara, the Secretary of Defense, was
building a summer retreat outside of Aspen. Joining forces
with local liberals and immature artists, they advertised a
march to his house, to be followed by a love-in at the local
park. But they compromised and publicly stated there could
be no booze or drugs: Just love and rock for peace. They
walked to McNamara's house and gave him a peace poster
especially designed for the occasion, I think by Tom Benton, a

local freak with streaks of madness. They returned grateful for his acceptance of the poster and danced wildly on the lawns with children and cookies.

Hunter and I had been at it for twenty-four hours. When I had last passed out, he had written something on my bare back without my knowledge. We purchased a bucket full of drink-size bottles of booze and decided to crash the love-in and come to the aid of the people.

Wearing but a bathing suit and a headband, people stared, gaped and laughed at me as I passed out the refreshments. When the head hippie bawled me out for being a poor sport, Hunter and I grabbed him, threw him to the ground and measured the length of his hair with a carpenter's "T" that I had brought just for the occasion. He tried to laugh it off. (In those days, it was a sin for Hippies to get uptight.) "Hey, man, what'd you want to do that for?"

"Can't you just see it, man," I replied as I measured. "Here I am in, say Frisco, and someone says, 'Ever heard of Chuck Mason?' And I say, 'Oh, you mean the cat with seventeen and a quarter-inch long hair?'"

We let him go when I saw some nuns playing with kids. I ran over and asked them to dance. Neither replied. People started running up to me and taking pictures of me, usually from my back. I asked Hunter what was going on. He acted innocent. I was dancing with a tall, skinny chick when out of the blue someone struck me in the back. I swirled and saw a fat-assed broad swing away at me. I pushed her and said, "What the fuck's got you, baby?"

"You, you...you beast! You dirty, filthy son of a bitch!" She swung again and I ducked. I finally got someone to tell me what it was. Hunter had written "Fuck the Pope" on my bare back.

We drove away cussing at them. Driving downtown I kept shouting out the window, "Here come the hemorrhoids, here come the hemorrhoids!" Every time we saw a girl, Hunter would stop, I'd run out and ask if I could measure her legs, or her hands, or whatever struck my fancy, with my ruler. We dropped more acid and decided to get serious, for the bastards had bugged us enough! We went to his house, got a tear-gas bomb and a six-foot bow with steel arrows. We returned to town, went to the *Daisy Duck* and dared anyone to fuck with us, carefully placing the bomb and bow in front of us. When

Phil started *giving* us the drinks, and no one would accept the
challenge, we got bored and decided to find the apartment
where Eric Severied, the newscaster, was staying. Hunter had
run into him the night before and the dirty old man had asked
him if he knew any chicks. "Do I look like a pimp?" Hunter
kept asking me as we drove from place to place. "I'll throw the
bomb and you keep watch. If anything moves, shoot it," he
instructed me.

Of course, we never killed him. Instead we found a couple
of sisters who thought we were cute and blessed us with their
company until they realized how hopelessly insane we were
when we dropped our fourth cap and lugged in our second
case of beer for the evening's entertainment.

The fourth day of our lost weekend, Sandy, Hunter's wife,
finally kicked us out of the house. I barely recall telling
Hunter he'd be cold wearing only bermudas in New York as he
walked down the gangplank leading to the airplane at the
Aspen airport. Wearing a woman's hat I'd stolen earlier and
carrying a small flight bag with a bottle of Old Fitzgerald and
a '44 magnum, Hunter took the prize. That weekend he flew
off to New York after instructing me to tell Sandy he'd gone to
San Francisco. I didn't see too much of him thereafter. His
wife, naturally, blamed me.

I got a job as a construction worker and cleaned windows
for a couple of weeks. When they fired me, I learned another
trade as a plumber's assistant which I stayed at for a month
until they found out that I wasn't being too careful: The way I
felt, it didn't seem like such a big thing for me to fail to con-
nect those wires between the walls; to fail to screw on the pipe
under the house; to leave a pipe out completely in the attic;
after all, I only neglected to follow the instructions when it
was too hard, when I bruised my knuckles or when I was in a
bad mood.

When the mountains turned to an autumn of yellow and
orange I knew my days were numbered. Feeling serious, one
day I decided it was time to find real work, a job more com-
mensurate with my station in life, as the ads say. I had
stopped looking for chicks. It had become perfectly clear to me
that the pretty blondes simply weren't going to ball me, for
whatever reason. I'd meet many who thought I was super,
particularly when they found out I was really a lawyer and a
friend to Hunter. But they weren't dumb, they could smell my

death coming. They knew, as women always know, that if they made it with me, that in the cold of winter, after I'd split, they'd be marked with the sign of the beast and no white man would have a thing to do with them. So they offered tons of friendship, but no ass. Instead I continued to read and play my clarinet in the woods, and in October I once again put on a suit and a tie.

I went to the office of the district attorney to seek employment, perhaps as a law clerk. He wasn't in. I rode my bicycle to the City Hall where I thought there might be some clerical job. I walked into the wrong office. The Chief of Police told me he had nothing to offer and hinted I could find suitable work in California. I went home, took off my suit and tie and burned them.

That night I went to a bar and the bartender refused to serve me.

"I'm going to put it to you straight, man," he said very dryly. "Just tell me...are you a narc?"

Aspen is the most paranoid town I have ever known. Despite the fact that everyone, including the mayor and the district attorney, is a junkie, they suspect all strangers of being federal narcotics agents. When the stranger is also of a different race, the suspicions turn into conclusions. But what is one to say when asked that stupid question? If you are, you can't admit it; if you're not, they won't believe you.

I laughed at him and walked out. Three bartenders refused me service that night. I bought a bottle, drank it at my pad by myself, and went out to break a few windows just to cool off.

The local head Nazi, Guido, had a sign in his restaurant window. It had annoyed me right from the start, reading: No Beatniks Allowed.

I threw a rock through the thing, took the sign and gave it to a friend at a Halloween party as a going-away present, along with a clipping from the local rag. The Aspen Times quoted Guido to say that "he had been invaded by numerous beatniks." Billy promised to throw it into the middle of the Atlantic on his way to Europe.

The following week Hunter returned and asked me to meet him for drinks. I told him of the paranoia and later he found out that their suspicions were aroused when two local funhogs had seen me going into both the prosecutor's and the

chief's offices that day I had sought serious employment. I
refused to deny the accusation and no longer frequented the
bars. My loneliness increased.

When the snows fell, I cried. It was my first experience
with silent, white death. I roamed the hills and soaked up the
soft wetness of that first snow. I was so taken with the emotion of the snow I called my son, Marco, in San Francisco and
told him to get ready: that I'd be there in a couple of days to
pick him up. Together with a wild Irishman, Tim, the brother
of John, the poet, we raced at a hundred all the way to Frisco
in twenty-one hours and consumed a lid of grass, a fifth of
Scotch, two bottles of wine and several dozen bennies before
we crashed into *Trader JJ's*. Nothing had changed!

After three days in the city, I knew then for sure I'd left it
for good, it seemed so dull. With Marco in the back, we drove
like hell back to Aspen and found a storm waiting for us.
Everything was white. While we were unloading the trailer, a
friend of Tim's came up and told him his house had burned to
the ground while we were away. He went instantly amok and
struck me in the face when I refused to let him drive the car
I'd borrowed.

The last time I saw him, he was running down the alley,
falling in the slick snow, shouting to the heavens with his fist
clenched like King Lear.

My pad in the Aspenleaf Building overlooked the main
drag and up, up to the gargantuan mountain of white that
attracts skiers and their retinue from all over the world. As
the new year approaches, they come in droves and make the
otherwise sleepy town into a Sunday afternoon, pro-football
stadium. Surely the worst of man comes out when he is away
from his home on vacation. The ugly American is ugly even in
America. He dons new clothes, new money and new anticipa-
tions of perversions with the swagger of a man who has
already conquered the native. It does not matter that the
native is of his same class in every respect, the tourist is a
beast, a bore and a barbarian that should be exterminated as
a matter of law.

Drunks, rapists and junkies roamed the street beneath
my window at all hours. On occasions I threw snowballs at
them. But usually, I sat and smoked, listened to records and
read heavily. Dylan Thomas and Konrad Lorenz kept me from
going stir crazy. Lorenz in particular awakened something

within me that had not moved since I had first come in contact with Jesus, some thirteen years before...I began to seriously question my existence, my relation to other life forms and, most importantly, my identity; while all the others, including my son, skied.

I had met an Olympic ski champion from France, known to me only as Frenchy, who got on well with Marco. He taught Marco, who has the guts of the devil himself, in one day the use of the equipment. The second day, according to Frenchy, Marco rode the ski lift to the top of the mountain, reserved only for the experienced adults, and shot himself down the ten-thousand foot expanse with the abandon of a drunken racer. I placed him in a school and before he left, two weeks later, he'd acquired a reputation by and all for himself...a true son of the brown buffalo.

The day before Christmas, I was broke. I had no job. There were no jobs for the likes of me. The snows were falling every day and the muddied streets filled with rich tourists. The few jobs were taken by the locals who had proven themselves in past seasons, or by those who could fit the descriptions in the ads. I was not then, nor have I ever been, "clean-cut." It was simply impossible for me to support myself and my son. The last paycheck I had already given to Marco for his ski lessons and equipment. In desperation, I sent a telegram to a cousin in Los Angeles I'd not seen in ten years. "Held in contempt of court. Thirty days or 150 dollars. Help."

We ate cold cuts and other necessities we both shoplifted. Outside, the icy winds registered twenty below zero. It literally took the wind out of you. It was too cold to walk, my bicycle wouldn't move in five feet of snow, and my car had long since been towed to the dump.

A short, weird friend, Bernard, entertained us with stories of orgies on the high seas in rich men's yachts. He shoplifted toys and taught Marco how to build model racers which he claimed to have driven. Bernard was a versatile man, a man for that season in Aspen: he could do anything with his hands. His mind, like mine, wandered to thoughts of a better life. We stayed up nights planning an escape from the snow. We dreamt of sandy beaches and girls without tops.

One day he had found an ad in a sportsmen's magazine. It advertised the sale of used, rebuilt sailboats somewhere in the Bahamas. Bernard would put a motor on it and we would sail into the sunset of the Caribbean to smuggle and trade with the natives. But first we had to find enough money to get there.

He decided to work as a waiter for a month. I would meet him when we had gathered our resources, and off we'd be to the land of the sun. But I had to wait the will of the gods and find food. The rent I had not paid for two months, so I decided to send Marco back to his mother, wait for the money from my cousin and get through the holidays without completely cracking up. But Marco insisted he remain until the new year, with or without money to spend.

I sat and drank cheap wine I'd stolen, and ate bread and cheese that Bernard had taken from some girl's house, as the hour approached. He had taken Marco into the woods and I remained alone with my records and books and hatred of all I saw from my windows. I could see them frolicking below on the sidewalk in their fur coats and Austrian ski parkas. Their drunken laughter and wild abandon in my hour of need stirred my brain. The entire town was crowded with smartly dressed ski bums, foul-smelling longhairs and plain, old, Okie-looking funhogs. They, together with the rich tourists from throughout the country, took their fun quite seriously at this high-class ski resort hidden high in the Rockies. Drugs and hard rock was their total trip. They were heavily into the hip scene, an amalgam of indifference, non-pain and non-involvement. No one read newspapers: they would never catch themselves watching t.v. or listening to anything but music on the radio...and this was the year of the riots, when the cities began to go up in flames. Theirs was a cool world of white acid and middle-class awareness without knowledge of confusing facts: they romped and fell and stomped and belched with a sense of completeness under powdered snow, slick skis and pretty girls snuggled in bright parkas and colored glasses. I despised them on Christmas Eve of 1967 as I never had before. And I despised myself even more for seeking their company.

But still the word from the gods did not arrive. I could make no decision of what to do, where to go or whom to seek for comfortable companionship. Those I'd known in the summer and fall were now with their own kind on the slopes or in the bars that did not cater to me. Even those who had shown a certain friendship no longer invited me to their parties and merely waved at me if they saw me on the streets. They had simply tired of me, of my calling attention to their predicament and of my foul moods. They denied the issue was race or social class, but only with a word. None would deal with the issues that my simple presence presented: they accepted me, to the extent that they did, simply because I was interesting to have around and to a degree because their idol, the town's super freak, Hunter, had at least taken me on as one of his many competitors for the title.

When Marco returned he brought the message. He told me he wanted to give gifts to certain friends he'd made at the ski school. When I told him I had no money, he simply said, "I can take things without being caught."

With a drunken smile and a stirring of my soul, I said, "Let's go, Chooch. Let's get rid of everything we can get. Let's give away everything we don't need."

We wrapped ourselves in the clothes we'd purchased from the Thrift Shop and went into the streets as thieves. We shoplifted jewelry, trinkets, art objects and various sundry bits of glittering paraphernalia. We returned to the pad, wrapped the gifts and drank more wine. With the madness fully set in my swirling brain, we made the rounds to the homes of persons who had at one time or another befriended us. We gave them rich gifts without value, trips for their memories of wild Indians in the snow. They were embarrassed, of course, for not having thought of us, but the drinks and the drugs calmed us. We went from house to house and the dawn's light found us with our sacks empty and my brain completely shot.

As soon as the stores opened on Christmas Day, we went shopping again. Returning to the apartment to wrap the booty, we saw a delivery truck parked in the alley. Without a word, we both ran, slipped and fell, got up and just as the truck was pulling away, I jumped into the rear and hauled off a case of liquor. Marco quickly covered it with his coat. We carried it to Bernard's and drank good Scotch for an hour. The three of us then filled a five-gallon bucket with a dozen bottles, walked to the main drag in the center of town and stood on the corner like Salvation Army creeps. Whenever we'd see someone who caught our fancy, whether known to us or not, we'd give him a bottle of Scotch. When the bottles were all gone, we went to visit a girlfriend who on occasion had spent some time with us.

We gave Judy a *Magical Mystery Tour* album we'd stolen. Without batting an eye she kissed me and handed me a plug of hashish someone had layed on her earlier. The four of us went to a bar-restaurant for lunch and drinks. Standing in line I saw a recent bald-headed arrival to Aspen who billed himself as a talent scout and cartoonist for *Playboy*. I walked up and handed him a boiled-egg holder, wishing him a happy, etc. We left after a few beers and walked in the now falling snow to a bar while Marco went skiing. The waiter in *The Pub* was perhaps the ugliest Okie I've seen, but an apparently decent fellow. When he brought us our drinks, I felt compelled to give him something for thinking ill of his looks. I reached in my pocket and the plug of hash came out. I slipped it to him with a hearty handshake and he couldn't answer; the hash was worth, perhaps, a hundred dollars. Later he invited us to his house. We left the joint and drove in someone's car to the waiter's house. I was very loaded by this time. We stopped on the way at a liquor store where I bought two cases of short dogs, i.e. pint-sized Thunderbird wine. A party was in progress when we arrived; I gave everyone in the house a pint for Xmas. After an hour or so, we returned to Judy's apartment and I put her to bed.

Walking out, I spotted a communal refrigerator in the hallway. I found two bottles of champagne and two frozen ducks. I took them, and with Bernard still waiting in the car, I ran up the steps to a lawyer's office next door. I had once asked him for a job as a clerk. He was the same one who had suggested I return to California and practice my trade there, if in fact I was an attorney.

I walked hurriedly beyond the secretary's desk, burst into his office and slapped a bottle and a frozen duck in front of him. "Merry Christmas, Lenny," I shouted. His mouth simply stayed open as I ran out.

The last thing I remember is eating the breast of the second duck and talking to Bernard about how much ass we'd get in the Bahamas come spring.

Two days later my parents arrived to take Marco home. Sometime during my drug frenzy I'd called them, and while Marco and I were playing Santa they drove from California to take the kid away from his crazy father. I felt relieved when they drove away, knowing from experience I was in the midst of another crackup. My father just shook his head, and my mother sighed when they saw the completely unkept and almost destroyed apartment.

During the following week, into the new year, I remained constantly and consistently drunk and stoned to the point that it is now impossible to recall any of the events. I search through my notes and my memory, but all I find are glimpses of strange, long-haired people wandering in and out of what became a halfway house, a crash pad for any freak, thug, runaway teenybopper or junkie. I seem to sit in the corner and observe the parade, the charade, the nightmare of strangers in your house, out of control, observing you without a word. It seems that I tolerated them only so long as they kept the drugs coming. Several hard-faced junkies with XKEs and Porsches moved in, bringing methedrine, needles and foulmouthed chicks with them. It seems they wanted me to drive the stolen cars to Mexico, where I told them I could sell them to a smuggler I had met in Aspen. I simply don't remember what happened to them.

To my most humble surprise, I received a telegram with a hundred and fifty dollars. Quickly, I checked the Greyhound and found one leaving for Glenwood Springs within the hour. I bought a ticket and called Sandy, Hunter's wife. I asked her to meet me at the station. When she came, together with their son Juan and their Doberman Pinchers, I gave her the very last of my possessions: A wooden idol, a god of the San Blas Indians of the Caribbean which they'd given me in 1956 when I visited their islands as a friend and Baptist missionary.

"Tell Hunter he'd better have this. He's going to need it more than me if he's to remain here."

She kissed me and the dogs barked. They were the only seriously, decent people I'd known in Aspen on that trip. All the others I condemned for one reason or another that no longer matters, since, as we shall see, I have since returned to take the cup away from him.

I got on the bus and fell asleep immediately. Twenty-four hours later I was in Juárez, Mexico, intent on finding Victor, the Mexican cook I'd worked with in Aspen. He had promised to teach me the smuggling business.

Con Safos 2/7 (1971): 34-46.

DRAFT:
THE REVOLT OF
THE COCKROACH PEOPLE

The week after McIntyre got the ax, I first encountered death as a world of art.

It is early one morning when the family of Robert Fernandez arrives. The sign outside the basement office only announces *La Voz*, but these strangers come in asking for me. Via the grapevine, they have heard of a lawyer who might help them. Nobody else is around. It is just them and me:

"We gotta have somebody to help us, Mr. Brown. The deputies killed my brother."

A hefty woman with solid arms and thick mascara burnt into her skin is talking. She says her name is Lupe. She is the spokesman, the eldest child in a family of nine. The woman beside her is the mother, Juana, an old nurse. Juana is still in shock, sitting quietly, staring at Gilbert's paintings hung on the wall. John, Lupe's husband, sits on her other side. His arms are crossed, bright tattoos over corded muscle. He wears a white T-shirt and a blue beanie, the traditional garb of the *vato loco*, the Chicano street freak who lives on a steady diet of pills, dope and wine. He does not move behind his thick mustache. He too sits quietly, as a proper brother-in-law, a *cunado* who does not interfere in family business unless asked.

"Why do you say they killed your brother?" I ask.

"*Porque son marranos!*" Juana cries out, and then falls back into silence. Aztec designs in black and red meet her glazed eyes.

I ask for the whole story...

Robert was seventeen when the weight of his hundred and eighty pounds snapped the bones and nerves of his fat brown neck. He, too, lived in Tooner Flats, a neighborhood of shacks and clotheslines and dirty backyards. At every other corner, street lights hang high on telephone poles and cast dim yellow glows. Skinny dogs and wormy cats sniff garbage cans in the alleys. Tooner Flats is the area of gangs who spend their last dime on short dogs of T-Bird wine, where the average kid has eight years of school. Everybody there gets some kind of welfare.

You learn about life from the toughest guy in the neighborhood. You smoke your first joint in an alley at the age of
ten; you take your first hit of *caraga* before you get laid; and
you learn how to make your mark on the wall before you learn
how to write. Your friends know you to be a *vato loco*, a crazy
guy, and they call you "*ese*," or "*vato*," or "man." And when you
prove you can take it, that you don't cop to nothing even if it
means getting your ass whipped by some other gang or the
cops, then you are allowed to put your mark, your initial, your
sign, your badge, your *placa* on your turf with the name or initial of your gang: White Fence, Quatro Flats, Barrio Nuevo,
The Jokers, The Bachelors, or what have you. Your write it
big and fancy, scroll-like, cholo print. Graffiti on all the stores,
all the garages, everywhere that you control or claim. It's like
the pissing of a dog on a post. And underneath your *placa*, you
always put C/S, "*Con Safos*," that is: *Up yours if you don't like
it, ese!*

There is no school for a *vato loco*. There is no job in sight.
His only hope is for a quick score. Reds and Ripple mixed with
a bennie, a white and a toke. And when your head is tight, you
go down to the hangout and wait for the next score.

On the day he died, Robert had popped reds with wine
and then conked out for a few hours. When he awoke he was
ready for more. But first he went down to Cronie's on Whittier
Boulevard, the Chicano Sunset Strip. Every other door is a
bar, a pawn shop or a liquor store. Hustlers roam freely across
asphalt decorated with vomit and dogshit. If you score in East
Los Angeles, you score on The Boulevard. Broads, booze and
dope. Cops on every corner make no difference. The fuzz, *la
placa, la chota, los marranos, la jura* or just the plain old pig.
The eternal enemies of the people. The East LA Sheriff's Sub-
station is only three blocks away on Third Street, right alongside the Pomona Freeway. From the blockhouse, deputies
come out in teams of two, "To Serve And Protect!" Always
with thirty-six-inch clubs, with walkie-talkies in hand; always
with gray helmets, shotguns in the car and .357 Magnums in
their holsters.

The *vato loco* has been fighting with the pig since the
Anglos stole his land in the last century. He will continue to
fight until he is exterminated.

Robert had his last fight in January of 1970. He met his
sister Lupe at Cronie's. She was eating a hamburger. He was

dry, he told her. Would she please go to the store across the
street and get him a six-pack on credit? No, she'd pay for it.
Tomorrow is his birthday so she will help him celebrate it
early. Lupe left Robert with friends. They were drinking cokes
and listening to the jukebox. Robert liked mayate music, the
blues. They put in their dimes and sip on cokes, hoping some
broad, a ruka, would come buy them a hamburger or share a
joint with them.

I know Cronie's well. I live two blocks away with three
cousins. I know if you sit on the benches under the canopy
long enough, someone comes along with something for the
evening's action. This time the cops brought it.

By the time Lupe returned with a six-pack, two deputies
were talking with Robert and his friends. It all began, he told
her when she walked up, just because he shouted "Chicano
Power!" and raised his fist.

"The cop told me to stay out of it, Mr. Brown. I told him
Robert is my brother. But they told me to get away or else
they'd arrest me for interfering, you know."

Juana says, "Tell him about the dirty greaser."

"Oh, yes... We know this pig. He's a Chicano. Twice he's
arrested Robert," Lupe says.

"Yes, Mr. Brown!" Juana could not restrain herself. "That
same man once beat up my boy. He came in one day, about a
year ago, and he just pushed into the room where Robert was
sleeping. He dragged him out and they held him for three
days... They thought he had stolen a car... But the judge
threw the case out of court. That pig hated my boy."

Robert had been in jail many times. He's spent some time
at the Youth Authority Camp. But he's been off smack over a
year now. He still dropped a few reds now and then. And yes,
he drank wine.

The cops took him in from Cronie's, they said, to check
him out. They wanted to see if the marks on his arms were
fresh. But anyone could tell they were old.

Lupe appeals to John:

"That's the truth, Brown," the brother-in-law says. "Robert
had cleaned up. He even got a job. He was going to start working next week."

"And we were going to have a birthday party for him that
Friday," Juana says.

The deputies took Robert and told Lupe not to bother arranging bail. They told her he'd be released within a couple of hours. They thought he might just be drunk, but mainly they wanted to check out his arms. They said for her not to worry.

An hour after he was arrested, Robert called his mother. The cops had changed their minds, he said. They had booked him for Plain Drunk, a misdemeanor. The bail was set at five-hundred dollars.

"He told me to call up Maldonado, his bail bondsman. Robert always used him. I could get him out just like that. All I had to do was make a phone call and then go down and sing, you know? The office is just down the street. I didn't even have to put up the house or anything. Mr. Maldonado always just got him out on my word!" the mother cries.

Juana had called the bail bondsman before she received the second call. This time it was a cop. He simply wanted to tell her that Robert was dead. He'd just hung himself. And would she come down and identify the body.

"He was so cold, Mr. Brown. He didn't say he was sorry or anything like that. He just said for me to wait there and he'd send a deputy to pick me up," she says bitterly.

"I went with her," John says. "When we got there I told the man right away that they'd made some mistake. I told him Robert had just called.

"Then they brought in a picture. And I said, '*gracias a Dios*,' I knew him. It wasn't Robert; it was somebody named Sanchez. But that lieutenant said there was no mistake. He said the picture just didn't come out too good... But Juana told him, 'Well, I should know. He's my son.' And I told him Robert wouldn't do a thing like that. He'd never kill himself. He was *católico, Señor Café*. He even used to be an altar boy one time. And he was going to get married, too. He was going to announce it at his party. I talked to Pattie and she told me. She said they were going to get married as soon as he got his first paycheck."

"Pattie is pregnant," Lupe says. "You might as well know, Mr. Brown."

"So what happened after that?" I ask.

"We had the funeral and they buried him last week," Juana says.

Lupe says, "We just got the certificate last night. It says he killed himself. Suicide, it says."

"That's a goddamn lie," John says. "Excuse me... But it is."

"How do you think he was killed?"

"I know," Lupe says. "At the funeral...you tell him, John."

"Yeah, I was there. I saw it."

Doris, another sister, had discovered it. At the funeral, while the others sat and cried, Doris had gone up to get her last look at the body. She bent over the casket to kiss him. Tears from her own eyes landed on the boy's face. She reached over to wipe the wetness from his cheek when she noticed purple spots on the nose. She wiped away the tears and the undertaker's white powder came off his face. It was purple underneath. She called John over and he verified it. They began to look more closely and noticed bruises on the knuckles.

"We told the doctor at the Coroner's Office," John finishes. "But he said not to worry about it. It was natural, he said."

"Anything else?"

"Just what Mr. de Silva told me," the mother says.

"Who's that?"

"You mean...the Andy de Silva? The man who makes commercials? Chili Charlie?"

"Yeah, that's Mr. de Silva."

I know of him. He is a smalltime politico in East L.A., a bit actor in grade-B movies who owns a bar on The Boulevard. And he considers himself something of a spokesman for the Chicano. He served on Mayor Yorty's Chicano Community Board as a rubber-stamp nigger for the establishment. He and his cronies, the small businessmen and a few hack judges, could always be counted upon to endorse whatever program the Anglo laid out for the Cockroaches. He had been quoted in all the papers during our uprising against the Church. He had agreed with the Cardinal that we were all outside agitators who should be driven out on a rail.

"What did Andy say to you?" I ask.

"Well, I don't even know him. I used to go to his meetings for the old people. Anyway, he called me the next day after Robert died. He said, 'I heard about your boy and I want to help.' That's how he started out. I was so happy to get some-

one to help I told him to do whatever he could. He said he was
very angry and he would investigate the case. He said he
would have a talk with the lieutenant and even with the captain if necessary."

"What happened?"

"He called me back the next day. He said he had checked
it all out and that the captain had showed him everything; the
files and even the cell. He said not to make any trouble. That
Robert had hung himself."

"Did he say how he knew about it?"

"Yeah. I asked him that, too," John says.

"He said his nephew was the guy in the cell with Robert."

"His nephew?"

"Yeah, Mickey de Silva... He's just a kid like Robert. He
was in there for something... Anyway, Andy said his nephew
told him that Robert killed himself."

"But we don't believe it," Lupe says fiercely.

"Can you help us, Señor Brown?"

I pick up the phone and dial the office of Thomas
Naguchi, the Coroner for the City and County of Los Angeles.

"This is Buffalo Z. Brown. I represent the family of Robert
Fernandez," I tell Naguchi. "And we want to talk with you
about the autopsy... Your doctor listed it as suicide. However,
we are convinced that the boy was murdered. We have information unavailable to the pathologist conducting the autopsy.
I plan to be in your office this afternoon. I'm going to bring as
many people as I can and hold a press conference outside your
door."

"Mr. Brown. Please, calm yourself. I can't interfere with
the findings of my staff."

"I'll be there around one."

I hang up and tell the family to go home, call all their
friends and relatives, and have them meet me in the basement of the Hall of Justice. They thank me and leave. I then
call the press and announce the demonstration and press conference for that afternoon. I know my man. And since Naguchi
can read the newspapers, my man knows me. The afternoon
will be pure ham.

Naguchi has been in the news quite a bit. He was charged
with misconduct in his office by members of his staff. They
said he took pills, that he was strung out, and hinted that perhaps he was a bit nuts. After the assassination of Robert

Kennedy he allegedly said he was glad Kennedy was killed in his jurisdiction. He was a publicity hound, they contended. He was removed from his position of County Coroner. He hired a smart lawyer and challenged it. The Civil Service hearings were televised. The white liberals and his own Japanese friends came to his defense. He was completely exonerated. At least he got his job back.

A month prior to the death of Fernandez, both the new City Chief of Police, Judd Davis, and the Sheriff of LA County, Peter Peaches, announced they would no longer request Coroner's Inquests. The publicity served no useful purpose, the lawmen stated. Since the only time the Coroner held an inquest was when a law enforcement officer was involved in the death of a minority person, they contended that the inquest merely served to inflame the community. Naguchi made no comment at the time of this statement, although his two main clients were emasculating his office.

When we arrive at the Hall of Justice, the press is waiting. The corridor is lined with Fernandez' friends and relatives. The television cameras turn on their hot lights as I walk in with my red, white and green briefcase, the immediate family at my side.

"Are you making any accusations, Mr. Brown?" a CBS man asks.

"Not now, gentlemen. I plan to have a conference with Dr. Naguchi first, then I'll speak to you."

I hurried into the Coroner's Office. The people shout "Viva Brown!" as I close the door. The blonde secretary tells me Naguchi is waiting for me. She opens the door to his office and ushers me in.

"Ah, Mr. Brown, I am so happy to make your acquaintance."

He is a skinny Jap with bug eyes. He wears a yellow sport coat and a red tie and sits at a huge mahogany desk with a green dragon paperweight. The office has black leather couches and soft chairs, a thick shag rug and inscrutable art work. It seems a nice quiet place. He points me to a fine chair.

"Now, Mr. Brown, I'd like you to read this." He hands me a typed sheet of white paper.

I smile and read the paper.

The Coroner's Office announced today that it will hold a
second autopsy and an inquest into the death of Robert
Fernandez at the request of the family through their attorney, Mr. Buffalo Z. Brown. It will be the first time in the
history of the office that an inquest is being held at the
request of the family.

Thomas A. Naguchi
County Coroner

I looked into the beady eyes of Mr. Moto. He is everything
his men say. "I've been wanting to meet you, sir," I say.

"And I've heard about you, Mr. Brown. You get a lot of
coverage in your work."

"I guess the press is interested in my cases."

"Would you be agreeable to holding a joint press conference?"

"Sir, I would be honored... But one thing... If we have
another autopsy, the body will have to be, uh..." I am coy.

"And who will perform the autopsy?"

"I assume the family will want their own pathologist."

I looked down at his spit-shined loafers. I shake my head
and sigh. "I just don't know... The family is extremely poor."

"I understand, sir. I offer my staff, sir."

"Dr. Naguchi...would it be too much to ask you, personally, to examine the boy's body? I know you are very busy..." It
is my trump card.

"I would be honored. But to avoid any...problems, why
don't I call up the Board of Pathologists for the county. I will
request a panel. Yes, a panel of seven expert pathologists. It
will be as careful and as detailed an autopsy as we had for
Senator Kennedy. And it won't cost the family anything...I
have that power."

I stand up and, walking over to him, I shake his hand.

"Dr. Naguchi, I'll be glad to let you do all the talking to
the press."

"Oh, no, Mr. Brown, it is your press conference."

He calls his secretary and tells her to bring in the boys.
When they arrive with their pads and cameras, he greets
them all by their first names. He is better than Cecil B.
DeMille. His secretary has passed out copies of his statement.
He tells them all where to sit and knows how many lumps of

sugar they want in their coffee. Then he introduces me to them and stands by while I speak.

"Gentlemen, I'll make it short... We have reason to believe that Robert Fernandez died at the hands of another. The autopsy was inconclusive and we have since found some new evidence that was not available to Dr. Naguchi's staff... The Doctor has graciously consented to exhume the body and hold a full inquest before a jury. On behalf of the family and those of us in East L.A. who are interested in justice, I would like to thank Dr. Naguchi."

After the press leaves, I reassure the family and all the arrangements are nailed down.

The following Tuesday, I again enter the Hall of Justice. Above me are Sirhan Sirhan, the mysterious Arab who shot Kennedy, and Charles Manson, the acid fascist. Both await their doom. I am told to go straight down the corridor, turn right and the first door to my left is where I'll find Dr. Naguchi and his seven expert pathologists. The light is dim, the hard floors waxed. Another government building with gray walls, the smell of alcohol in night air.

I open a swinging yellow door and immediately find myself inside a large dark room full of hospital carts. Naked bodies are stretched out on them. Bodies of red and purple meat; bodies of men with white skin gone yellow; bodies of black men with blood over torn faces. This one has an arm missing. The stub is tied off with plastic string. The red-headed woman with full breasts? Someone has ripped the right ear from her head. The genitals of that spade are packed with towels. Look at it! Listen! The blood is still gurgling. There, an old wino, his legs crushed, mangled, gone to mere meat. And there, young boys die too. And there, a once beautiful chick, look at her. How many boys tried to get between those legs, now dangling pools of red-black blood?

Don't turn away from it, god damn it! Don't be afraid of bare-ass, naked death. Hold your head up, open your eyes, don't be embarrassed, boy! I walk forward, I hold my breath. My head is buzzing, my neck is taut, my hands are wet and I cannot look away from the dead cunts, the frizzled balls, the lumps of tit, the fat asses of white meat.

I have turned the wrong way. Backtracking, I find the room with Dr. Naguchi and the experts.

The doctors wear white smocks. They smoke pipes. Relaxed men at their trade. They smile and shake my hand. In front of us, the casket is on a cart with small wheels. On a clean table we have scales and bottles of clear liquid. There are razor-sharp tools, tweezers, clips, scissors, hacksaws, needles and plenty of yellow gloves. The white florescent light shines down upon us. It reminds me of the title of my first book: *My Cart for My Casket.*

"Shall we begin, gentlemen?" Dr. Naguchi asks the experts.

The orderly, a giant sporting an immense mustache, takes a card and a plastic seal from the casket. He booms it out to a gray-haired fag with sweet eyes who sits in a corner and records on a shorthand machine.

"We shall now open the casket, Coroner's Number 19444889, Robert Fernandez, deceased."

We all gather close to get the first look.

The body is intact, dressed in fine linen. Clearly, Robert was a bull of a man. He had big arms and legs and a thick neck now gone purple. Two experts lift the body and roll it on the operating table. It holds a rosary in the hands. The orderly removes the rosary, the black suit, the white shirt, the underwear and brown shoes. The chest has been sewn together. Now the orderly unstitches it. Snip, snip, snip. Holding open the rib cage, he carefully pulls out plastic packages from inside the chest cavity. I hold my breath.

"Intestines." The meat is weighed out.

"Heart... Liver..."

A Chinese expert is making notations of everything. So is the fruity stenographer.

There is no blood, no gory scene. All is cold and dry. Sand and sawdust spill to the table.

"Is this your first autopsy?" a doctor with a Sherlock Holmes pipe asks me. I nod.

"You're doing pretty good."

"He'll get used to it," another one says brightly.

When the organs are all weighed out, Dr. Naguchi says, "Now, gentlemen, where do you want to begin?"

Sherlock Holmes asks, "Are we looking for anything special?"

"Treat this as an ordinary autopsy, Dr. Rubenstein. Just the routine," says Naguchi.

"Circumstances of death?"

"Well, uh...Mr. Brown?"

"He was found with something around his neck."

"Photographs at the scene?"

"No, sir," a tall man from the Sheriff's Department says.

"That's the issue," I say. "The body was found in a jail cell. The Sheriff claims it was suicide... We, however, believe otherwise."

"I see."

"We have reason to believe that the boy was murdered," I say.

"Nonsense," the man from the Sheriff's Department says.

"Now, gentlemen, please..." Naguchi oils in.

Dr. Rubenstein is obviously the big cheese. He comes up to me and says, "You think there was a struggle before death?"

"It's very possible."

He ponders this and then announces: "Gentlemen, we will have to dissect wherever hematoma appears."

"What's that?" I ask.

"Bruises."

I look at the body closely. I noticed purple spots on the face, the arms, the hands, the chest, the neck and the legs. Everywhere. I point to the face. "Could that be a bruise?"

Rubenstein answers. "There's no way to tell without microscopic observation."

"You can't tell from the color?"

"No... The body is going through decomposition and discoloration...purple spots...is normal. You find it on all dead bodies."

"Are you saying we have to cut out all those spots?"

"That's the only way to satisfy your...yes."

"Well, Mr. Brown?" says Naguchi. "Where do you want us to begin?"

I look around at the men in the room. Seven experts, Dr. Naguchi and a Chinese doctor from his staff, the orderly and the man from the Sheriff's...they want me, a Chicano lawyer, to tell them where to begin. They want me to direct them. It is too fantastic to take seriously.

"How about this? Can you look there?" I point to the left cheek.

Without a word, the Chinese doctor picks up a scalpel and slices off an inch of meat... He picks it up with the tweezers and plunks it into a jar of clear liquid.

"And now, Mr. Brown?" says Naguchi.

I cannot believe what is happening. I lean over the body and look at the ears. Can they get a notch from the left one?

Slit-slit-slice blut!...into a jar.

"Uh, Dr. Rubenstein?... Are you sure there's no other way?"

He nods slowly. "Usually, we only try a couple of places... It depends on the family." He hesitates, then says, "Is the case that important?"

"Would you please take a sample from the knuckles... here?"

No trouble at all, man. Siss-sizz-sem...blut, into another jar.

The orderly is precisely labeling each jar. Dr. Naguchi is walking around like a Hollywood mogul. He is smiling. Everything is going without a hitch. He touches my shoulder.

"Just tell us what you want, Mr. Brown... We're at your service."

"Would you please try the legs?... Those big splotches on the left."

"How about the chin?"

"Here, on the left side of the face."

"What's that on the neck?"

"Try this little spot here."

"We're this far into it... Get a piece from the stomach there."

Cut here. Slice there. Here. There. Cut, cut, cut! Slice, slice, slice! And into a jar. Soon we have a whole row of jars with little pieces of meat.

Hrumph! Yes, men? Now we'll open up the head. See where it's stitched? They opened it at the first autopsy. See the sand fall out from the brain area? Yes, keeps the body together for a funeral. No blood in here, boy. Just sand. We don't want a mess. See that little package? That, my lad, is the brain. I mean, it was the brain. Well, actually, it still is the brain...it just isn't working right now. Yes, yes! Now we pull back the head. Scalp-um this lad here. Whoops, the hair, the full head of hair, now it lays back, folded back like a Halloween mask so we can look into the head...inside, where the stuffings for the...Jesus H. Christ, look at those little purple blotches... You can tell a lot from that, but you got to cut it out... Then cut the fucking thing out, you motherfucker! This ain't Robert no more. It's just a...no, not a body...body is a whole...this is a joke... Cut that piece there, doctor. Please!

Uh oh! Now we get really serious. If he died of strangulation... We'll have to pull out the...uh, neck bone. Go right ahead, sir! Pull out that goddamn gizzard.

Uh, we have to...take the face off first.

Well, Jesus Christ, go ahead!

Slit. One slice. Slit. Up goes the chin. Lift it right up over the face...the face? The face goes up over the head. The head? The head is the face. Huh? There is no face!

What do you mean?

The face is hanging down the back of the head. The face is a mask. The mouth is where the brain... The nose is at the back of the neck. The hair is the ears. The brown nose is hanging where the neck... Get your goddamn hand out of there.

My hand?

That is the doctor's hand. It is inside the fucking face.

I mean the head.

His hand is inside. It is pulling at something. What did he find in there. What is it?

He's trying to pull out the...if we put it under a microscope, we'll be able to make some strong findings. It's up to you...

Slice, slice, slice... No dice.

"Give me the saw, please."

The goddamn face is gone; the head is wide open; no mouth, nose, eyes. They are hanging down the back of the neck. God! With hammer and chisel in hand, the Chinese doctor goes to town. Chomp, chomp, chomp... Hack, hack, chuck, chud, chomp!

Ah! Got it!

Out it comes. Long, gizzard looking. Twelve inches of red muscle and nerve dripping sawdust. Yes, we'll dissect this old buzzard, too.

How about those ribs? You want some bar-b-que ribs, mister?

Sure, ese. Cut those fucking ribs up. Chomp 'em up right now!

"How about the arms? Is there any question of needle marks?"

Yes, they'll claim he was geezing. Cut that arm there. Put it under your machine and tell me later what I want to hear. Tell me they were old tracks, you sonofabitch... And try the other one.

Why not? The body is no more.

Should we try the dick?

What for? What can you find in a peter?

Maybe he was raped, for Christ's sake. Or maybe he raped someone. How should I know? I just work here.

I see the tattoo on his right arm... God Almighty! A red heart with blue arrows of love and the word "Mother." And I see the little black cross between the thumb and the trigger finger. A regular *vato loco*. A real *pachuco, ese*.

And when it is done, there is no more Robert. Oh, sure they put the head back in place. They sew it up as best they can. But there is no part of the body that I have not ordered chopped. I, who am so good and deserving of love. Yes, me, the big chingon! I, Mr. Buffalo Z. Brown. Me, I ordered those white men to cut up the brown body of that Chicano boy, just another expendable Cockroach.

La Gente (November-December 1973): 4-5, 12.

TO WHOM IT MAY CONCERN
[A Solicitation]

I am paralyzed. I've heard the electrification and cannot move from my desk. I try to think, but all that happens is a conglomeration of horses running in circles immediately above my head, about four inches above. They go nowhere. They merely circle to confuse.

They've all ran out. I'm the last to leave. I've sat here for a full minute trying to set my circles straight, while outside my window on the seventh floor the wail of the siren rolls wave-like over the tall concrete structures. All is sound out there. The commotion awaits my movement. The world enveloped in electrical confusion is divesting itself of humanity, and every mass and all energy shrieks as if above the feathered white streaks a huge ear can receive them. What a childish fantasy! There is neither color nor voice to still the pandemonium, wild now in permanent gray.

Within the past hour, before we were electrocuted, before the first Conalrad, I told my son, "I'll bring you a present tonight."

"A brake, dad. And a cable-car hat. A big one."

"A brake? What's a brake?" I asked.

"To stop the cable cars. A brake," he said in his condescending manner of speaking to me. He has yet to learn that humans cannot so perfectly communicate. He is impatient. He has much to learn.

He wants a big one. He is still a child; five years has he loved me 'best', and I him. "Make it a big one," were his last words. Even with imminent destruction outside, irony curves my mouth...just the corners, lightly and immediately for a moment.

We have all awaited those waves, the idiots' panacea, that now mount and no longer crest. For He had electrified us; some by ears, some by eyes, none by the flesh. We all knew! He told us enough times. They both told us many times. They electrified us through ears and eyes many times. Their men told us to prepare; they warned us even as the prophets of old warned men of the death surely to come. And we, like the men of old, heard the words, understood the words, believed the words, but because we could not feel the words, because there was no precedent in the whole of human experience, we did not move...except to continue Their power. We are totally unprepared.

As I leave my concreted prison wherein I have worked at some salvation all the days of my life, I cannot see any one thing in the streets. For there are no colors to serve as background and thus my perception is flattened. But even if there were colors, how could I perceive, how could I comprehend the movements of electrified gigantic ants, flurried as they are helter-skelter away from what each thinks is point-zero? How is a man who is accustomed to what until now had posed as seeming orderliness to act?

Things curse and things shout, they strike me, they kick me, willy-nilly they run like idiots chased by spitting snakes. Do they cry? They think they cry, for water cannot be found to moisten them where their eyes once were. But do I deceive myself? If I misjudge, it is not out of hostility, for truly I would that enough water were created by them to drown the fireball that surely will fall within the hour. But all I can see is a grayish dryness, mouths agape grasping a moisture not to be found in the air here.

I am struck. I have fallen. I raise myself and my hand slides on spittle. I am kicked down again. I arise and continue my journey to my son without panic. This I had prepared for myself. I had refused to heed the warning, not out of laziness, but because I did not believe them, for I most certainly did; but I did not act because to do so would have been my suicide, for I would then have been still-dead, and it was necessary for me to live, if not for myself, for my son. But I most certainly prepared myself not to panic, for in the end, I reasoned, the only preparation that can possibly have absolute effect without death is to prepare oneself not to panic at the day of point-zero.

I edge through the alleys. My son awaits me. The cars have now taken to the walkways for feet, but it is foolish for they cannot budge the hordes of ants. They try to be bulldozers and snowplows. They make their cars as tanks in battle. They plow through the ants, but they cannot budge them, there are too many. They will kill all even before the fireball falls. Fools!

Every horn in every car shrieks. The ants aim into the streets like salmon rush headlong into the rapids. I have in as many minutes seen ten ants squashed, their packages and purses still clutched to their breasts like the Egyptians entombed. But I have seen no blood for the same reasons I see no tears; the liquid gushing on the concrete is like all else...gray.

In their confused foolishness I see some awaiting a bus, their necks stretched angrily at the massive front of autos. They look to the sky. I am proud of my behavior. I have not once lifted my head, for I know the fireball will fall upon all of us...none shall escape the wrath to come!

In fifteen minutes I have seen and felt and been touched by more death and blood and arms askew than in a whole war. And this war has not yet formally begun. In His electrification message to us it was announced: The dangers of which I have on numerous occasions spoken of are at hand, people of Amerika... Prepare now for invasion... All units have been alerted to retaliate... But I am, however, hopeful that...

The ants who remained to hear Him out will die.

The law of probability is dead. It no longer is. This law which is a basic assumption (so basic that it is a law of all behavior, physical, social and psychological) no longer exists. It has never occurred to anyone to plan, to build or to live without this most fundamental of assumptions in operation, else all would have been chaos even as the world now is. To see it now inoperative in the social and psychological behavior of ants is more provocative than to see the law of gravity without effect; for our generation has lived to see the moons conquered and controlled. But it is not until now that we have seen the simple phenomena of fear terminate the basic control of behavior in humans... Simple at birth but years in gestation, for Those Two conceived in narcissism and over the years nurtured Their mania of the ego to perpetuate their sinful conception of whoredom and have now given birth to the devil of fire that already is eating my brain. My heart of flesh died when the electrification commenced.

The sirens, the bells, the whistles, the horns, the screams and the shouts cannot be less terrible that the weeping and wailing and gnashing of teeth awaiting us all. There is not one good ear in the city and surely there is not one calm and conscious nerve in the entirety.

The man ran the stairs and pushed himself against the door. The boy sat surrounded by toys. He smiled quietly at the father.

"Dad, my Nana left. What are those foghorns? Is it New Year?" He held a red crayon in his little and long hand.

The man rushed to the clothes bureau and jerked the drawer open throwing things into a leather pouch.

"Federico, hurry, get a knife...get a knife and... From the kitchen get a knife. Run!" He could not coordinate his slow, faltering speech with his wild bodily movements.

"But, dad..."

"Hurry! I'll tell you about it later. But hurry for now!"

The man stuffed a can of milk and a bag of raisins into the pouch. The fantastic din reached through the red velvet curtains, reverberating against the glass elephants on a shelf, tinkling them one against the other. Doors crashed against walls. There was no resolution of closed doors to quiet the logically oriented mind.

The man took the boy's hand and ran out of the building.

The sky was ominous with white vapor splintering at the edges like plumes, softly melting together because there were an abundance.

They ran the hill and others ran around them. The boy fell and the man did not wait to apologize. He dragged his hand as if it were the furled mouth of a burlap sack.

Down the hill they ran and he quickly was thankful for the cobblestone. The pouch shot out of his hand. He could not stop in time. He kicked it and they both fell. The boy's mouth spouted blood. He screamed and lay on his back. The man brushed his own elbow, wiping the blood on his lap.

"You son of a bitch!" He belched at the sky with uplifted arm. He thought to himself, I must be still; each and every man if he is to live must find his own silence even in the turmoil lest he die before his turn.

He lifted the boy and took off his belt. He tied the belt around his back and hung the pouch from it. He squatted and motioned to the boy to climb on his back. The boy closed his eyes in shame. He carried him and felt his son's hot tears and thick blood on his neck.

"Federico, be a big boy. A real big boy. Please," he implored as he held the cold pipe railing with one hand, climbing down the steps leading to the wharf.

The boy reached his head around his father's and said looking from around, "Why are we running, dad? Is there a fire? Is that it, dad?" The boy almost cried begging for an answer.

"As soon as we get to the beach I'll tell you, son. Now we have to hurry. We're going to the beach... You remember those caves we found by the bridge?... Remember that time we were fishing?..."

"But why so fast, dad? I don't see any fire engines or fire."

The boy touched the man's cheek. The man pressed his hand on the boy's hand and wanted to lick it.

The bay was green and gray and filled with craft. Loudspeakers bellied electrified messages to the private craft putting out, ordering them to clear the way for the warships destructive and fearful in their very color and shape. Even the boats were crashing into one another.

Foghorns and ships' bells and electrified voices vied against themselves in their echoes, all at their optimum to be understood. But none listened to the other. Each with their own salvation at hand struggled for as many right of ways as there were heavens in mind. Even as it had been written at the beginning of the century, all turned their bows to the mother of us all... the sea.

The man's feet sunk in the white-brown sand. He kneeled and the boy jumped to the sand he loved so well and without hesitation picked up a handful. The man wiped the boy's lips and chin clean of blood.

"Now, Federico... Now we must run to the bridge. I want you to run all the way. We can't stop. We have to get there before... Son, there is a war. An airplane is coming to drop a bomb... Do you understand?"

"Why, dad? What did we do?" he asked simply, his face brown like the sand at his feet. His tears had caked his cheeks. His hair was short, like bristles of brown fur, and his eyes squinted with the devil while his thin lips parted, sardonically showing wisps of irony enameling his square white teeth. His forehead wrinkled much too dark for a boy five-years old and the hairline was of a grandfather rather than of a grandson.

"I'll tell you the whole story when we get to the caves, son... Now we must run."

He took the boy's hand and squeezed it, remembering the many times they had raced on this same beach when the fog crowded at the water's edge like a jealous neighbor hiding his garden of roses behind a tall fence.

The boy jerked his hand away. "Will you promise to tell me the whole story—big—dad?"

"Yes, Federico, I promise. But run now."

The boy's eyes twinkled showing his profound maturity in their squint. "Do you want to race, pop?"

The man tightened his teeth and cursed the world. Immediately he was forced to return to the here and now by his son's challenging sarcastic eyes. The man closed his eyes, saying to himself quietly: This is my last time to calm myself. After this one time I must think nothing of it; it will only slow me and thus hurt him.

He shot his eyes open and shouted to the green water with all his force, "Fuck you, Mack!"

Before the boy could question the outburst, the man shoved his right foot before him as if to cheat on the starting gun. With his teeth showing like white tombstones, he said, "If I beat you, you have to tell me the whole story."

They ran around the people who were now rushing away from the beach to the wharf. The warships had fired warnings into the clouds to muscle their orders, and thus in fear and anger they ran like frightened ants escaping the onslaught, screaming and cursing and menacing their fists to the gray ships.

But the bomb fell on the city before the boy and his father reached the caves. The boy beat the man because a log for tying ships splintered like dry straw and cut across the man's right leg.

Before he fainted he hobbled into the cave with the boy, whose nose immediately poured blood when the sky turned black.

When he awoke he saw the boy's face white and yellow with blood freely flowing over his mouth around the corners of his sardonic lips. The eyes still naturally sarcastic stared at the man.

"I guess we didn't make it, son. We didn't run fast enough... Or the plane just flew faster than we ran."

"Dad, my ears hurt. I have sand in my eyes." But the boy would not cry. He belched and then vomited without warning on the man's waist.

I know that the fireball has now burned the city. I know. I guess His hopes were not hopeful enough. I wonder what happened to Them. I wonder if they are in caves like we are? Was it all as colorful as the slick beautiful pictures in Life magazine? Probably not. That's a camera seeing. Eyes, those that remain at last, see nothing. I've not seen a color since the electrification... Damn!

I lay dying and my son is dying before my very eyes and I make jokes. Is my brain all burned out? I wonder if all the loudspeakers and all the sirens were electrocuted to death? I hope so, those god-damned, noisy things bursting eardrums! They must have been. I can't hear a thing. Or have I lost my ears, too?

Here big boy Federico is puking his little brown stomach onto mine and I cannot move to keep myself clean, as if it really mattered... Those crazy, stupid bastards!

But I must hurry. I must tell him the story before I faint again. For when the darkness cuts me off again it will be forever this time.

I didn't think we had so much blood between us, he and I. Maybe those stories I told him about our kingly blood were true, there seems to be so very much of it. A billion years it took to produce this blood of ours... Fornication after fornication, food upon food and water and air and work and play, sex and love, birth and death and marriage and adultery and books and schools and beautiful thoughts and kindly pictures and now in a second, in the twinkling of an eye, it's all destroyed. World, dear sweet, crazy world! Whatever possessed you to perpetrate such idiocy upon yourself? You've consumed yourself, perversion that you are. It's unimaginable. Your crime is the greatest since the creation. It is our original sin made anew.

But, Oh dear God, I must talk to my big boy before I die, before he dies.

The man groaned and vomited. He could control neither his bowels nor his bladder and so his clothes darkened with feces and urine. He sat in his dung like a lamb before the slaughter. Each breath burst hot needles in his heart and he knew the boy suffered the same agonies.

"Federico, can you hear me?" The man coughed in his blood.

The boy nodded, his forehead brooding and black with blood now.

"Do you still want the story? Or shall you tell it?"

The boy nodded again. "But I beat you, dad." The boy in a super-human effort reminded the man. "You promised you'd tell me if I won."

"Son, the bomb fell...I am very sick...I told you before about dying. Remember all the things I told you about dying, son?"

The boy raised his hand to his nose and wiped away a handful of clotted blood. "I didn't think it was like this, dad."

The man belched and vomited again. "Son, it didn't have to be like this. I didn't want it like this for you."

"You said there was nothing bad about it, dad...I don't like this. I'm too hot and it hurts inside my head. I feel a fire in my eyes, dad."

"Son, oh, son...I meant death, after you die. There is nothing bad after. It was against religion I taught you. I meant to tell you it is a sleep without dreams. Not even good ones. It's just a simple and prolonged sleep. There is no pain... It is the dying that hurts, that we have reason to fear... Son, my blood is about all gone. If I faint again before you do... If I go to sleep... Son..."

⌒

What can a father do? If I die before I wake, what then? What of him?... Jesus, what shall I do? I can't leave him all alone, can I? A man cannot know if his son lives after he dies. How long can he live? A minute more? An hour? A day? Then what? Have I the right, the power? Can I really kill him to save him? Would that he would kill himself after my death if he suffered. But children know nothing of death, or suicide. It is only men that kill, that seek out death. Children want life, to them it is good. Children destroy, but they do not kill. This is their purity, their innocence. Their destructiveness men confuse with their own evil, but in truth their destructions are but the smoking and drinking of men who also need a way out.

Now the time has come for death, which I do not fear. But how can I die unfearful knowing that he still lives in his suffering, knowing he will be frightened to death if he has to stay with a dead body after the sun sets. Can a child of five wander into the darkness alone with only the light of a burning city to find his way? Surely he will die very soon. Either of radiation or of starvation or of fear, but die he must because Those Two have lost themselves in delirium.

What then shall a father do? Of a truth it is better put:

Greater love has no man than to take another's life whom he loves!

—

The man spoke softly to his son. "Federico, give me the bag, the knife is in the bag."

The boy vomited blood with yellow bile on the blade as he put it in his father's hand.

"Son, Federico, my big boy... I will faint and die very soon. I must do something first because it will be too late after. I have told you many times that death is nothing. It is only the dying that we fear and that because it is the only thing that hurts, that we do not understand. And I have told you that to kill is bad because no man should take away that right which each man holds as his own. It is only the killer that suffers after the death... Federico, try to feel my words... Soon all the pain will be gone..."

"Oh, I don't think so, Manuel... I hurt too much," the boy cried in his pain.

"Son, if I die before you, then you will be alone... I believe it would be better for you if you went with me."

"Where, dad? I'm too sick to move. I want to sleep. I hurt very much inside my face." The boy held his stomach and his throat gasped seeking wind to push up what remained of the bile burning brightly within his once brown stomach, now white- and yellow-blotched.

"Son, I believe if I die you should... You would be better with me. You can't live by yourself. No one can do that. You're very sick, you cannot remain alone... Do you understand?"

The boy shook his head slowly. Blood dripped from his eyes. He rubbed it into his now completely red face.

"Father, please help me. I hurt, I hurt all over... Please, father, please make me feel good," the boy cried.

The man stretched his hand around the boy's neck and brought him on his chest. He pressed his lips on the prickly brown head and licked it with his warm tongue.

The boy turned his face to his father. His eyes were now completely filled with red blood.

"Father, please, please...I can't see. It is so dark and cold... Please, dad, save me."

"Federico, be a big boy for the last time now. I love you, my wonderful son."

The father killed his son and died himself before he could cry for his boy's death.

[After 1966]

THE WORM DIETH NOT

I

"Hey, you, what the hell you doing here?" The man yelled as he rushed to the boy.

"Turning a bolt. Why?" The boy smiled before the man reached him. When the boy had entered the barn to prepare the tractor for the day's run, he had heard rats scampering in the rafters and among the ladders against the walls. When he heard the scampering of their tiny feet he whistled at them to warn them, to shoo them further back into the rafters where the spiders had spread their work intricately from rafter to rafter.

The boy smiled now because the short man's feet scuffling on the cement floor as he rushed toward him reminded him of the rats scampering among the ladders.

The man grabbed the wrench from the boy's hand.

"What you mean, 'why?' I'm asking you what you doing around here. Who told you to mess with this here tractor?"

"Mess? I have to get the tractor ready for work. Mr. Preston always wants the tractor checked before it goes out into the field."

"Look here, you. I told you yesterday Preston don't live here no more. I'm the boss here now. I ain't told you to do nothing round here. So you got no business messin' round here. You just turn yourself right around and go through that door and be on your way."

Fernando Garcia, the boy, wiped his hands on a rag. "Mister, I don't know who you are and it seems you don't know who I am. I do know that Mrs. Preston, who happens to own this ranch, told me to start work today. So if you got some gripe, why don't you go see her. I have work to do." He reached for the wrench the man was holding. The man drew it away.

"I guess you just don't savvy English, do you, Mex?" He grabbed the boy's arm and began pushing him. "When I say get, I mean get!"

Fernando Garcia crushed the toe of the man's boot with the heel of his brogan.

He screamed and dropped his hands as the boy ran for the door. The man flung the wrench at him. It hit the door as the boy rushed through.

"You greaser, you better run! Don't let me catch your black butt round here no more!" The man yelled after him, his weight on his left leg, his right foot barely touching the cement.

The woman, tall in black slacks, opened the door for him. When the woman saw the boy's lower lip protruding and covering the upper one, she remembered that the previous day she had said to him, "Why Fernando, each summer when I see you for the first time, you look more and more like your father," whereas now he looked only like Fernando, the boy, the young, silent, black-haired, black-eyed Mexican boy, furious now in his silence. He followed her into the house without a word.

"What's the matter? You look mad enough to kill." Then she smiled. "Or has someone tried to kill you?" The words came out slowly, fully pronounced. Her long legs, seeming more extended now by the black slacks she wore, moved always with deliberation, with precision.

"I was getting the tractor ready for work when that man, the short one with the stupid moustache, told me to get out."

"Damn! I forgot. It's my fault, Fernando. I forgot to tell him about you yesterday. I'm sorry." She saw his annoyed expression become a smile and she thought that she would like to touch his cheek.

The five hollow tubes painted gold (the boy had seen them when he entered) sounded their chord. "I guess that's him," she said. They met him at the door.

He was short and thin, but he gave the appearance of being fat. A thin, reddish moustache hung from under his nose. His hair was beginning to thin; the boy could see the man's scalp. It was a colorless blond, with vitality, like a child's watercolor painting of the sun.

The woman nodded her head. "The boy already told me. I'm to blame, I guess; I should have told you yesterday. He came to see me after you had told him about Mr. Preston no longer being here, and I gave him the job. You see, he's worked for me for such a long time, I guess I think of him as being part of the place." She smiled, as if the matter were settled. The man did not return the smile.

Each was waiting for the other to speak. Finally the foreman spoke. "Well, ma'am, it's like this: I done hired me a driver already. Fact is, I hired him over a week ago. Now I've known this driver for quite a spell. I know what he can do; I know what he will do." His eyes had not once glanced to the boy since he had entered.

"But you see, Bill, he's worked here for ten years." She thought for a moment before she continued. "You can give some other job to your friend."

"Well, I don't rightly know, ma'am. I done told him to start tomorrow; ain't no need to start today anyhow."

"Can't you see him and tell him there's been a change?"

"It ain't that, ma'am; question is, what would I tell him? That the job's been given to...someone else?"

"Well, what are we to do?" Although she looked at both of them, she was not really saying that to them, to either of the two. She had lived long enough in this valley to know what the man meant, but had not said. She really meant, "What are we to do?" Her husband, the one who was no longer there, had told her, "I can trust them; that's why I hire them." And yet, she had thought during the winter months, he ran off with one! She had heard men speaking in bars; you can't trust them anymore, they're getting too big for their own good; specially them dark ones. Just look at their eyes, a white man can never tell what they's thinking...yeah, you got to watch out for them, they'll rob you blind...and they sure is lazy, that's why they need a siester...far's I'm concerned they's stupid, that's why they can't learn American.

Not that she was actually thinking of all these things now, but she had heard these same things over and over until she did not have to think of them specifically, the mere presence of the foreman was enough. With her eyes she asked the boy the question again. She thought it strange now that she had not thought of the boy or his father during the winter months when the fog crept around the walled garden and the owl hooted in the orchard after her husband had left her, running away with the Mexican woman.

"Well, ma'am, if you want to know, I'll tell you the truth."
There was a certain sobriety in the man's entire composure.
One could not tell which way he was looking. His eyes seemed
to have no direction, though they were open wide and staring
forward.

"Now, I don't mean anything personal, but it's just that I
always found it best to work with people of my own race. I just
get along better with them. I can understand them, I can
depend on them. As I said, there's nothin' personal, but to be
honest with you, I can trust them, that's all." He stopped and
took a breath. "Now I don't know this here boy; he probably is
a good worker. I hear that many of them is good workers, but
I just prefer to work with my own people."

*

Without knowing it, and without willing it, the boy's face
concentrated on the man's boots that were brilliant and pointed like plow blades. He was conscious of their heaviness, as if
they wanted to close. Within his body he felt an emptiness, a
longing that ached to be filled...

*

Shouts, laughter, whistles and chaotic sounds made havoc
of the acoustics in the auditorium. Teachers with notebooks
ran from one side of the room to the other while the orchestra
was practicing "Pomp and Circumstance"... A woman raised a
megaphone. She told the boys to assemble at one end of the
hall and the girls at the other end. They laughed and pushed,
for it was all a game to them. Still holding the funnel to her
mouth, she told them to arrange the tallest at one end and the
shortest at the other, graduating from one extreme to the
other. After many arguments, and near fights, the noisy group
settled the important things: it was to stand for the record
that so and so was taller than so and so, because Miss Gardner, the teacher, whose body pleaded for a girdle, (it would
have been to her advantage, for when she walked in the halls
the boys crowded against the walls and snickered. She did not
know that they were laughing at her pot belly which supported two unnecessarily long breasts) had stood him to the right
of this one or to the left of that one.

"That's it. Now all the boys walk straight ahead and take the girl that is directly in line with you. Yes, yes, that's it, the tallest with the tallest and the shortest with the shortest."

It was easier for the boy to believe in a miracle than simply a coincidence. That he should be paired with Gretchen, the freckle-faced German girl who had shared her lunch basket with him during the annual school picnic, was more than just a coincidence; it was a miracle! But before he could speak to her a complete silence closed on the group like a lid. The band still played, but the graduating grade-school students held their tongues. The principal had entered and was talking to the teachers, who had rushed to him the moment he set foot in the door. He spoke to them and then left as suddenly as he had entered.

Miss Gardner raised the megaphone to her mouth once again. In a normal tone, for she was also the drama teacher, she said, "Excuse the interruption, children. Let me see now, we want to get this just right. Uh, Pablo, you trade with Billy, you're a little tall for Shirley...yes, that's better. And, Marco, I think you're more Rosario's size. Why don't you trade with, let me see, Freddy...yes, that'll be closer to it." The boy, Fernando, still lost in the thrill of the miracle, was not aware of the list; that is, he was not conscious of it, but he sensed it. And finally she called his name. He was told to march with Josephina; and the emptiness in his body was filled: there was room for a bull, but not even a single ant could crawl into it.

The boys who had been asked to change marching partners knew that Miss Gardner would never make a movie actress, even though the rumors said that she had already had offers. These same boys also knew that they could not say so much as one word, for to do so would be an insult to their partners, the girls whom they would marry someday, the girls who would become women and give them many sons. These same girls they would someday ask, "Remember when we had to march together because old man Wilkie told Miss Gardner?"

~~~

The boy looked at the woman and wondered if she were going to give him the job; the job that had been his for so long.

The woman said to the foreman, "If that's the way you feel, I suppose that's your business. All I know is that I already promised Fernando a job. I just don't know what to do about it." They had not moved from the entrance hall. Empty vases stood in the corners; someone, or something, had painted them carelessly. The boy looked at the two vases. He had not yet spoken.

"I'll tell you what I'm goin' to do. Now I ain't goin' to hire none 'cept my own, but since you already promised him a job, I'll back down this once and let him have one. He can pick the fruit."

"Oh, no, we can't do that. I promised him the job on the tractor; it's been his job for seven years. I don't know what to do... What do you think, Fernando? Would you like to try picking this summer?"

He stood with his feet apart, for support. When she spoke he looked up, but only for a moment; he did not want them to see the emptiness that he felt. Because his skin was like the desert sand, they could not know that he was blushing. If it was to be seen, they would have to look for it in his eyes. They became like little almonds from their heaviness...

≈

"Would you like to stand next to Josephina? I think you're just a trifle too tall for Gretchen," Miss Gardner said.

"Are you Spanish, little boy?" Two old women had picked him up once when he was thumbing a ride and had asked him that question. "Oh, you're Mexican. Well, how nice! My daughter has a Spanish lady that helps her around the house. She makes the best food! Why, you know, you speak English so well, one would think you were an American. I've always said I wished I could speak two languages."

Although the boy was only ten years of age, he knew it was not a question. He felt compelled to pretend that a question had in fact been asked. This pretension, or rather his disgust for pretension, is what now made him spread his legs apart for support. If he were sitting, he would clench his fists for the same reason.

≈

"Well, what do you say?" The foreman looked at the boy for the first time. "'Course it's harder than driving, but a good man can make himself some money if he works. 'Course there's some people that are just too soft to pick, but it's up to you's far's I'm concerned."

"It's picking them here or picking them somewhere else. I'll pick peaches here." He rubbed his palms with his thumbs.

The woman saw him looking down at his hands. "What is it, Fernando?"

"Nothing," he said. He let them fall.

The woman squinted her eyes. Then she threw her head back.

"Oh, I forgot! It's your hands," she said.

"What's the matter with his hands?" the foreman asked.

"Nothing! I said nothing is the matter with my hands," Fernando Garcia said.

"But why not?" Mrs. Preston said. "It is something. I forgot all about that. Oh, my God, what'll we do? Why didn't you say something? He's a musician, Bill. He plays the guitar. They have to be very careful with their hands. Their fingers have to be very good."

~~~

When she and her husband bought the ranch, she made a vow. She did not tell him of her vow. She had said she would work in the field for ten years, then she would retire to the quiet of her house. Each summer, when the heat became unbearable, she would remind herself of her vow. Each winter as they waited to see if the frost would damage their crop, she told herself that it would not be this way always. This secret vow of hers is what gave her the courage to continue working alongside her husband even though they had no life together. But those ten years left their mark. When they passed, she found that they had left her tired. These ten years were the cause for the feeling of tiredness that came over her when she looked in the mirror, or when she read the magazines; the magazines with the pictures of young girls wearing tight-fitted dresses, their eyes accented with blues, their eyelashes long and perfect. Even the words in the ads made her feel the tiredness of the ten years of work in the orchards. She read them after her husband had fallen asleep. Once, when they were first married, he caught her reading and said to her, "Jesus, ain't it too late to be dreaming?"

One year led to two and then to three, and on to ten. And her one consolation, her great compensation for her husband's insult, was that now she could be those things that she had read about, that she had dreamed of throughout that ten-year period when her only hope was her secret vow.

The same winter that he left she began to use their shampoos, their creams, their paints. She was wearing the dresses already this summer, and had ordered more. The house had been painted and redecorated that spring. Even the cars that the models sat in, even this she had already acquired. She pulled the skin back under the eyes when she looked in the mirror. With patience, with care, she massaged the pink lotions into her face. The plucking of the hair under the lip and above the lip, the new brassieres, the new hair styles, all these things had already begun before this present summer. She had said that she would leave all the work to the foreman; now she would retire to her house. Now she would rest and enjoy the life she had been unable to while her husband had lived with her. He had been so blunt about things that she could not enjoy life, she could never relax, she could never feel free of his critical eye, his mocking speech. He was as brutal as he was blunt. He always hid his thoughts from her, he would not speak to her about what he thought, what he felt. Instead, with an animal indifference, he grabbed her, as a drunk grabs a prostitute, and he kissed her and bit her, even as a rapist does his victim. If only once he had mentioned the word love, then she might have excused him. But because he neither mentioned it, but rather mocked the idea, nor even stopped to think of it, she was left with only her tiredness and her secret vow. When she faced the mirror, naked and alone, she gazed at her body as if it were a thing apart from her, a thing unbelievable. When she saw the brown curls of hair pressed against the white bathtub, the hair which plugged the pipes when it collected in a dirty ball, she knew then without question that she hated the whole idea. Her husband would crawl into bed, still smelling of the fields, and would breathe deeply, tired and indifferent. Then without a word he would pounce on her. The cigarettes he smoked left a stain on his fingers and on his tongue; a brown, or a dirty yellow. Once she asked him to wash his mouth before he came to bed. He replied, "You shit don't smell good neither!" When it had ended, he would jump from the bed and run to the bathroom, there to scrub himself. She would sit on the bed and think of the boys whom she used to beat in horseshoes when she was a girl; the young boys whom she had joked with, before whose eyes she wagged her tail. The blonds and the redheads, the ones with horses and the ones with motorcycles. The very same ones whom she laughed at when they undressed behind the trees, their buttocks showing. Her husband would always be asleep, and snoring, when she returned from the bathroom.

"His hands!" Before the obnoxious laugh burst forth, for one single second, there came to the foreman's face an expression of incredulity; a sober, serious, blank look that was broken when the air gushed out from his mouth.

The boy and the woman waited for the laugh to cease. Their eyes were fixed together. They could not move so long as he laughed, as if he had jelled them.

"Shut up, Bill! Shut your damn mouth!" She wanted to, with one slash, with one great sweep of her hand, clear the whole of her thoughts.

"What do you mean? What do you mean, 'shut up?'"

"Just that! Shut up! I've had enough! The boy will pick the peaches, if he wants to, that's all."

"Well, ma'am, I don't appreciate no one tellin' me to shut up."

"Forget it, we've said enough. I said he can pick if he wants to."

And with that the boy nodded his head and walked out of the hall. He looked at the empty, still vases in the corner and wondered why they had been painted at all. His waist, thin as a young girl's, remained almost static, while his legs followed the direction of his feet.

"Well?" she asked him.

"Nothing, ma'am. I guess I'll be going now." He walked behind the boy and stood smiling as he saw him drive away in his Model A.

He had told the men at the bar, "Don't you worry none, her well ain't gone dry yet. It's been a long time between drinks for her, just you give me a little time." They laughed when he told them that; they shook their heads and rubbed their chins. He lived in a cabin behind her house. The previous night he had seen her through the window. As she stood above the sink, rubbing the creams into her face, wearing only a white slip, the blood in his body rushed to his stomach. His hands were clenched and he thought of knocking, but he could think of nothing to say to her if she should answer the door. And more perplexing was the problem of what he would do if she did open. There was no question of what he wanted to say, what he wanted to do, of course. He waited while the long branches of the eucalypti shuffled against the roof of the red brick house and while the moon rode high above the trees. Soon she turned off the lights. He hurried into the small town and told his friends that he would have her before the last peach was picked.

II

Rather than return to his empty house, which would be quiet except for the ticking of the clock, the boy drove to the river. He changed into his swimming suit. He sat next to the water, alone and with his guitar in his arms, plucking it slowly, delicately, listening to his own music.

His birth had been his mother's death. Manuel, his father, had crossed the Mexican border into Arizona. His wife, pregnant with the boy, walked at his side. She helped carry their few possessions. They traveled mostly at night because the scorching sun nauseated her, causing the life within her to stir. "Let us go to the new country," he had told his young bride. "Maybe there we can find a new life. The men who have been there tell me that in that country a man is repaid for his labor. A man cannot live on promises; he needs food and the things that make his life tolerable. I love my country, my people, but all I see in the future is the same life that my fathers have lived; a country should have something new, something better for each generation. Surely we will not lose our heritage, but rather, we will gain the riches of a new country."

She went with him and did not once complain of the journey. Her dark eyes followed him and did not turn from him. She warmed him with her body in the early mornings when the dew of the cactus fell to the sand forming tiny puddles. When the nausea came, she only stepped to the side and did what she had to do. She sat by the fire and listened to him talk of the things that he would provide for her, and her child, when they reached the new country. She sat silently, and when the fire began to die, she arose and threw another dry cactus branch into it.

They arrived when the peach season had just begun. At the labor camp they were given a tent and a kerosene stove. There was no time for rest. They were told that they must begin work that same day. When they were out in the orchard she told him that she must return to the tent. At the end of the day he ran back to their tent. As he approached the tent he heard the wail of a newborn child. Even before he entered the tent he saw that the women who were crowded around were wearing black shawls over their heads and carrying the beads that only sad people use. As he pushed aside the hanging door of the worn and bleached canvas tent, he remembered the words of parting that his father had given to him: May God go with you, my son.

⌐⌐

The long, brown fingers rolled up; the thumb, rigid but flexible, pushed down on the strands of thin wire. One finger followed the other and the thumb chased them all. The palm patted all the wires and struck against the black box.

The boy did not see the river carry the driftwood. When he played his guitar he was in his own world of self. The river lifted a gnarled and yet smooth piece of wood above the water level, and then bobbed it back under. The water seemed to be toying with it. The wood approached the boy, who was lost. He could have reached out and pulled it to the river's edge, but he did not. The river carried the wood further down, away from the boy to its destiny.

⌐⌐

A friend had given him the guitar; more precisely, it had been willed to him by this friend. His friend was an old man who wore a patch over his left eye. The women of the *barrio*, the Mexican neighborhood, had told him to cover his eye. They told him that unless he put a cloth over the eye they would not buy his corn. There was a hole where the eye had once been; it was a gruesome empty hole which had become pink in the center and purple at the edges.

"Old man," they said to him, "don't you know you'll frighten our pregnant women? It is *mala suerte*, bad luck, for a woman with child to be frightened. You know that." They shook their heads with great seriousness when they reprimanded him, while he tended to his business, arranging the corn in his cart, wiping the dust from his tomatoes. He always nodded to them when they spoke to him like this, like a man does to a child who has asked him a foolish question.

"And the children? You must not tempt them with that ugly hole. Of a truth it is ugly, you know that. They see you and they laugh at you. You know as well as we that it is a great wrong for children to mock their elders, but we must be careful not to put temptation in their path. That is the duty of the fathers. So cover it, *viejo*, cover it or don't come around here anymore!"

Before each speech, for this is how the old man spoke, he gave a short chuckle if he was speaking to women or children. Had he done this only with women, one might have suspected him of being bashful before them, but since he did it with both women and children it remained as part of the mystery of the old man. No one had ever seen him with a clean-shaven face, yet his beard always appeared to be but a three- or four-day growth. If he bathed, no one knew that either, for his face was forever streaked with tobacco juice, with dirt and sweat; that is, with the earth, for he was a toiler of the field. He planted and he grew vegetables: corn, chiles, tomatoes and squash; and if you were to ask him if there were any other vegetables, he would say, "Of course, there is one other vegetable. The bean. The Pinto bean. But that is the meat, the basis of the meal. I deal in delicacies. I am, as you might say, an artist. Anyone can grow the bean; why it can almost grow of its own accord. But the corn? Eh? That is a different matter, is it not? No, my friend, the corn is quite another thing. And have you seen wild tomatoes? Without the touch of the human hand, the human spirit, a wild tomato is lifeless. It is colorless, dry. It is, in fact, not a tomato."

His vegetable cart rolled along the streets on two large wheels. It was a small wooden cart painted orange. One of the wheels was white; the other was black.

The boy's guitar was black. It was solid black. The boy thought of the old man now. He remembered how during the summers the old man would stop at their house after his selling. When Manuel, Fernando Garcia's father, would arrive, the old man would offer some of his corn that he had not sold. Manuel would accept it, thank him and then invite him to stay for supper. Each day they did this, each day they went through this formality. Because the boy knew little of manhood, of the pride, the propriety that each man must have if he is to remain a man, he wondered even now as he sat by the river strumming the black box, why they should have retained this formality over the years. I knew, he thought, that Huero would give us the corn to assure himself of a meal, and he knew it and my father knew it; why then, was it necessary to go through all that for so long, for twelve years? It must be a part of age, maybe this is what happens with age, he thought.

After the meal of fresh corn, green squash, and a small piece of meat fried and then boiled with onions and tomatoes, they would go outside and sit by the willow tree next to the garden. The ground was hard and cooler than the air. They sat with their arms around their legs, waiting for the sun to fade behind the mountains.

"A little tobacco, Manuel?" the old man grunted as he somewhat ostentatiously pulled the pouch from his pocket. He mixed his tobacco with chopped, dry corn leaves.

"No, *viejo*, thank you so much, but I fear it is too strong for me."

The old man wrinkled his eyes and chuckled. He took a long time to untie the string of the dirty pouch made old with sweat.

"Here, would you like to try some of mine? It is not the real thing, like yours is, but maybe you'll like it for a change."

The old man shrugged his shoulders. "Well, Manuel, if you would like me to try it, I will. Of course, I prefer mine; it is the real thing, you know."

They would sit and smoke quietly. Occasionally the boy would ask a question or two, but while they had their first

pipeful, for the most part, they remained silent. The boy
would lean back, using his arms for a pillow, and count the
stars, pointing them out with his finger.

"But why do you waste your time with the stars?" the old
man asked. "They are not real. Not the way we see them. Look
at them. They look like pinpoints of light, do they not? But
what are they? They are great masses of fire, or they are pinpoints of light. Why have they been made so? To confuse us, or
to scorn us? Who knows? I'll tell you, no one knows. That is
why I say that they are not real. No, Fernando, you should not
waste your time on the stars. On the moon, yes, but the stars,
no. Look at the moon. Is she not a reality? She is beautiful,
no? Is she not more beautiful than even my corn?"

"Why do you call it a woman, Huero?" the boy asked.

"Why? Why do we call the sun a man? Since the beginning of time we have called things by their names. We say *la
luna*, and we say *el sol*. Why? Because that is what they are.
But I am speaking of the moon, this June moon. As you know,
there are twelve of them. Eleven of them are women, as you
say, but one of them is a man. I say that the April moon is a
man."

"A man? How is that, Huero?"

"It, the April moon, is a man like the other eleven are
women. The April moon is *el ojo de Dios*, the eye of God. It is
the only good moon. It is the only time that God looks down on
this earth. The corn must be planted when God looks at us.
That is why we plant our corn in April."

When the old man began to talk in this manner the boy
quit counting stars. He shut his eyes in such a way that the
stars became long needles of brightness. "It's been over a week
since you played for us, Huero. If you play for us I promise to
help you irrigate your corn this week."

The old man looked at the boy's father. "I would, son, but
I am so tired from the day that I doubt if I could even lift the
guitar." He inhaled and exhaled deeply, to show his tiredness.

Manuel smiled and asked, "And if you had a glass of wine,
viejo? What then? Would it give you the strength?"

"Oh, one can never tell, Manuel. Sometimes a glass of
wine is not enough for these old bones of mine. You forget that
I am an old man now."

"Why don't I just bring the whole bottle out then?" He
arose from the ground and went into the house. He returned

quickly with the bottle of red wine. He pulled the cork and handed the bottle to the old man. Huero held his palm before him. "Nay, my friend, you first."

"No, no. You are our guest. Please. Drink from it."

"If that is your pleasure." He raised the bottle to his mouth and took a small taste. Then he lifted it higher and let it pour in, some running down his chin. He returned it to Manuel and he in turn drank from it.

"Do you feel like playing your music now, Huero?" Fernando asked.

"Not yet. Let me rest first. It was a very hard day."

"What is it, Huero, didn't the wine make you feel better?"

"When you are as old as I am you do not feel better. Not even wine does that. You feel different, but not better. Old men have but one feeling. When they get old, they feel old. Nothing changes that."

Manuel chuckled and shook his head. The sun had set now. They could hear the crickets. The mosquitoes from the nearby river buzzed near their ears. Manuel had never seen the old man swat at an insect. It must be that he is deaf, Manuel would joke with himself. The boy and his father, as Huero talked, constantly swatted at the mosquitoes, but the old man was impervious to them. He is both blind and deaf, Manuel thought.

"*Viejo*, it seems you are extra tired tonight. Why don't you tell Fernando a story?"

"If I tell it, I tell it for you also, Manuel. Or have you learned so much that you cannot learn more?"

"Huero, tell us how you lost your eye. Please tell us. And don't do as you always do. This time, tell us truthfully how you lost it," the little boy pleaded. Fernando Garcia was ten-years old when Huero told this story.

He began the story as he refilled his pipe from his own pouch. His elbows resting on his knees, his back slumped like a drunk over a bar, he spoke quietly, monotonously, almost as if he were bored with his own story; but of a truth he was not; if they had been able to see his eye they would have known that he was not bored, that as a matter of fact his one great joy in life was to entertain these two, the boy and his father. They were his only friends, and they knew how to listen. The boy lay flat on his back, and Manuel clasped his legs tightly and rocked slowly with the tempo of the story.

"You want me to tell you of my eye. Not the one I have, but the one that is no longer there. Well, we shall see if I can remember. It happened before you were even born. But you only want to know how it happened. Maybe I should tell why it happened. But you are too young now, Fernando. I will only tell you how it happened. Then you can tell all the boys in the *barrio* that you are the only one who knows of my eye."

"No, Huero, I promise. I will keep the story only for myself."

"Very well then. I will proceed with my story."

"As you know, every story must have a history, even as every stalk of corn must have a kernel before it can exist. The story of my eye, then must have a history. The question is, how far back into history shall I go? My eye came from me, but I came from my fathers, and they came from their fathers, so on and so on. In a sense, every story must go back to the beginning of time; every storyteller must be able to answer and account for the beginning of time. This then, of course, leads to religion. In other words, no storyteller can practice his trade unless he has religion. Or at least knows of religion. But already I am straying from my story. I must decide at what part of the history of my eye my story begins. Well, I think it should be enough if I begin the story with my grandfather. My story opens when he was only a young man. Let us say he was twenty-five. And though I am not quite certain, let us say that my grandmother was seventeen at the beginning of my story. They had not married yet. In fact, they had only met that day. My grandmother, her name was Martina Mercado, was the daughter of a very rich man. He was of such great wealth that on each holiday he could afford to give gifts of food and clothing to all those who lived in the village. They say he could ride a horse better than any man in the state and that he could fell a flying eagle with one shot. Furthermore, he owned so much land that his one great wish was to explore all of it; I am told that when he died, and he lived to be more than seventy years of age, he had not yet seen all his land. Of his wife, I know nothing, except that she only went outside her house on very special occasions, such as during the season of the Lord's birthday, which is to say, Christmas. My great-grandfather

was not a believer. People say he was a heretic. That he open-
ly cursed the church and fought with the priests. In fact, it is
said that they had to get a new priest once a year because this
man, my great-grandfather, had written to the Pope saying
that if he did not send a different priest every year, he would
force them to do so by killing anyone who remained there
more than the year. I do not know if it is true, but this is what
I am told. Well, he had not allowed by grandmother, Martina,
to go to the school in the village. Each year, the new priest
would come to his house and beg the man to send his daughter to the school, but he would say, 'What for? She does not
need to learn to write; only those who wish to advance themselves need to learn to write. My daughter has no need for
that.' And he would say no more. The priest, mindful, it
seems, of how much it would mean to his church and school if
this rich man's daughter would attend, pleaded with him, but
he would say no more, only that. He was a man of very few
words. Well, on this day of which I am speaking the new
priest came. He arrived, at the house tired and thirsty from
the long walk wearing his long white robe. He was a volunteer
to that mission, for the head priests, having heard of the trials
that befell those who went there, had made it a rule to send
only the volunteers. He had wanted to go to a leper colony on
one of the islands in the Pacific, but because of his young age
and lack of experience, they suggested this place in the state
of Durango. When he arrived the servants told him that Don
Mercado was out in the fields, and that he would have to wait
the whole day if he wished to see him. He waited outside,
drinking from the well near the vineyard, and there is where
he met the young girl Martina. She asked him of his business;
though she knew of course, for as I have already told you this
happened every year. She was so accustomed to speaking with
the servants that she had learned their ways; that is, she was
actually teasing the young man. He was embarrassed, for he
was sweating and he knew his face was covered with dust.
More than that, his skirt was longer than the one she wore.
He had never liked the idea of wearing skirts, but what could
he do? If a man wanted to be a priest and serve God, how else
could it be done unless one wore a skirt; a longer skirt than
those the women wore at that? He blushed and he tried to
make his voice sound older and serious by making it deeper.

"'I am here to tell your father to send you to the temple of God.'

"The young girl lifted herself onto the edge of the well and dangled her nose in the air and said, 'No one tells my father what to do. If I were you I might ask him, but I would certainly not tell him.'

"And when she put it that simply, the young man realized that in this house he would not be able to use the fear of God to aid him in his argument. So he laughed. Then she laughed, and from then on they were friends. She took him into the house and fed him and showed him the house and barns and animals all that day.

"When the father arrived that night he found them in the large room where he kept all his books. Because the young priest was smiling and because his daughter was smiling, the man invited the young priest to stay on for supper.

"After they had eaten, he took the priest into that same room again with all the books. They drank a glass of wine and smoked cigarettes. Then without any warming, the old man said, 'Well, young man of God, what have you come for?'

"The young man had already planned his moves, for as he talked to the young girl, who, by the way, was the most beautiful girl in the whole state, a young exciting girl just coming into womanhood. As I was saying, as he had spoken to the girl that day he had realized that he must not try to force the man to send his daughter to the school, but rather, he must try to convince him, as I will show you by what he said:

"'I have come to help you, señor,' the young priest said.

"'To help me?' and he went into a great laugh, a laugh of contempt.

"'Yes, to help you.'

"'So now they teach them how to make jokes. Before they only taught them how to scare people, but now they teach them to be funny men. Well, maybe it is better that way, for of a truth your whole religion is funny.'

"'I do not come to make jokes, señor. I come to help you. Listen, Don Mercado, I know. I have heard from the people in the village that you need help, and for that I have come.'

"'You have been here but a week and already you are like the others before you. Already you listen to the gossip of the peasants. Why must they always gossip? Can their lives be so filled with boredom that they must spend all their rest hours talking about the things that we greater men do? Yes, it must be that. ¡Ay, qué pobre gente! But I try to help them, do I not? Or have they not told you that? Have they not told you that I give them food and clothing many times throughout the year?'

"'Yes, Don Mercado, they have told me that. But they have also told me that you cannot read.'

"Don Mercado quit laughing. 'And what is that to you?' His voice was suddenly angry.

"'I know that a man as great as you is concerned with his land, with all his property, his money and his cattle, his horses, and so forth.'

"'Yes, that I am, but what has that to do with you?'

"'Do you have to pay taxes?'

"'Yes, of course.'

"'And when you sell, do you not sign certain papers?'

"'Pues, ¿cómo no? Every man must sign papers of sale.'

"'They tell me in the village that you are thinking of trading with the Army now, is that so?'

[After 1966]

THE LITTLE HOUSE

After my father had been in California for several months and had earned enough money working in the canneries, he sent for us. My mother and I rode the Greyhound from El Paso to the little town of Burneyville in the San Joaquín Valley, where my father had prepared a home for us. At nearly every stop my mother tried to convince me that I'd like California as well as Texas by buying me ice cream, my favorite food. It had taken me nine long years to build up my reputation as a leader in our neighborhood, and leaving the city just when I had become interested in a little redhead was a thing I felt could have no substitute. But the ice cream did, I must confess, help me to get used to the idea. After many hugs and slaps on the rump at the depot in Burneyville, we got into the dilapidated Ford with wrecked fenders and my father took us to our new home.

Had he known the traumas that the neighborhood which he had picked would inflict upon me, I'm certain, unless he was of a sadistic bent, he would never have rented the duplex in *el barrio*. *El barrio* is what Mexicans call the Mexican part of town, as opposed to Okie Town. Okie Town is, of course, the part of town where the Okies live.

I was too young to be concerned with the decor, the size or even the poverty of the duplex; what I was interested in was the neighborhood. My father had assured me in his letters that there would be plenty of kids to play with. Of course, it was just one of his tricks to get me to come to California without giving my mother, whom he thought he always had to protect, too much trouble.

We arrived on a Sunday and were too late to go to church, so my father (because, as I see it now, he wanted to be alone with my mother) told me to give the place a "once over."

With the eagerness that only a young boy who has just arrived in a new environment can have, I ran out of the house, slamming the screen door, and, like a madman, gesticulating wildly and screaming loudly, I went toward the first sight of interest.

At first I thought it was a playhouse, or even a small house for little people; but neither of these suppositions satisfied me, so I walked slowly and quietly toward the miniature house to find out just what it was. I peeked through a crack between the boards. Immediately, after my eyes had focused upon the object inside, my head felt slightly dizzy and my stomach suddenly became empty; only a feeling of terror remained...the kind one gets when he sees a snake.

I had had enough lower-class morality pumped into me to create guilt at that moment, but, I suppose, not quite enough to make me turn my head or close my eyes. I continued to stare, boldly, and tears even rolled down my cheeks from holding my eyes wide open. It was a wonder of wonders, fascination upon fascination, and I could no more take my eyes off the object inside than I could fill the emptiness of my stomach at that moment...I tell you, I was staring at a bare ass!

I had not realized that I had been holding my breath all this time, when suddenly I inhaled loudly and the owner of the posterior, upon being startled, threw down the comic book she had in her hand and quickly began inspecting the entire room to see where the noise came from. I continued to be fascinated and refused to run away even though I still had a chance. Then she discovered me; or rather, she saw my eyes and screamed. Her voice startled me out of my fascination... now I had to act!

Something came over me; I felt a great weight upon my heart. It was not exactly a weight, it was more like a heavy pounding of fists upon me. Guilt had fallen on me because I had been discovered. I had been caught, and so, as if to ease the guilt by retaliation against the fists of the angels, I picked up a handful of dirt and threw it in through a small window at the top of the miniature house.

This naturally made the young, dark-skinned girl scream even louder. I was about to pick up another handful when I noticed a kid standing outside the other half of the duplex. I knew then that my crime had not been perfect. I became so frightened that the pounding stopped; it seemed to me as if the angels decided to leave me to my folly and let the threat of hell bring out the fear of God in me. I had never achieved any fame in the neighborhood in El Paso for being a speedy runner, but this time I'm certain I must have broken some kind of record. I thought that if I ran fast enough, somehow, time cou-

pled with distance would obliterate vision and the witness to
my crime would not be able to remember whom he saw. I ran
around the block and felt quite silly and a little frightened
while doing it, for I had been told that in El Paso if the cops
ever saw you running, they would arrest you. I found a tree
across the street from our house and climbed to the top. I was
contemplating the object of my crime and the wickedness of it
and had almost decided on the practicality of either suicide for
me or death for the witness when I heard my mother calling
me to go and eat.

After we had eaten, my mother and I complained of the
sweltering heat which, as you know, gets quite high in the
San Joaquín Valley, and so my father took us swimming. The
river was crowded with people on both sides. The people were
noisy and their paper bags, empty beer cans, pop bottles and
bread crusts cluttered the beach.

I was anxious to meet the kids who were playing in the
water. My parents wanted me to stay with them; they told me
I didn't know how to swim well enough to go play with the
boys. I sat between them, silently, and spacing my breathing
so I would have to inhale deeply every so often. The loud
exhale was timed with the movement of my eyes toward the
boys. My lips were puffed and my eyes were downcast. This
made it quite plain that I wasn't enjoying myself. After fifteen
minutes of this, they gave me permission to go. Without a
word, I jumped up and ran to the bunch of boys and girls who
were playing in the water and appeared to be my age and
nationality.

I stood on the beach, waiting to be invited. I looked at
them, smiling when one would glance at me. I drew lines and
circles in the sand with my toes. I knelt directly in front of
them on the beach and started digging a hole in the sand
while they continued to play tag with a rubber ball. The mosquitoes bit me, and the sun lay heavily on my naked back, but
they didn't even notice me. Once their ball was thrown out of
the water close to me. I crawled quickly to it, hoping that this
would lead to an introduction or invitation. As I was about to
pick it up, one of the bigger ones yelled, "Hey, leave that ball
alone!" I was so embarrassed I didn't even look at him.

I walked further down the river toward a clump of trees
that had benches and tables underneath. There I saw another
group of kids. They were playing football, a game that I had

played in El Paso. Again I became excited with the hope that I might meet some kids. It had been five days since I had spoken to a person my own age and that was hundreds of miles away from Burneyville.

I had been standing there only several minutes when a blond-headed, freckle-faced boy came up to me and asked me in his southern drawl, "You all want to play?"

Without thinking (for the boys playing were all bigger than me) I said yes. He interrupted the game and told the other boys that we both wanted to play. The captain of one side stepped up to me and asked, "Can you all play this here game?" I looked up at him and just nodded my head. I was neither shy nor inhibited, but the new environment made me feel somewhat lost and, therefore, I didn't say a word. All the players looked at me suspiciously; that is, they, too, didn't say a word...they just stared.

The captain said, "What's the matter, kid, don't you all savvy English?" He stood taller than I and kept alternating the ball from one hand to the other. It was not until several weeks later, after I started school, that I found out that these boys were what the Mexicans called Okies. At that moment all I knew was that I wanted to punch him in the jaw. He had several large, white pimples on his face and I wished I could break them and watch the junk run out. I hated condescension, especially linguistic condescension.

I said, "Yeh, sure I can play. Which side do I play on?"

"You can be on the other side. You all look kinda small to play on my side."

The captain from the other side, shrugging his shoulders, said I could be on his team if I didn't get in the way. But how could I help it? The very first play, a player from the other side with buck teeth and limpid blue eyes that looked like slits in a jack-o-lantern stuck his entire palm against my nose and pushed me on top of the ball carrier: unfortunately, the ball carrier happened to be my captain. This naturally caused him to give me a look of warning. I know that teamwork and discipline are essential to any group, but for some reason his long hair and bony face looked as repugnant as the other team's captain with the pimply face. In my mind, while lying on the ground, having been pushed by the jack-o-lantern, I saw myself intercepting a pass or recovering a fumble and running for a touchdown; then walking up to both of them and spitting in their eyes. But, sad to say, this was only in my mind. Meanwhile, ol' slits-for-eyes kept pushing me and stepping on my toes. By the end of the game, I had received a bloody nose, skinned shins, and, also, I couldn't help hating those three boys.

My captain blamed me for losing the game; the other one laughed at me for "trying to play with us men;" and the buck-toothed one (who by this time had snot coming out of his nose) simply sneered with superiority.

We had just finished when a heavy woman with a black dress and no lipstick told the boys to form a line around the table for ice cream.

All this time not one of the boys had spoken to me. I couldn't understand why. I didn't think I had played that bad, and even so, could a silly game be as important as that?

The boys eagerly scrambled around the table and I was left alone several yards away. I stayed, hoping they'd invite me, but they had forgotten me. They were too busy eating and talking. I don't mean literally that they'd forgotten me; I mean it sarcastically! They would look at me and hurriedly bend their heads over their plates filled with ice cream, or else turn their heads sharply and talk and laugh loudly. Because they knew that I wanted to be with them, for the second time that afternoon I felt embarrassed; only this time it hurt deeper, because it was the second time. I walked slowly back to where my parents were, stopping before I got there to wipe the tears from my face. The huge lump in my throat refused to leave, so I walked back with it showing. It must have been showing, for the minute my father saw me, he asked me what had happened.

I refused to tell him at first, then he promised to buy me some ice cream, so I relented. That's how we operated; always bribes. He'd either give me or take from me whenever he wanted something from me. The older I grew, the more I realized how childish it was to act that way, but I could never decide if it was he or me who was the child and if being childish, since I got my rewards and he his information, was a bad thing. I don't think I ever found out.

By the time we arrived at the house, he had talked me into another of his "deals." Since loneliness seemed to be my problem (according to him), he was going to take both mother and me to meet our next-door neighbors. The image of the wit-

ness to my crime of that morning suddenly appeared before
me. He was standing outside the door of the other half of the
duplex, looking at me with a mocking grin that said, "We'll
meet soon." There was nothing I could say. I had told him that
I wanted to meet some kids; how could I tell him that the boy
next door would not do because he was the one witness to my
crime. All I could do was pray; a little habit I had picked up in
El Paso. Whenever I was in real trouble I prayed. I don't just
mean a hope, or a wish, I mean a real prayer, and not the kind
you find in books either. I had decided at an early age that
although I didn't really know if there were such persons as
Jesus or Mary or Joseph, nevertheless, just in case there were,
my chances of getting what I wanted would be greater if I
prayed. For if I didn't pray, even if there were such persons, I
wouldn't get what I wanted, but if I did *pray* and there *were*
such people, I'd get what I wanted; and if there weren't, all I'd
lose would be a few words. So I prayed. As you can see I had
an involved philosophy, and this was probably the reason for
many of my childhood traumas. But I was not one to turn my
back on truth simply because it was involved and intricate.

While we were eating supper there was a loud yell and
the sound of a dish thrown against the wall. A loud voice,
harsh and deep, and coming from the room next to ours, pro-
claimed emphatically in the Spanish idiom, "If there can't be
pork meat, there shan't be *any* meat!" Father said that the
man who was hollering (and who was my witness's father)
was a very good man at heart, but that when things didn't go
his way he'd lose all control of himself. From all his yelling
and banging of dishes, I could see why my father had arrived
at this conclusion. All this noise simply because the mother
had not bought pork.

I was quietly eating my tortilla and beans, thinking about
how much I should offer as a bribe to the kid next door when
out of the clear blue sky it hit me. It was as if the devil himself
had thrown a burning fork into my heart, for I felt frightened
like earlier in the day, only this time instead of wild fists it
was a steady rhythmic crescendo like the beat of a tympani.
"What if the girl happens to be related to the boy, like his sister, for instance? And what if the boy tells the girl and the girl
tells the father? If the old man blows up about no pork meat,
what will he say, or do, about a nasty, criminal youth like me
who goes around looking at young girls like his daughter

when they're in the john?" I can't say I actually thought all that; as I said, it just all fell in my lap in one split second.

I said to my parents that I had to go to the bathroom and was excused. I went outside and into the outhouse (my father had told me that the little house was also our bathroom) and felt like the criminal returning to the scene of the crime. The first thing I did when I walked in was to see if anyone was peeking through the cracks, and then I wiped the seat off and killed three spiders by burning them with a match. I know that some people would think that an outhouse is no place to pray, but at that moment I was not concerned about God's sense of smell; all I wanted was that He or the Holy Virgin, I didn't care which one, either not have the girl be the boy's sister, or else, if she already were, to have the boy not tell her who had thrown the dirt. I wanted to ask the Holy Virgin that she take me back in time to that morning so I could not do what I had already done; however, I felt that was going a little too far; there's reasonable faith and then there's ridiculous faith. I professed the former.

It was dusk and the sky had turned orange when I came out of the little house. I felt more relieved than when I had entered for both obvious and subtle reasons. There was no logical reason why God couldn't answer at least part of my prayer.

My father took us next door. Their apartment was like ours except that they seemed to have more food. There were two sacks of flour, two of beans and a five-gallon tin of lard in the corner of the kitchen. The front half, because it was the only part with a floor, was the living room and bedroom. These were not the first things I noticed, of course.

A tall, heavy, black-haired man with a mustache the shape of a pocket comb met us at the door. He shook hands with my mother but only gave me a nod...I felt like running away. The mother came out from the kitchen (as I have already described the floor plan, you know she didn't come out, she simply came forward) and also shook hands with mother. She looked at me, smiled, and wiping her hands on her dirty apron which hung about her fat belly like a flour sack, said I looked like her boy and that he would be back shortly. I wanted to ask if they had a daughter, but decided against it just in case they did, and just in case the father knew about my nasty habit. I expected him to strike me at any minute, without warning, so I kept my feet flat on the floor so as not to lose my balance if he did.

I thought, "Maybe the father knows but is too ashamed to tell the mother or to mention it to my father," when they started talking about the canneries and El Paso (and other things which, of course, bored me).

Because the old man didn't look at me and hadn't said a word to me, because he had such a loud voice, the kind the fatter type of priests have, and because he blew his top when there wasn't any pork meat for supper, I sat quietly, almost mousy like. I didn't crack my knuckles or breathe loudly as I usually did when I was bored with the conversation. I chewed the inside corner of my lip and waited.

I would know when the boy entered if the girl was his sister, since if she were, she was probably with him. I started making plans for a break. I wouldn't be able to go out the front door because Hitler (the man with the mustache) was sitting close to it. The window was out of the question because it had a wire screen. After scanning the entire room like a criminal with sharp, somewhat squinted eyes, I finally decided that my best bet would be to make a quick break for the rear door. The two women were sitting in the middle of the room and would be able to reach me, but I'd yet to meet a woman who I thought was stronger or more intelligent than I. I could outfight them and outsmart them any day of the year...including my mother.

I had no sooner made up my mind when, upon hearing some noise outside, that is, above the crickets and the frogs which infest the entire San Joaquín Valley, the other said, looking at me, "Oh, here they come now." She said it happily; as if I wanted to meet them! I was now assured of my punishment, for having said "they" could only mean one thing: the boy and the girl. For one second my mind got the idea that maybe God would somehow create a heavy mist or fog around me as He had done with the Jews in the Old Testament; but this seemed unlike Him. He only did those miracles for the Jews and the Popes and the Saints, never for dirty-minded people like me. Besides, it was too late. They had already entered the room.

The boy entered first. He looked me straight in the eye and said, "Hello." I swallowed my excess spit and was about to answer when the girl stepped in front of him. I rose quickly, not because of politeness, but preparing for my escape. She, too, looked me in the eye and said, "Hi."

I couldn't speak. I poised myself for the flight. My heart beat harder and faster than it had that morning during my crime. My mother asked why I didn't answer. Father gave a mocking laugh, the kind that fathers give instead of rubbing index fingers in mockery as young kids do. This was father's way of saying, "You're embarrassed because a pretty little brunette walked into the room." He was a man who would rather laugh, or look, or make funny sounds with his tongue instead of waste words... how little he knew!

Hitler, in his big voice, a voice that by this time had so threatened me simply by its resonance that I hated the sound of it, said, "John, Martha, this is Manuel."

They had both put down their grocery bags (which I'm sure contained a lot of pork) and stood between me and the rear door. I still didn't know if anyone knew, with the exception of John. His constant straight-looking into my eyes was a warning to me. This is the way nine-year-olds communicate intimacies: with their eyes. I didn't want to look at his accusing eyes, nor did I want to look at the victim of my crime. I kept silent and I think my fists were clenched in case I was suddenly attacked by the father or anyone.

The girl broke the silence between us. The older folks continued their boring conversation. Now they were talking about the lack of rain which had caused the poor peach season.

The black-haired one said, "Do you want to go outside and play?"

I looked at her with my eyes squinting. Then I looked at the boy. He was just standing and still staring at me. He refused to answer my questioning eyes. I quickly thought that even though she was bigger and probably older than I, I would have a better chance for escape outside the house.

"Well, do you or don't you?" she asked sharply. I could see this girl was not one to toy with.

"Sure," I answered, somewhat defiantly. If she was planning a fight, that was okay with me, so long as her old man wasn't involved.

Walking outside, I first thanked God for not letting Hitler know about it, and at the same time I hoped for strength to whip the girl. This, I didn't have to pray for, since she was *only* a girl.

As soon as we got outside, John looked at me once more and said, without batting an eyelash, "See you later, Mr. Peeper." With that, before I could say a word, he ran off. I was left alone in the semi-darkness with the girl. A street lamp cast lights and made shadows all about us.

"What do you want to play?" the girl asked.

"Doesn't matter," I answered.

We couldn't decide on any games so instead we sat in the middle of the street under the light and talked. She asked me about El Paso and about the schools and about the niggers (she had never seen one except in the movies). She was full of questions, this one. Every time she asked one, she would wrinkle her forehead and cross her arms.

I told her about the boys at the river and how they had not invited me to play tag. She said she knew them and that most of them lived in *el barrio*. "Ah, they're just dumb Mexicans," she said matter-of-factly, throwing the words off with an obvious tone. "All the guys around here are a bunch of creeps," she continued in the same tone. "They think girls, Okies and new people are worse than cowshit." She said that word as natural as if she used it every day of her life, which I wouldn't doubt if she did. "They don't even let me swim with them after school. And just because some of them don't wear their trunks. The dopes!"

She kept on talking about this and that until I could stand it no longer. I kept believing and not believing. First she knew, and then she didn't. My hands were getting tired from being clenched, and this waiting for the bell was driving me nuts. I wanted her to get down to brass tacks. I'd had enough of this pussyfooting around. And yet, there was no way to really know if she knew. She was still telling me about the "creeps" when I finally jumped up and, taking a step back, said in my high voice: "Do you know or don't you? Just tell me, will you?"

She looked at me again, wrinkling her forehead and crossing her arms. "Do I know what?" she asked, with an inflection of the voice that asks the other person not to speak so loud.

"You know what," I shouted. This dirty black-haired, black-eyed female was beating me. These were the times when I doubted my belief in my superiority over women.

"Oh," she laughed, almost giggling, "you mean about the dirt?"

Did I mean about the dirt? She knew darn well I meant the dirt. This, I knew, was her way of striking. But there was no more to say. If she knew, we'd either fight or else I'd simply leave. I was about to either run away or cuss her and was still wondering what she planned to do, when she rose from the ground and, looking at me with her big, black eyes twinkling and smiling, said to me, "John told me this morning, but I don't care. You're the first guy to even throw dirt on me. The other guys around here don't even know I live here. The creeps!"

Who was this girl? Was it God helping me or had I simply met a girl who was nutty? On the way to California my mother had told me that there were a lot of crazy people out here, but I didn't think I'd meet one that soon. Certainly not the first day and living practically in the same house. I guess it really didn't matter to me what her mental state was, for to me the prognosis was more important than the diagnosis. So long as I could forecast her behavior, why should I worry about the cause of it. Needless to say, I was quite happy with the outcome of things, and to settle it forever in heaven as well as on earth, I confessed the entire wicked affair to a fat priest to whom Martha introduced me.

[Circa 1970]

TELEPLAY:
THE CATALINA PAPERS

It begins in the foyer of the auditorium: Each participant in the experiment must, upon entry, present his social security number. No refreshments will be allowed. No talking. No touching. A pencil and pad are given to each viewer. Uniformed guards will enforce the above rules. Music of Montavani *is piped into the lobby and the auditorium prior to the curtain call. Inside the auditorium: Curtain is down. Flags of all nations surround the seats. Onstage, at either end, stands the flag of the United Nations.*

ACT ONE

Enter man with pipe in mouth, crew cut, tweed jacket: Ivy League. He carries notebook and pen. Crosses to center-front. He calls mutual, ad lib, *greetings to his "friends" in the audience: Hi, Sam, etc.*

MAN: (*Harvard accent.*) Men...ladies. (*Ad lib.*) Quiet down please... (*Etc. Indicating sound man in projection room.*) Turn off the music, Harry. (*Pause one full minute. Then music stops.*)

MAN: That's fine. Thank you. (*Beat.*) Now, ladies and gentlemen... (*Annoyed with noise.*) Please... The sooner we get started, the more time you'll have for your lunch. (*Smiles.*) Or whatever.

FIRST WOMAN IN AUDIENCE: (*Chummy.*) How long's this going to take, Bob?

BOB: (*Pleasantly.*) Oh, hi, Harriet. (*Beat.*) Well, assuming... (*Indicating projection room.*) Harry's crew—he's up in the computer room...if they've really gotten all the bugs out...I'd say an hour.

SECOND WOMAN IN AUDIENCE: We get overtime for this, don't we?

BOB: (*Forced smile.*) Come on, Marge... You've volunteered. (*Beat. Seriously.*) Besides, you'll recall your contract with Eden-Oak requires you participate in these demonstrations.

SECOND WOMAN IN AUDIENCE: I was just kidding, Bob.

BOB: (*Pause.*) Anyway... Ladies and gentlemen, you've been asked to view this demonstration pursuant to the regulations of The Agency... As you know, the rules provide for an objective viewing of all our demonstrations by personnel not directly connected with the particular experiment... Each of you are to spell out your comments on the forms we've given you... The Agency wants your opinions, primarily on whether the demonstration should go into a permanent location... They've tentatively approved the project. (*Beat. Coyly.*) Of course, the Agency will greatly rely on your opinions before reaching its final conclusion as to the total funding of the proposal. (*Chuckles.*) So...let your..."conscience" be your guide. (*Chuckles.*) It *is* a billion-dollar scheme! (*Bob puffs on his pipe. It is out. He lights it, carefully. Beat.*) The scenario itself... (*With pride.*) It is the creation of Doctor Empringham, our distinguished Nobel recipient...Dough has been working with the men in the Think Tank for some time now, as most of you know... His main purpose in this is to devise the means whereby man can be made to reproduce and perpetuate himself under conditions of total confinement... This demonstration, however, will simply deal with the initial problem of getting a man, any man, from a random selection—he has devised a process, primarily through drugs and hypnosis, whereby any man can be compelled to participate in the experiment.

MAN FROM AUDIENCE: (*Jokingly.*) Say, Bob...are you trying to tell us Dough's developed a super aphrodisiac?

WOMAN FROM AUDIENCE: So that's what they do in the Think Tank.

BOB: (*Slightly perturbed.*) Please, please... We'd like to get started. (*Beat.*) No, Doctor Holt, that's not what I mean... (*Seriously.*) What you will see today are the effects of a process which gives the participants a different history, a temporary change in the memory banks... In fact, most of you will recognize these specimens... Each of them works in the Institute... They will possess different characters and personalities, which were selected at random from the general population. (*Beat.*) The whole purpose of today's scenario is to demonstrate that man will subject himself to the experiment—that comes later; that given the conditions of total dependence as the sole means of survival, he will ultimately subject himself to the experiment of controlled reproduction for purposes of perpetuation of the human race. (*Jovial. Beat.*) But, frankly, you need not concern yourself with the purpose of the experiment... I've explained simply to make it more meaningful for you... Your only concern is to give us your opinions on the workability of the demonstration; that is... (*Lecturing.*) One, that is, have we succeeded in changing the personality of the participant, and, two, will this new personality ultimately follow the instructions of the computer?... That's all... Let us begin.

Lights go out and there is silence for two minutes.

Curtain rises. Lights overhead on right-rear-middle stage of soft orange-yellow; slowly increasing its intensity for thirty seconds until it become a naked yellow of intense heat to see: Mohave desert of white dunes, dry plants with yellow-orange-brown desert flowers. Young Woman, sits combing hair: She is twenty-four, almond eyes, oriental, beautiful. She wears a Mexican blouse and skirt, with a Mexican leather purse. She takes a handkerchief from the purse and carefully wipes her brow: A girl of gentleness and sophistication. Occasionally she licks her chapped lips. She stares. Enter from right-rear stage: A Man, tall, thirty-years old, broad-shouldered, tanned, blond Anglo. He wears khaki pants and shirt with brown brogans. A holster with a knife hangs from his belt. Man crosses, slowly, to Young Woman, who does not blink or turn: She is in a subtle state of shock. Man observes her, walks around to her point of view, since she will not turn to face him. He stands in front of her for several beats. Young Woman finally acknowledges his presence: Looks up.

TALL MAN: (*Carefully.*) You hurt?
YOUNG WOMAN: (*Flat.*) Dizzy... Thirsty.

TALL MAN: (*Beat.*) Me too. (*Beat.*) Nothing around here.

YOUNG WOMAN: (*Pause.*) Where are we? (*He stares at her for a full pause. He looks all around him, full circle. Sighs.*)

TALL MAN: (*Ironically.*) Sure doesn't *look* like Catalina.

YOUNG WOMAN: Catalina?

TALL MAN: (*Decidedly.*) I woke up back there...two hours of walking...everything looks the same...I guess the boat must have collided pretty hard.

YOUNG WOMAN: (*Confused.*) Boat? (*Shakes her head to clear the fog.*) What boat?

TALL MAN: The boat, the excursion...to Catalina.

YOUNG WOMAN: Excursion?... What are you talking about? (*Softly.*) I wasn't on any boat.

TALL MAN: (*Beat.*) I'm sorry, but...I *saw* you on the boat.

YOUNG WOMAN: (*Nervously.*) I don't understand. I wasn't on any boat... I was going... (*Shakes her head.*) I was...I'm a teacher. (*Beat. Anxiously.*) School. I was in school! (*She stares desperately at him for a long pause.*)

TALL MAN: I see.

YOUNG WOMAN: (*Pause. Pathetically.*) I don't remember.

TALL MAN: (*Patiently.*) It must have been a big crash. People get into a state of shock. Nothing serious. Post trauma. They can't remember things...for a short period. It happens, very common. (*Beat.*) But you *were* on the boat: An excursion, left San Pedro this morning... It was headed for Catalina. (*Beat.*) I suspect we're on the other side of Avalon.

YOUNG WOMAN: (*Sighs.*) I really don't remember...hardly anything. (*Beat.*) You're really sure?

TALL MAN: (*Smiles.*) Look... We're not lost, believe me. (*Looks up at sun pleasantly.*) First, we'd better find some water. Who knows how far it is to the other side. I'm sure they've got a rescue squad looking for us, but you never can tell how long it'll be. (*Reaching for her hand.*) I think we'd better get to it. (*She takes his hand, stands, and immediately her knees buckle. He grabs her, an arm around her waist. Pause.*)

TALL MAN: Okay?

YOUNG WOMAN: Yes, thank you. (*He nods his "welcome" and picks up her purse and hands it to her. She thanks him with a nod of her head.*)

TALL MAN: (*Smiling.*) My name's Scott.

YOUNG WOMAN: (*Relaxed.*) I'm...Patricia Sun.

SCOTT: Cecil Scott...but call me Scott. Only my mother calls
　　me Cecil. (*They laugh and begin to cross to left-rear stage.*)

PAT: We're going to?...

SCOTT: We'll be there by sundown, you watch...Avalon...
　　You know... (*Beat. Singsong.*) "I met my love in Avalon."
　　(*They laugh as they exit.*)

Lights go off. Long pause.

BOB: (*Offstage—over microphone.*) Uh, ladies and gentle-
　　men...Harry's got a slight problem with the trans-
　　former... (*Beat.*) While we're waiting... (*Proudly.*) I take
　　it you recognized Suzzie—from accounting. (*Beat.*) And of
　　course, that was our famous Dr. Thompson, chief of the
　　Think Tank... What's that, Harry? (*Beat.*) Fine, let's con-
　　tinue.

Long pause. In darkness, we hear the following voices.

NEGRO CONVICT: (*High, whining, rapid.*) I *still* believe the
　　Man put us here!

JEWISH WHORE: (*Bronx accent, low, raspy, sarcastic.*) Crap!
　　Get off that! What man?

HIPPIE: (*Hip, slurred.*) Could be the Pig. I can dig it!

*Lights suddenly go on: Bright, shocking yellow, high noon!
Scene is generally same as previous topography, except different location.*

*Negro Man is tall, thin, hair cut G.I., wears blue denim
prisoner's outfit. On his left front breast pocket is stenciled:
County Sheriff, W. Crook. On the back of his shirt is stenciled:
Prisoner. W. Crook is an ex-con, his movements are suspicious,
his talk is patterned with inflections of the con, the jazz musician, and of late, the black militant.*

*The Hippie is short, medium weight, long-haired, white.
He wears leather bell-bottoms, cowboy shirt, a medallion of
ten-penny pressed nails with a skull and an inverted sailor's
cap with a dime store policeman's badge pinned to the center.
He nods, snaps fingers, talks rapidly, can't ever sit still, must
inspect everything around him...antsy, antsy. His name is
Bernard.*

Jewish Whore is María, a bisexual woman getting fat with short, black hair. She wears paint-splattered pedal pushers and a smock with a print of Beethoven's *face on the front and one of* Snoopy *on the back. She is an artist, of the old beatnik school. She is vulgar and nuts and mimics celebrities constantly living in the fantasy world that she does. Despite her vulgarity, she is a warm, friendly, dirty, foul-mouthed bitch.*

MARÍA: Kee-rist! You two are paranoid!

CROOK: (*Superior.*) Paranoid, sheeet! You just don't know, you white folks don't know what it's like.

MARÍA: (*Annoyed.*) Oh, crap, not *that* again...your Old Black Joe bit's getting stale, Crook.

CROOK: Woman, you sure got some mouth there.

MARÍA: (*Unafraid.*) At least my head's on straight... Boy, you really are nervous!

CROOK: What the hell you expect? Look at us! (*Beat.*) I ain't uptight without reason, you know... Every time I found myself in some predicament—and I been in some bad sit-u-a-tions, let me tell you...it's always been some jive from the Heat.

MARÍA: (*A truce.*) I'll go along with that... The heat, that is. If I don't get some water soon... (*Southern belle.*) Why I'm just going to wither up and dry away. (*Begins to stand.*)

BERNARD: Yeh, man, the sun's a bummer.

CROOK: (*Pause. Looking at sun.*) You better sit some more. Already used up too much energy. (*Condescending.*) This kind of heat can kill white folks, cause you didn't know. (*María sits, then shakes her head at this. They sit silently, sweating, staring.*)

BERNARD: (*In reverie. Pause.*) You know, I can't even re-member where I was going... It's weird, but all I remem-ber is *leaving* the pad.

CROOK: Pad, eh? (beat) Now, me, I was in the joint. (beat) That's *all* I remember. Don't know even if it was yester-day or today.

MARÍA: (*Putting him on.*) Or *Tomorrow.*

CROOK: (*Perplexed.*) Huh?

MARÍA: (*Flippant.*) *Tomorrow*... You know, the flick.

BERNARD: Oh, yeh. Groovy, man.

CROOK: Flick?

BERNARD: A movie, man... The bomb falls, three people left in the City. Really wild.

MARÍA: No, that was... something else, with Belafonte and... that mousey chick... *I'm* talking about the one where everyone disappears except three people on an island.

BERNARD: (*Snapping fingers.*) Oh, yeh... Yeh... The last people on earth.

CROOK: HEY! What the fuck's a *show* got to do with us?

BERNARD: (*Sheepishly.*) We're just messing around.

CROOK: You people *are* messed up bad!

MARÍA: (*Beat.*) Okay... (*Changes tone, mood to matter-of-fact.*) So it's not a movie... so you tell me. What the hell's going on here?

BERNARD: (*Pause. Confidentially-absurdly-paranoid. Looking around for cops.*) I think we're into an acid scene... Must be a freakout... a bad trip.

CROOK: (*Annoyed.*) What the fuck! From movies to dope. JESUS! (*Beat. Points to stenciled name with thumb.*) See this? Now this ain't no costume, partner... I'm telling you, I was in the *joint* before I woke up here... Now, I know you wasn't in no joint. Not with your hair... And she sure ain't in no prison. Not in that outfit.

BERNARD: Well, man, it sure feels like it to me... (*They sit and stare into the desert, avoiding each other's face.*)

Enter young Blonde from right-rear stage.

CROOK: Hey, dig! (*The young Blonde crosses to them, her hips swinging freely in leather mini-skirt, proud breasts shaking decidedly in tight, red, sleeveless blouse.*)

BLONDE: (*Absurdly cheerful.*) Good afternoon. (*The three heave, their eyes popping at her entrance.*)

MARÍA: (*Lustful. María always has a deeper, serious, more sensual voice for the women.*) What have we here? (*The Blonde nods to them and waits for an invitation.*)

CROOK: (immediate hots for the broad) Sit down a spell. (*Blonde crosses her feet, sits yoga like, without use of hands. She sighs, exhausted!*)

MARÍA: (*Beat.*) Are you okay?

BLONDE: (*Sighing.*) I am now. (*Shakes head and smiles, relieved.*) I've been walking for, it seems, hours... I saw your tracks back there... (*Breathes deeply, controlling herself.*) It's been... The heat... (*Beat.*) I don't know quite how to put it... But to tell you the truth. (*Beat.*) I'm really glad I found you, cause...I'm lost. (*The three look at one another with embarrassment.*)

CROOK: (*Quietly.*) Hate to disappoint you, girl...but fact is, we're lost, too.

BLONDE: (*Pause.*) You mean...

BERNARD: (*Interrupting.*) We don't know where we're at... That's right.

Blonde begins to whimper. Crook takes a handkerchief from his pocket, inspects it for dirt, hands it toward her. The Blonde looks at him, hesitates. María takes it and gives it to her. Crook steps back, hurt, embarrassed. Blonde blows her nose, very gentle-like, her little finger sticking out. Suddenly, Blonde starts to cry. María puts her arm around her back, hand on ribs.

MARÍA: (*Motherly.*) It's okay, dear. You'll be safe now.

CROOK: (*Obscene. Poking Bernard in his ribs with his elbow... Winks at him.*) Safe?

The Blonde finishes crying. She looks at María, as if for the first time, with her arm around her. She is embarrassed, but doesn't know how to avoid it. María doesn't bat an eye.

BLONDE: (*To María.*) Thank you...I guess I *look* like a child. (*She moves out from her embrace, carefully.*) I'm sorry... It's just that... To tell the truth...I thought I was... All alone.

MARÍA: You're not by yourself, kiddo, it was the same for us; we *all* about had a heart attack when we ran into each other.

CROOK: (*Pride hurt.*) Where do you get that "we" shit. Not *this* man.

BLONDE: (*To María.*) What does he mean?

MARÍA: Ah, don't pay him any attention. All he sees are conspiracies.

BLONDE: (*Confused. To María*) Conspiracies?

CROOK: (*To Blonde. Indicating María.*) All she sees in movies!

BLONDE: (*Utterly confused.*) Movies?

MARÍA: (*Snaps.*) Oh, for Christ's sake, Crook! I said it's *like* a movie. (*To Belinda.*) You know, like all those weird doomsday flicks.

BLONDE: (*Beat.*) Oh, I see... You mean, our *situation*? (*Beat.*) like, On The Beach?

MARÍA: Exactly, Or, like *Tomorrow*.

BLONDE: (*Beat.*) *Tomorrow*? Never heard of that one... Has it been on T.V.?

BERNARD: (*Breaking in.*) Yep...Channel 13, last year... Channel 7, Channel 5, and...

CROOK: (*Interrupting.*) HEY! HEY! (*All the others turn to him, slightly frightened at the outburst.*) What's wrong with you people?

MARÍA: "People"!

CROOK: Here we are, lost, no food or water, and all you do is talk make-believe... Motherfucker!

BERNARD: What else is there?

CROOK: Lots, Jack, lots.

MARÍA: Like what?

CROOK: Like...we got to figure things out.

MARÍA: Oh, Christ!... Another lecture on reality from "the brother"?

CROOK: You bet your fat, Jewish ass, bitch! (*The Blonde jerks back and stiffens.*)

MARÍA: (*To Blonde.*) Don't pay any attention to him, dear. (*Crook stands and starts pacing around the group.*)

MARÍA: (*To Blonde.*) By the way, my name's María.

BLONDE: Belinda Smith.

CROOK: (*Lecturing. To Bernard.*) Now you mentioned T.V., right?

MARÍA: Right on, brother! (*Crook ignores her. María sighs, looks at Bernard, points her index finger at her temple, swirls it around, indicating Crook's "insanity".*)

CROOK: Now, correct me if I'm wrong: (*Points to his stenciled name on shirt.*) But as you all can see, I've been "out of circulation."

MARÍA: So?

CROOK: (*Ignoring María. To Bernard.*) Now, the number of the channel depends on the town you're in, right?

MARÍA: Brilliant!

CROOK: (*To Bernard.*) Now you mentioned, what was it: Channel 13? (*Bernard nods.*)

BELINDA: What in the world is he talking about? (*María shrugs, rolls her eyeballs like a "minstrel", indicating Crook's insanity.*)

BERNARD: He's just tripping... (*To Crook.*) Yeh, man. Thirteen: Lots of flicks.

CROOK: (*Nods proudly.*) Ex-act-ly! (*The others look at one another, in despair, wondering if Crook is not really insane.*)

BERNARD: "Exactly"?

CROOK: (*Proudly.*) Uh, huh!... Where I've been, there *ain't* no Channel 13.

MARÍA: (*Short, boisterous laugh.*) Well! How do you like them apples?

CROOK: (*Continuing.*) Now one *sure* way of finding out where you are is to figure where you've been... And where I been, there weren't no number 13. (*There is silence for a long pause. The three others suddenly realize he is making sense.*)

MARÍA: Okay...I'm from the Bronx.

CROOK: The Bronx?

BERNARD: New York.

CROOK: You're from New York?

BERNARD: No, man, *she's* from New York.

CROOK: I thought she said the Bronx.

BERNARD: Same place, man.

CROOK: (*Annoyed.*) Well, shit! How am I supposed... (*To Bernard.*) And you?

BERNARD: Well, you know, man...I trip. But I been holding down in Venice lately...near the beach.

BELINDA: I'm from Beverly Hills.

MARÍA: (*Silly. With a short bump and grind.*) Oo, La La! Belinda smiles.

CROOK: (*Beat. Thinking.*) Least it's *mainly* Southern Cal... but... (*Indicating María.*) How'd she get here?

MARÍA: Oh...I'm staying around L.A. *now.* That idiot shrink won't let me split. (*Boisterous laugh.*) Won't he throw a fit when I don't show up for my session!

CROOK: (*Really pissed.*) Motherfucker! (*Beat. To María.*) We got business, woman! Less you want to make it on your own...

Voices, ad lib, of Scott and Pat, are heard offstage. Crook turns toward sound.

CROOK: You'd better. (*Beat.*) Hit the dirt. (*Hissing.*) Hit it, damn it! (*All four clumsily lay flat on their stomachs, looking toward the top of the dune.*)

Lights over four are dimmed. Enter Scott and Pat from right-rear. The dune separates the two groups. Scott and Pat freeze.

SCOTT: (*Whisper.*) Shh...I heard something. (*He takes his knife from his holster.*)
SCOTT: (*Pause. Hesitantly.*) Hello?
CROOK: (*Pause. Stronger.*) Who's there?
SCOTT: (*Pause.*) Well... Me and a lady. (*Beat.*) We're looking for water.
CROOK: Just the two of you?
SCOTT: Yes. (*Beat.*) We need help. (*Scott places the knife back in the holster.*)
CROOK: You don't say... Well, just you come and join the *other* lost sheep, brother.

Lights go off. Long pause.

Curtain down.

Offstage we hear sounds of computers ticking, electronics. Bob enters, in front of curtain. Familiar pipe and pad in hand.

BOB: (*Apologetic.*) We're still having some difficulty with the transformer... Please be patient.
WOMAN FROM AUDIENCE: Bob, is that Julie?
BOB: (*Jovial.*) With the smock? Yes, Julie Rand, from the Bio Lab.
MAN FROM AUDIENCE: Doctor, what I'd like to know... Did these individuals...pick the characters?
BOB: You mean did they, "try out" for the parts?
MAN FROM AUDIENCE: Well... Yes. What I'm trying to understand... is there any relationship between the real person from the institute, and the character?
BOB: (*Beat. Superior smile.*) Only insofar as the part is representative of the whole...that is, each man will find something of himself in every man.
WOMAN IN AUDIENCE: But surely...the participant...who is it, Crook?

BOB: Brother Crook.

WOMAN IN AUDIENCE: Yes...I mean, in real life—I don't recognize him—

BOB: Sorry... That's Ralph, uh... He's one of the guards here.

WOMAN IN AUDIENCE: What I mean...In real life, he's actually a Negro?

BOB: Well...yes. To *that* extent the selection of participants is not at random... And the same goes for Suzzie...and you'll see him later on...there's a... (*Pronounced in English.*) Joe Angel... Uh, I mean... (*In Spanish.*) Angel, José Angel... We did seek a Mexican to play...to adopt that selection.

MAN IN AUDIENCE: Who'd you get?

BOB: We couldn't get one from the Institute...there aren't any...not males, anyway... So we found a volunteer in one of our subsidiaries, a Mr. Razo. He's a social worker. (*Beat.*) But, please, ladies and gentlemen...no more questions. We've got the computer ready... By way of explanation... The difficulty is in the time extrapolation... You see, time is accelerated from the demonstration; that is, relative to our time... Nine to one.

MAN IN AUDIENCE: How 'bout when the computer...goes off?

BOB: (*Beat.*) Well...that's one of the problems... We can only guess at this point... It appears that—you notice from the previous difficulty... It seems that time accelerated quite rapidly... So, let's continue.

Lights on: soft orange lights, for it is dusk now. Exit Bob.

Curtain up. Same scenery as in previous scene. The group is sitting with their arms and hands around their legs, shivering, obviously cold, looking at Bernard. Bernard carefully selects the proper stick or twig for his "model" structure, which is a campfire, while on his knees.

MARÍA: That thing gonna work?

CROOK: Not 'fore we freeze our balls off!

SCOTT: (*Nicely.*) Don't bother Bernard. He's creating a masterpiece.

MARÍA: (*Mocking.*) Oh, he's an architect!

PAT: (*Joking.*) Bernard can do anything!

BELINDA: Catalina's finest!

CROOK: (*Jealous.*) Sheeet! (*Bernard, the architect, selects the final piece, places it gently on the top.*)

BERNARD: Voila!

SCOTT: Here, here!

All, except Crook, ad lib applause, hooray, etc. Enter from left-rear stage, Man with beret. Only his head shows over the and dune. He only stares at the group throughout the following.

BERNARD: (*Excitedly.*) Okay, Scottie... light it!

SCOTT: (*Offering cigarette lighter to Bernard.*) Heck, no ... it's *your* creation.

BERNARD: (*Refusing lighter.*) But it's *your* idea. I'm just a mechanic.

MARÍA: And he's modest, too?... Whew!

PAT: Bernard's an artist. (*Scott again offers the lighter to Bernard.*)

MARÍA: (*Reaching for the lighter.*) I'll light the damn thing!

Lights are rapidly becoming dimmer. The sun has set. A full moon comes out. We can see the silhouette of the Man in beret's head.

BERNARD: (*Comically. "Shooing" her away.*) Down, woman!

SCOTT: (*Jokingly. To María.*) To the kitchen, wench! (*María grabs for the lighter, but Scott pulls it away.*)

CROOK: (*Sour grapes.*) She ain't learned her place yet! (*María gives Crook "the finger", puckers her mouth obscenely.*)

MARÍA: (*To Crook.*) Screw you, buster!

CROOK: (*Indicating María.*) That one needs a good horse-whipping.

SCOTT: (*Handing lighter to Crook.*) You do us the honors, Brother Crook. (*Crook takes lighter and kneels to light fire. He snaps lighter several times throughout the following, without success, ad libbing a shit, fuck, etc.*)

BELINDA: (*To María.*) The "kitchen"? How provincial!

MARÍA: John Wayne types! (*Puffing and beating her chest.*) Me Tarzan! Uhg, uhg! (*The three women laugh.*)

CROOK: (*Snapping lighter.*) God damn machine!
BERNARD: (*Reaching, itching to get his hands on it.*) Let me.
  (*Crook tries it two more times then disgustedly hands it to
  Bernard. Bernard inspects it carefully, toying with it
  intensely, over the following.*)
PAT: God! I can barely feel my feet!
BELINDA: (*Joking.*) Maybe Bernard will have to amputate.
MARÍA: What'll he do with my frozen butt?
CROOK: Stick a banana in it...then we'll sell it for a nickel.
MARÍA: And you'd be the first one in line, sucker! (*Crook jabs
  a thumb in the air at María.*)
BERNARD: (*Fingering lighter.*) Um...um... Uh, huh! I've got
  it!

  *All five ad lib a hooray, etc. Silent pause, concentrating on
Bernard.*

BERNARD: (*Quietly. Beat.*) We're out of flint.
MARÍA: Shit!
BELINDA: Are you certain?
SCOTT: He knows.
PAT: What'll we do? (*Beat.*) Really, I'm freezing!
MARÍA: (*To Pat.*) At least you got a bra.
SCOTT: (*Beat.*) It can still be done... Right, Bernard?
BERNARD: (*Brightly.*) Yeh, right! (*Soberly.*) Uh, what do you
  mean, man?
SCOTT: To put it simply: Can you start a fire with sticks?
MARÍA: Can't you guys cut the clowning?
BERNARD: (*To Scott.*) I've never tried it.
SCOTT: Me neither, but I've seen it done...Vernon Kenecht,
  the youngest Eagle Scout in history—he also taught me
  how to...about the birds and the bees...
MARÍA: For Christ's sake!
SCOTT: Okay, okay... Look, Bernard, old buddy... You said
  you were a sailor?
BERNARD: I've sailed.
SCOTT: And a mountain climber?
BERNARD: I've been up a few, yeh.
MARÍA: Oh, Jesus, save me from these imbeciles!
SCOTT: Well...then I know you can do this little thing.
BERNARD: (*Picks up two sticks, looks at them. Pause.*) If Ver-
  non Net can do it...
SCOTT: Ke-necht. It's German.

BERNARD: Yeh, well...if some friggin' Nazi can do it... (*BERNARD begins to rub the two sticks over the following dialogue.*)

The moon is the sole light now.

BELINDA: (*To María.*) I don't think I'll last.

MARÍA: (*Putting her arms around her.*) You'll make it.

CROOK: My, my! Ain't that pretty?

SCOTT: It's a good idea...Pat? Why don't you get between Crook and me? (*Pat moves between them. Bernard is rubbing furiously, ad libbing a damn, fuck, etc.*)

PAT: If you don't mind.

CROOK: Mind? (*Beat.*) Whew! You know it's been *two years* since I snuggled with a woman.

MARÍA: (*Singsong, like a football cheer.*)
    If you can't get a woman
    Get a jailbird man!
    Right, Brother Crook?

CROOK: (*Angry.*) You got a big mouth, Mike.

PAT: I don't get it.

CROOK: Ah, she's talking 'bout the punks they got in the joints.

PAT: Punks?

CROOK: You know...homosexuals.

MARÍA: Right on, brother!

BERNARD: Son of a bitch!

SCOTT: Don't give up the ship, buddy! (*Pause while Bernard rubs.*)

MARÍA: Now I know how Jack London felt.

BELINDA: Jack London?

MARÍA: *To Build A Fire...* Remember?

SCOTT: At least he had matches.

PAT: But how could it be so cold after the heat?

MARÍA: Same as on the moon...or so they say.

BELINDA: That's right. What was it the astronauts said?

MARÍA: Jack Armstrong said...

SCOTT: (*Interrupting.*) *Neil* Armstrong.

MARÍA: (*Short chuckle.*) What's the difference?

PAT: Wasn't that a comic strip?

MARÍA: The All-American Boy.

SCOTT: (*Looks up at moon. Beat.*) Only one thing wrong.

CROOK: What's that?

SCOTT: We *can't* be on the moon. (*Points to moon.*) 'Cause there it is. (*All six turn toward moon.*)

PAT: (*Screams!*) Look! (*The Man in beret jerks head down and exits.*)

SCOTT: What is it?

PAT: (*Hysterical.*) Didn't you see it?

MARÍA: Slow down, kid.

SCOTT: (*Puts arm around her.*) Tell us.

PAT: It looked like...I don't know... A man...with a...cap or something. (*Scott rises and crosses to right-rear stage.*)

SCOTT: There's nothing here.

PAT: (*Indicating left-rear.*) Over there! I saw it. (*Scott crosses to left-rear stage. Back to audience.*)

SCOTT: Hello! (*Beat.*) Anybody there?

MARÍA: (*Beat.*) What is he doing?

PAT: Just...staring at us!

SCOTT: Hey, you!... Are you *there*? (*Scott turns and crosses to group. Bernard throws one of the sticks to rear stage.*)

SCOTT: I can't see anything.

BELINDA: Maybe it was an animal. (*The men look at one another for long pause. The women look at the men looking at one another and sense there is something wrong.*)

MARÍA: (*To men.*) Cat got your tongue, children?

BERNARD: (*Beat.*) I don't think it was an animal.

PAT: Why not?

SCOTT: It would have made a noise, or something.

MARÍA: Come on, what is it?

BELINDA: (*To Bernard.*) Why don't you think it's an animal?

BERNARD: (*Forced smile.*) Well, you know, man... Like this isn't their trip.

MARÍA: Cut the shit, will you!

SCOTT: (*Pause.*) All right... (*To Crook.*) I guess we should tell them.

CROOK: Okay by me.

MARÍA: Jesus Christ!

BERNARD: (*Beat.*) What we're trying to say, is... There aren't any animals around here.

BELINDA: You mean on *this* side of the island?

BERNARD: Well...yeh.

MARÍA: Wait a minute!... On *this* side?

PAT: (*To Scott.*) There *are* on Avalon? (*Pause.*)

CROOK: (*To Scott.*) We'd better tell them, man.

BELINDA: I swear to God, I'm going to...

MARÍA: (*Interrupting.*) Will you boys forget your male egos for one minute, for Christ's sake?

SCOTT: Okay, okay. (*Beat.*) When we went out this afternoon... (*Indicating the men.*) We didn't see anything.

BERNARD: Nothing.

CROOK: That's right. No animals, no birds...nothing.

PAT: (*Beat.*) Scott...we *are* on Catalina?

SCOTT: (*Pause.*) "For sure?..." I can't say... Seems more like—just a desert.

BELINDA: (*Spoiled.*) But you told us!

SCOTT: I know. (*Beat.*) We looked for signs of life...anything.

MARÍA: Now that you mention it...I haven't seen...not even a bug.

BERNARD: There's nothing green around here... The wood...it won't spark.

SCOTT: (*To Bernard.*) It won't?

BERNARD: It's weird, man!

PAT: What about the *thing* I saw?

SCOTT: We'll have to wait till morning.

CROOK: Could be the moon playing tricks on you.

MARÍA: (*Insinuating sex.*) "Tricks!"

CROOK: You *know* what I mean.

MARÍA: Yeh, I sure do... That's *all* you got on the brain: Tricks of the trade.

CROOK: Takes one to know one.

BELINDA: God, what are we going to do? I'm really hurting inside.

SCOTT: Maybe tomorrow we'll run into something.

MARÍA: Yeh...like what?

SCOTT: Food, water...who knows.

MARÍA: And we can have a picnic?

SCOTT: Well...

MARÍA: But how can we do that?

SCOTT: What?

MARÍA: A picnic?... How can we have a picnic without ants?

PAT: María!

MARÍA: No, really...I've always been told you can't...

CROOK: (*Interrupting.*) Motherfucker!

SCOTT: Hey, guy!

CROOK: No, fuck it, man! I've had it! These people are nuts.

MARÍA: Our squash is rotting.

CROOK: (*To Scott.*) You see? See what I mean?

MARÍA: Oh, get him, will you? (*To Crook.*) And you're so *straight*?

CROOK: Clowning around, all day long! Jesus, what's wrong with you people?

MARÍA: "*You*" people, "*you*" people! What the hell are you? An ape?

CROOK: (*Viciously.*) Look here, you dumb cunt!...

SCOTT: (*Interrupting.*) Hold it, you guys.

CROOK: (*To Scott.*) Get her off my back!

SCOTT: (*Calm.*) Sure, man... She's just nervous. (*Seriously.*) We all are.

BERNARD: If I just had a joint.

BELINDA: I'd settle for a cigarette.

SCOTT: (*To Crook.*) It's to be expected. We're all a little scared. (*Beat.*) But we've got to relax...

BERNARD: Keep our cool, man.

CROOK: I can't, not...

MARÍA: (*Interrupting.*) I can't do anything else.

CROOK: (*Shakes his head.*) Augh!

SCOTT: I've always noticed...the people that get through these things...they just relax.

MARÍA: As old Coop would say: "Yep".

BERNARD: *One* joint...that's all I'd ask for.

PAT: A nice warm bath.

MARÍA: In the nude, with a hamburger...

SCOTT: And a bottle of beer.

CROOK: (*Grabs his head with both hands.*) God almighty!

Silent pause as they dream. Offstage, from a long distance, we hear a long grito [Mexican yodel]. The six react with instant fright.

BELINDA: Oh, my God!

BERNARD: Holy shit! What *was* that?

SCOTT: Shh. Listen. (*Silent pause. We hear another long grito.*)

SCOTT: Sounds like an animal.

BELINDA: Or a bird.

MARÍA: No...it's Superman.

CROOK: Shut the fuck up!

SCOTT: Listen. (*Silent pause.*)

PAT: You know what it sounded like?

BELINDA: What? (*They all turn to Pat.*)

SCOTT: Tell us.

PAT: Well, I'm not sure...

CROOK: Come on, girl!

PAT: (*Beat.*) I think it was a *grito*.

MARÍA: (*Beat.*) A what?

PAT: *Grito*.

MARÍA: They something you eat?

PAT: It's a...warhoop, a Mexican yodel.

SCOTT: You know...

BERNARD: You're putting me on.

PAT: No, really. They do it all the time. In country-type music.

SCOTT: Yeh... She's right. Mary-achi music. I've heard it.

MARÍA: Mary who?

PAT: (*Pronounced in Spanish.*) Maríachi...Mexican cowboy music.

CROOK: You talking 'bout...you mean, one of them crazy Chicanos is out there?

BERNARD: Chi-kay-nos?

CROOK: Metsikuns... You know... Like when they's tanked up on terquiler?

BERNARD: What a trip!... Acidland!... Freaksville!... (*Looks up to Heaven. Praying.*) Lord... What would a *Mexican* be doing out here?

MARÍA: (*Beat. Pure Jewish.*) So?... And what's a nice Jewish girl like me doing here?

Absolute silence for two beats. Scott gives a chuckle. Belinda and Pat follow suit. María giggles. Bernard and Crook laugh louder. Then all six go into hysterics. On and on for 60 seconds. The men slow down. The women are in hysterics, crying.

SCOTT: Okay, okay! (*The men stop. The women continue.*)

SCOTT: (*His first truly serious emotion.*) Enough! Damn it, stop it! (*Throughout next line, the women ad lib, will slow down, quiet down, a whimper here, one there.*)

SCOTT: (*Beat.*) We've had our guts out... Now that's enough... Pat?... (*Beat.*) If we don't stop, we're really going to crack. (*Beat. They stop. They listen to him.*)

SCOTT: I don't know what the hell's going on here... None of us do. (*Beat.*) Now we may, or may not, be on Catalina

Island. (*Beat.*) But I do know that for the first time since
we've been here...we heard a sound. Maybe a voice.
(*Beat.*) Only living *things* make noises... Man or beast,
doesn't matter... (*To Bernard.*) There is life. (*Beat.*) So
let's go and find out who's this..."Mexican." (*Scott crosses
toward rear-center stage. He waits.*)

SCOTT: (*Motioning.*) Come on! Let's go, Bernard... Crook?...
Let's make it! All of us!

All begin to rise, as lights go off.

Curtain down.

Enter Bob, in front of curtain.

BOB: (*Smiling, obviously pleased.*) Uh, ladies and gentlemen... You've been so cooperative, you really are an
excellent audience... Why don't we just get up and
stretch our legs for a minute or two...(*Indicating projec-
tion-room crew.*) The boys need a break, too.

MAN FROM AUDIENCE: (*Jokingly.*) That's right, Bob. You'd
better give them a break, or the Union will picket you.
(*BOB laughs.*)

WOMAN IN AUDIENCE: Say, Bob.

BOB: Hi, Lucille.

WOMAN IN AUDIENCE: I've been wondering.

BOB: (*Jokingly.*) That could be dangerous around here.

WOMAN IN AUDIENCE: No, seriously...I was thinking...
Are they, the, uh, "participants"... Are they on drugs
now?

MAN IN AUDIENCE: I go along with that, uh, Bernard...
They do seem to be under, well, like L.S.D. (*General
laughter from audience.*)

BOB: (*Seriously.*) Now, look...why don't we just stretch... We
can deal with those questions afterwards... We'd like to
complete the demonstration first... Put your comments,
questions, whatever, on the pad... (*To Harry.*) Harry,
how about some music.

*Pause. Then, music: twelve tone, violin and string bass,
with electronic counterpoint.*

Then, strobe light on curtain: controlled, electronically, by musical vibrations.

After three minutes, music and strobe stop suddenly!

~

ACT TWO

Curtain up.

Light of moon and campfire. Topography generally same as in previous scenes. Except that the footlights are the edge of the beach. We hear sounds of waves, the bay is the audience. The rear half of stage is a line of sand dunes.

A thirty-year-old man, José Angel, sits on a log by the campfire, roasting a single, three-inch fish on a stick. He is a Chicano, wearing a simple, short-sleeved white shirt, blue Levis and a brown beret, which he never removes. His movements are exact, taut. He appears relaxed, in control, but his insides contain a raging bull. He wears a Zapata-like mustache, which he constantly plays with, ad lib... Now he finishes roasting, blows on it, and eats it, bones and all in three quick bites... He wipes his hands in the sand. The log carries several conch shells, several carefully arranged bits of twigs, sticks and strands of seaweed... He dips his fingers in one of the shells, which contains seawater, as if it were a finger bowl and dries his hands by blowing on them.

Enter, all six. Only their heads show over the top of the sand dunes. They neither move nor make a sound.

José, resting on the log, stares at the moon. He takes a piece of pointed shell, and using it as a marker, makes notations on the log. He computes the time by looking at his wristwatch... This is repeated three times... Then he takes one of the pieces of twig and tastes it, rolls it around in his mouth, grimaces, then spits it out. He kicks sand over his spittle. With his head bent over, and from the corner of his eye, he sees the six, but remains ostensibly unaware... He places the twig to one side... He takes another twig and goes through the exact same tasting routine.

Crook holds the knife in his hand. We can see the glitter of the blade.

José Angel now tastes the seaweed. He spits it out loudly.

JOSÉ: *¡Chingado! (He kicks sand over the spittle.)*

CROOK: Hey! *(José continues to "taste" the next twig and does not glance up.)*

CROOK: Hey! You!

JOSÉ: *(His head down.)* Come on in, *ese.*

MARÍA: *(Pause.)* He doesn't *look* like a cowboy.

SCOTT: *(Pause.)* Let's go... He's uh, *invited* us.

Scott stands, where we can see his full body, and the others follow suit. They carefully cross toward José's campfire. José looks at them only for a glance, then begins to put more sticks on the fire. The six stand around him, hesitantly, with the feeling that they've intruded. Crook carries the knife in his hand, at his side.

SCOTT: *(To José.)* We saw your fire, heard the waves.

CROOK: *(To José.)* Say, how long you been here?

JOSÉ: *(To women.)* Why don't you ladies warm yourselves?

PAT: Thank you. *(The women get nearer the fire, and rub their hands over the flames.)*

BELINDA: I thought I'd freeze.

CROOK: *(To José.)* You, by any chance, got matches?

BERNARD: I tried rubbing sticks.

JOSÉ: *(Whisper. Looks up. To Crook. Indicating knife.)* Put it away. *(Crook looks at Scott. Scott nods in agreement. Crook hands the knife to Scott.)*

MARÍA: *(To José.)* Was that you we heard screaming?

JOSÉ: *(Nods.)* It was me.

BELINDA: *(Warming her hands.)* This is the nicest fire!

MARÍA: Thank the good Lord for simple blessings.

PAT: Beautiful wood.

JOSÉ: It's not wood.

SCOTT: What?

CROOK: Looks like wood to me.

JOSÉ: *(Pointing to desert.)* The bushes growing are. But this loose stuff, looks like driftwood. It's not wood.

BERNARD: Yeh, man, I told them. Something's weird about it.

CROOK: You trying to tell me this ain't wood?

MARÍA: (*Okie slang.*) He sure enough is.

CROOK: (*Beat.*) That *is* water out there? (*Points to audience.*)

JOSÉ: (*Looking at audience.*) Salty seawater.

MARÍA: Naturally.

SCOTT: Say...look, my name's Scott.

JOSÉ: (*In Spanish.*) José Angel.

CROOK: (*Reaching for his hand.*) I'm Winifred Crook.

MARÍA: Winifred?

CROOK: Folks call me Brother Crook. (*Crook and José shake hands briefly.*)

SCOTT: She's María, that's Bernard, Belinda and Pat.

PAT: (*Stretching her hand toward him.*) *Mucho gusto, señor Angel.* (*José smiles, takes her hand and holds it as he says.*)

JOSÉ: *¿Qué eres, Chicana?* (*The others stare at them, uptight to hear them talk in Spanish.*)

PAT: *Pues... Soy de East Los...Maravilla...pero soy Koreana. ¿Y tú?*

JOSÉ: *¿Maravilla?... También de East Los, de los Quatro Flats.*

MARÍA: Whew! Look at them go!

BELINDA: (*To Pat.*) You can really talk it...I didn't know you were...uh, Spanish.

Pat looks at José, both aware of the significance of the classification. They smile at one another, knowingly.

PAT: I'm not.

BELINDA: Oh! (*Embarrassed. Beat.*) Well, it's a *beautiful* language.

MARÍA: (*Implying shut up.*) Honey! (*Silent pause. They all stare at the fire.*)

SCOTT: (*To José.*) You don't by any chance have any water.

JOSÉ: (*Indicating audience.*) Just what's out there...but you can't drink it.

CROOK: Say, *hermano,* you got any food?

JOSÉ: (*Indicating the things on the log.*) You can try that seaweed.

BERNARD: Hey, man, you mind?

JOSÉ: Go right ahead.

Bernard takes a strand of the seaweed, looks it over, smells it, grimaces, then with a shrug, tastes it. Immediately he spits it out!

BERNARD: (*Choking.*) Augh! Fuck! Forget it!

MARÍA: (*Boisterous laugh.*) You'll never make a Chink.

JOSÉ: (*Beat. To six.*) Why don't you sit down? (*They all sit around the fire.*)

CROOK: Say, *hermano* Joe, you don't live here?

JOSÉ: Name's José... It's my campfire.

CROOK: Yeh, sorry.

SCOTT: What he means... You're not from around here?

The tempo of the dialogue is increased throughout the following:

JOSÉ: And you?

SCOTT: What?

JOSÉ: (*To Crook.*) How'd you get here?

CROOK: Well, I...

JOSÉ: (*To Bernard.*) Where'd you wake up?

BERNARD: I don't know, man, I...

SCOTT: (*Interrupting.*) Just a minute, Bernie.

José gets up suddenly. He reaches for more wood. The six tense at this movement.

SCOTT: (*Carefully.*) We're in a peculiar situation, Mr. Angel.

José feeds some sticks to the fire. He still retains a couple in his hand.

SCOTT: We had an accident...in a boat. You're the first person we've come across... So, naturally, we're curious.

JOSÉ: And what are your plans?

SCOTT: (*Perturbed.*) Why do you keep asking so many questions?

JOSÉ: And why do you?

SCOTT: Like I said...

JOSÉ: Yeh, I know, you're curious... And so am I. (*Beat.*) I'd like to know who put me here, just like you...

Belinda faints, falls back. María quickly grabs her in her arms.

MARÍA: Hey! Quick!

All but José rush to her, hovering over her. José quickly stands, crosses to the log, takes a handkerchief, dips it in the conch shell, then hands it to María.

JOSÉ: It's probably the change from hot to cold. (*He bends over and lifts her eyelids, touches her forehead.*)
JOSÉ: I think she's had a stroke.
MARÍA: Oh, Christ!
JOSÉ: (*To the men.*) Why don't you *vatos* come over here. (*He indicates right-front stage. Bernard and Crook look to Scott for the answer. Scott nods, stands, then they follow José to extreme right-front stage.*)

Dim yellow light over the huddle.

JOSÉ: (*Pause.*) I heard you people back at your site.
SCOTT: You're the one Pat saw? (*José nods. Crook looks suspiciously at Scott.*)
CROOK: How come you ran away?
JOSÉ: (*Pause.*) I didn't like what I saw.
SCOTT: (*Pause.*) I understand...I guess we look pretty...
CROOK: (*Interrupting.*) Fucked up! Just like I been saying all along.
BERNARD: (*To José.*) Hey, man... (*Indicating Belinda.*) You think she'll be all right?
JOSÉ: (*Beat.*) I don't know. It doesn't look good.
BERNARD: Man, this is getting too heavy... What the hell are we going to do?
JOSÉ: None of you know how you got here?
SCOTT: (*Beat.*) Not positively... The only thing I recall is being on a boat for Catalina.
BERNARD: And we're not even sure of that.
CROOK: I know I wasn't on any boat... (*To José.*) Just look at my clothes.
JOSÉ: (*Nods. Beat.*) We're *not* on Catalina.
SCOTT: (*Beat.*) You *know* this?
JOSÉ: (*Nods.*) Catalina is a populated island, with trees, water.
SCOTT: We couldn't be on the other side of Avalon?
JOSÉ: (*Nods.*) This is a man-made island. (*Silent pause for thirty seconds.*)
BERNARD: (*Fear in his voice.*) "Man-made"?
JOSÉ: The wood, it tastes like plastic.

BERNARD: Plastic?

JOSÉ: (*Nods. Beat.*) I've calculated the movements of the sun and the moon.

SCOTT: I *know* something's strange about that.

JOSÉ: There's no relation between my watch and the sun... Sometimes it goes steady, then it practically jumps ahead.

BERNARD: Man, I can't take this weird shit... It's getting...I don't know.

CROOK: (*To Bernard, fatherly.*) We've got to maintain, brother.

BERNARD: No, man...this is more than I can handle.

María screams. The men jerk their heads toward the women.

MARÍA: Get over here!

The men rush to the women.

They all stand gaping at Belinda who is motionless. María holds Belinda in her arms like a child, rocking back and forth. Pat cries. José leans over and puts his ear on Belinda's chest. He stands, nods, indicating that she's dead, and sighs, turning away from them, looking at the moon.

Bernard looks straight down at Belinda. He touches her face with both his hands.

BERNARD: (*With a sob.*) No, man, this is more than they can want. I've had it!

SCOTT: (*To María.*) You're sure? She's really... (*María simply nods and Pat cries.*)

CROOK: (*To José.*) What do they want?

JOSÉ: Us, what else?

CROOK: But what's going on here? (*Beat.*) I mean, they *had* me! What more can they want?

JOSÉ: Us, *vato.* The bastards want us, totally... They're just beating us down first.

Lights off. Long pause.

Curtain down.

Enter Bob—footlights go on—smokes pipe, casually.

BOB: Another slight delay, ladies...

WOMAN IN AUDIENCE: (*Interrupting.*) Bob! I'm confused! Are they, is she...

BOB: Dead?

MAN IN AUDIENCE: Oh, come on!

SECOND WOMAN IN AUDIENCE: I thought this was a *demonstration.*

BOB: It is.

SECOND MAN IN AUDIENCE: (*To Bob.*) Don't be absurd... If it were, she'd be dead.

SECOND WOMAN IN AUDIENCE: (*Controlled hysteria.*) Oh, come on! (*Beat.*) Bob, come on. This isn't *really* happening... Come on!

BOB: (*Relaxed. Long pause. Staring at audience.*) Perhaps it's the auditorium. (*Puffs on his pipe.*) We're ready to go on again.

Curtain up.

Lights. Early morning. Sun on horizon. Orange-gray.

Scene, same location, José's campsite. Belinda's body has been removed. Scott, María, Crook and Pat are lying motionless, asleep, in that order of half-moon circle. Bernard is further upstage, on his stomach, motionless, knife at side.

Enter José with several sharply pointed sticks. [n.b.: The men have nine-day growths of beard and mustache.] He sticks them in the sand near the campfire. He starts to gather sticks for the fire. Pat sits up and stares silently. María awakens.

PAT: (*Depressed. To José.*) Have you seen yourself?

JOSÉ: (*Normal. Pulls beard. Beat.*) Unless I'm completely... they've speeded up time about...I don't know...this is close to a two-week beard.

MARÍA: The son-of-a-bitches...my period's started... A week early!

Scott wakes up. Rubs his face, totally surprised.

SCOTT: Hey... (*Holding his beard.*) See this?

JOSÉ: Yeh, we know.

MARÍA: (*Looking at Crook.*) He's the same.

Crook awakens, sits up.

PAT: (*Rising and looking toward Bernard.*) I guess Bernard's the same.

JOSÉ: (*Quickly crosses to Pat, between her and Bernard. Gently.*) Forget Bernard.

All of them stare away from both José and Bernard, intuitively knowing the next line.

JOSÉ: He killed himself. Stuck the knife in his chest.

SCOTT: (*Slightly concerned.*) *My* knife?

MARÍA: What's the difference?

CROOK: Yeh. What's the difference?

José returns to the fire and feeds it sticks. Only Pat looks at Bernard's body, the others simply stare at audience. Long pause.

MARÍA: (*To herself.*) I don't even have to go to the toilet.

CROOK: (*To himself.*) Me neither. (*Long pause.*)

PAT: (*To herself.*) I'm not even hungry.

José stands and looks at the bunch.

CROOK: (*To himself.*) Me neither. (*Long pause.*)

SCOTT: (*To himself.*) I wonder if they'll really come.

MARÍA: Not before we all die...

CROOK: Or do ourselves in.

José is observing them. He is the only seemingly normal one. Long pause.

PAT: (*Not too convincingly.*) Shouldn't we bury him?

SCOTT: (*Looking at José.*) Well?

MARÍA: Shit, we could just move.

CROOK: Yeh... easier to take the fire further down.

MARÍA: No buzzards around here anyway.

CROOK: I'd eat one if there was.

MARÍA: I thought you weren't hungry.

CROOK: *I'm* not... (*Beat. Touching his chest.*) The body is.

MARÍA: Yeh, I guess I'd eat just about anything myself.

They all look at one another. They can't allow themselves to look at the body. Guilt is on their faces. They sense where the discussion is leading, so they stop. Long pause.

JOSÉ: (*Carefully.*) Yesterday... or whenever it was... I found a fish. Just a small one.

CROOK: What?

JOSÉ: *Before* you came.

PAT: Is that when you let out a *grito*?

JOSÉ: (*Nods a yes. Beat.*) There's just very little sea life... No crabs or things... I've only seen a few fish. Very small.

PAT: Can you... (*Indicating spear.*) Catch them with those spears.

JOSÉ: I doubt it. I was lucky.

MARÍA: (*Reminiscent laugh.*) Old Bernard probably could.

SCOTT: God!

MARÍA: (*To Scott.*) Well?

Crook begins to stare at Bernard's body.

JOSÉ: There is seaweed.

PAT: We can't eat that.

JOSÉ: We can use it for a net... Maybe we can weave a net to catch fish. (*Pause. No reaction from the group.*) With a net and the spears... maybe we can catch some fish.

Only Pat reacts.

PAT: (*Confused.*) But... if we've been here a week... or whatever... I thought people died if they didn't get water.

JOSÉ: (*Shrugs.*) I don't understand it either.

MARÍA: What difference does it make? (*Louder, with anxiety.*) What the fuck difference does it make!

JOSÉ: (*Ostensibly ignoring her anxiety.*) Maybe they've made... I don't know, some chemical change in us... We would be dead now, if it was two weeks.

SCOTT: I guess you're right... Maybe they've made our stomachs like... camels, or something.

MARÍA: (*Boisterous laugh.*) Camels!

SCOTT: Well, you know what I mean.

MARÍA: (*Exasperated.*) Ah, forget it. I was thinking about... Liz and Burton.

SCOTT: Come on, María!

MARÍA: (*Laughs.*) You remember that movie: Hump the hostess! (*Laughs. Beat.*) Well, this is Hump The Camel. (*Serious.*) If you didn't already.

PAT: (*Beat.*) What do you mean?

MARÍA: (*Nods, obscene smile. Indicating Crook.*) Ask him.

They all focus on Crook. He challenges their stare.

SCOTT: (*To María.*) What stuff you got now?

MARÍA: (*Beat.*) As if I didn't know.

JOSÉ: (*Impatiently.*) All right! Get it out.

MARÍA: (*Deadly serious.*) You think I don't know? You really
think we're all so stupid? (*Beat.*) You know god damn well
what I mean!

PAT: I don't.

MARÍA: (*Bitterly.*) No, honey, you wouldn't. (*Beat.*) God damn
it, I'm talking about Belinda. (*Beat.*) I'm talking about
why... (*Indicating Crook.*) he insisted... (*Indicating José
and Scott.*) they bury her.

JOSÉ: Don't be stupid.

MARÍA: You bastards think we're so dumb. I know you just
wanted...

JOSÉ: (*Interrupting.*) Shut up! Just...

MARÍA: (*Interrupting. Indicating Crook.*) Look at him! You
don't see *him* denying it! You crumbs! You sick bastards!

CROOK: (*To María.*) And what would you of done? (*Beat.*)
Stuck your finger up her ass?

PAT: (*Puts her hands over her ears. Screams.*) Oh, don't!

*María falls forward on her knees, lunging toward Crook,
like a vicious cat, hands clawing at him. He deftly steps to one
side and she falls flat on her face. Crook laughs mockingly at
her. He turns and steps away from her.*

CROOK: (*Disgusted.*) You people! Lying and make-believe!

*María is on her knees, takes one of the spears stuck in the
ground, and in one move lunges at Crook. José swiftly takes
two steps and simply kicks the spear out of her hand. Crook
moves aside, stepping toward Bernard's body.*

JOSÉ: (*To María.*) ¡Pendeja! (*María falls to her face, beats the
ground with her fists.*)

PAT: Please! María, please!

*Pat crosses to María, drops to her knees and strokes her
head in comfort. Crook looks down at Bernard's body, sees the
knife, picks it up, turns, and awaits further attacks. Crook is
ostensibly calm now. He plays with the knife in his hand, as in
defiance of all. Long pause.*

JOSÉ: (*To himself. Looking at audience.*) This is what they
   want. We're doing it just right.

PAT: José? (*José turns to her.*)

PAT: (*Pleading.*) Please... Why don't we bury Bernard?

SCOTT: She's right. We should.

JOSÉ: (*Looking at Crook.*) What do you say? (*They all concentrate on Crook.*)

CROOK: You know what I got to say.

MARÍA: Oh, God, not again.

CROOK: Stupid, bitch! You think I'm some punk?

PAT: (*To María.*) Please, we've had enough.

JOSÉ: (*To Crook.*) Yeh, I know what's on your mind.

SCOTT: (*Apprehensive.*) What? (*To Crook. Looking at knife.*)
   Hey, man, what is it?

CROOK: I don't know anymore about you people. (*Beat.*) I got
   to be in some fucking nightmare, that's all I know.

SCOTT: But we're *all* in it.

CROOK: (*Indicating María. Cynical.*) We're together? (*Beat.*)
   You see, Jack...that's the make-believe I'm talking about.
   Your kind always been saying we're together... Shit, all
   my life that's all I heard: To-geth-er! Always! When everybody can see we ain't never been no more closer than we
   are right now. (*Beat. Indicating José.*) Ask him. He
   knows. He's been through the same shit. (*They look at
   José. José nods, his hands extended, he indicates that he
   doesn't want to respond to this line. Long pause.*)

PAT: (*To José.*) Well, are we going to take care of Bernard?

SCOTT: (*To José.*) We should. (*Crosses toward Bernard's
   body.*)

CROOK: (*Wild gaze. Lifts knife.*) No! Just wait! (*All concentrate on Crook.*) Now...you just wait for a minute there.
   (*Beat. Becoming deranged.*) Now... (*To María.*) I'll admit
   I *thought* about the girl... What man wouldn't. (*Beat. To
   all.*) We're all gone, any fool can see that. (*To José.*) That
   fish thing, it's crazy. (*To all.*) And he knows it.

PAT: (*To José.*) José?

JOSÉ: (*Calmly.*) Let him finish.

CROOK: (*Beat.*) So, this is the way I figure it. (*Beat.*) If I don't
   get some food pretty soon... (*Beat.*) I'm gonna die. Just
   like that! (*He looks at them for a response.*) Well, you people can keep up your stores...but *this* man ain't going to
   die. Least not without trying something.

SCOTT: (*Perplexed.*) What're you getting at, man?
MARÍA: (*To Scott.*) Don't be so naive, Scott. Can't you see?
JOSÉ: (*To Crook.*) So you want to kill us, or eat Bernard? Which is it?
PAT: Oh, my God! You can't be serious!
JOSÉ: (*Carefully.*) He's serious.

Pat crosses to José. She grabs his arm with both her hands.

PAT: (*Hysterical.*) You don't mean that! *Please*, José! (*José puts his arm around her, but keeps his eyes on Crook.*)
CROOK: You cry all you want. All I know is…he's dead…I'm still alive.
SCOTT: And you're going to?… Hey, man!… You can't!
CROOK: To put it simple, brother…any man tries to stop me: He gets it, too. (*Long pause. All tense.*)
JOSÉ: That's exactly what they want.
PAT: (*Whimpering.*) I don't understand anything anymore.
JOSÉ: They put us here…no food, no water…we probably don't need water… They're trying to see who can live through it.
CROOK: I don't give a fuck no more… Reasons don't matter!
JOSÉ: You're right. (*Beat.*) But what'll you do after you finish off Bernard?
MARÍA: (*Sarcastic.*) He'll cross that person when he comes to him.
JOSÉ: (*To María.*) Don't! (*Beat. To Crook.*) Then what'll you do after you finish on Bernard? Start on us?
CROOK: I don't know! Maybe… Fuck it! You're just giving me reasons again.
MARÍA: What he's trying to tell you… Once a cannibal, always a cannibal.
PAT: Oh, God! What's happening to us?
JOSÉ: We've *got* to deal with this. (*Beat. To Crook.*) You're right about the Man, and you're right about the make-believe.
CROOK: That's what I've been saying.
MARÍA: On and on.
JOSÉ: But we've got to find the *reasons*.
CROOK: I don't want no reasons… I had too many of them!

José squats on his haunches.

SCOTT: (*To José.*) What reasons?

JOSÉ: (*Beat.*) The government, or whoever...they went through a lot of trouble, a lot of bread was spent in building this place... Now they didn't go to all this trouble just to watch us die... They aren't going to let us all die... (*To Crook.*) And you can bet they aren't going to let you kill us just to feed yourself. (*Long pause.*)

CROOK: (*Defeated.*) Then what do you make of it?

José nods, looks at the ground, doodles in the sand, thinking.

JOSÉ: (*Head down.*) We just have to wait. They'll come.

MARÍA: The bastards always do.

PAT: And then what?

JOSÉ: (*Looks up.*) They'll do with us what they want.

MARÍA: Like vegetables.

CROOK: Not me they won't! (*He holds the knife high in the air.*)

SCOTT: (*To Crook.*) I doubt if that'll protect us.

CROOK: Protect? Shit, man, I'm tired anyway. I'll use it on myself.

Long pause. Pat crosses to José and sits next to him. Crook sits and stares at the knife. María begins to "draw" in the sand.

MARÍA: Oh, well. (*Long pause.*)

JOSÉ: That's the ultimate protection.

CROOK: What's that?

SCOTT: The knife?

JOSÉ: Suicide. (*Beat.*) The last thing we can do...our only defense, fight... Whatever they plan to do with us...if we don't like it...we can all kill ourselves.

MARÍA: That'll be some movie.

They all ad lib, a smile, a laugh.

JOSÉ: That's one thing the bastards hate to do.

CROOK: What's that?

JOSÉ: Waste money.

PAT: God, how I know that.

MARÍA: You mean?

JOSÉ: (*Smiling, but not happy.*) Sure...if we all threaten mass suicide...they'll either let us go...or their experiment's a failure.

MARÍA: Or we...

CROOK: Do ourselves in... Why not?

JOSÉ: Sure. Why not?

Pat crosses to José. She touches his arm.

PAT: I don't think I could do it.

JOSÉ: Why not?

PAT: *Soy católica.*

JOSÉ: (*Sighs. Beat.*) *Y yo también...pero no importa.* (*José puts his arm around her.*)

MARÍA: Hey... (*To José and Pat.*) What are you two up to? (*José nods, smiles.*)

CROOK: It's called... They're tight.

MARÍA: I know, stupid!

JOSÉ: (*To Crook and María.*) You know, the way you two fight... One would think you had the hots for each other.

CROOK and MARÍA: Shit! (*The two look at one another, then laugh.*)

JOSÉ: See what I mean. (*Long pause.*)

SCOTT: (*To José.*) Hey, guy... You *really* believe it would work?

JOSÉ: (*Beat.*) It makes sense to me... If we can seriously convince them that we'd do it.

SCOTT: And what if the bluff doesn't work?

JOSÉ: (*Beat.*) Then we just have two choices: Obey them...or kill ourselves.

MARÍA: If only we had some popcorn.

CROOK: (*Pleasantly. Laughs.*) Woman, you are really something else!

MARÍA: Don't knock it, unless you've tried it.

CROOK: (*Beat.*) I just might do that. (*Long pause.*)

SCOTT: (*To José.*) How would we...do it?

JOSÉ: (*Pointing at spears.*) We could use those.

Scott crosses to spears, picks one up and fingers the tip.

JOSÉ: They'll work.

CROOK: Well...shit, give me one.

Scott picks up the bunch, hands two to Crook and two to José. Crook hands one to María.

CROOK: (*Smiling.*) Here's your poison, baby.
MARÍA: (*Southern drawl.*) Why, honey-child, I *do* declare! (*Long pause.*)
SCOTT: (*To José.*) You think they'll come soon? (*José shrugs.*)
PAT: I don't know if I'll be able to.
JOSÉ: No one does.
MARÍA: I guess it depends on... I don't know...
JOSÉ: (*Interrupting.*) Character?
MARÍA: (*Boisterous laugh.*) Yeh, that's it! And we got plenty of that!

They all laugh. Scott crosses to where María and Crook are and sits with them. Two-minute pause. Silence.

VOICE OF DOOM: (*Basso-profundo-computer. Offstage.*) GOOD AFTERNOON, LADIES AND GENTLEMEN, WELCOME TO EDEN-OAK RESEARCH INSTITUTE...

The five jump up, startled. They each hold their spears in front of them. Pat and María scream out.

VOICE OF DOOM: (*Offstage.*) There is nothing to fear... IF YOU WILL SIMPLY FOLLOW THE FOLLOWING RULES YOU WILL NOT BE HARMED... (*Pause.*)

Sound of tape running wild through recorder, a la Donald Duck, in extremely high-pitched screeching.
All lights off.
Sounds from audience: screams, shouts, laughter, hysteria.

BOB: (*Angry. Offstage.*) God damn it, Harry!... Can't you fix that fucking machine?

CURTAIN.

[Circa 1970]

NON-FICTION

RACIAL EXCLUSION

One million Mexicans live in Los Angeles County. Thirteen percent of the population, they constitute the largest ethnic minority in America's largest county; a local government which ostentatiously celebrates their dying traditions and ostensibly perpetuates their ancient, Hispanic/Indio culture but does not, according to recent arguments before a three-judge California Court of Appeal, protect and provide for them with equality under law in the selection of the county Grand Jurors which sat but a token three (3) of them in the past ten years.

Because an effective challenge to the composition of a Grand Jury results in a reversal or "quashing" of the indictment, and because the issue has never been successfully litigated in a California Court—it was denied in both the Huey Newton and the Sirhan cases—the legal ramifications are enormous. Where the further issue of racial discrimination in the selection process is attributed to the Superior Court judges in this day of judicial inquiry—see, e.g. Abe Fortas—the legislative overreactions could be extreme. Add to this that the defendants are militantly nationalistic Mexican Americans ("Chicanos") accused of conspiracy to organize and participate in the disruption of segregated Mexican-American high schools—a felony—in protest of an emasculating acculturation, and the possible political consequences simply boggle the mind of an already burning metropolis recently inflamed by a "racial" campaign for the office of mayor.

Once the owners and possessors of this City of Angeles, this "Spanish Surnamed" peoples with a unique proximity to their original homelands—only three hours to Mexico by Greyhound—continue to increase at twice the rate of the Anglo majority throughout the entire Southwest where, in one fast and furious year, they have without precedent adopted a nationalistic, militant posture all their own with a zeal and cry the Anglo assumed had died, if not with the grant of citizenship under the treaty of Guadalupe Hidalgo, at least with Zapata.

Whatever their elders and the more affluent may have
thought—the subjunctive is required in recognition of the
myriad opinions—for the young (13-25) Mexican American
and for the pre-Viet Nam veteran (26-40), their siesta ended
with the East Los Angeles walkouts of March '68. Living in
burgeoning barrios, collectively know as East L.A., and dropping out of their dilapidated, segregated high schools at a fifty
percent rate, thousands of these quiescent, brown "Chicanos"
organized and boycotted their schools during the first week of
March, 1968.

The myth of the passive Mexican blew up in this anxious
city's poisonous air as waves of mini-skirted, brown-skinned,
black-haired girls echoed in tandem the angry, clenched-fist
cry of these new *machos* in the *barrios*: *Viva La Raza! Chicano Power! Education—Not Eradication!* These were the new
gritos, the young, brown radicals (sporting cocky brown berets
and khaki field-jackets) exhorted their poverty-ridden, black-
eyed *camaradas* to yell to the *gabacho* (gringo) as they
marched to the School Board with their proposals previously
hammered out at ubiquitous community meetings over a six-
month period.

Throughout the spring and early summer of '68, their
demands were presented orally and in writing to a School
Board already burdened with "Black" demands and an apa-
thetic constituency becoming hostile to any demands requiring an increase in taxation or a loss in power. The list of
grievances were angrily stated both in simplistic generalities
and in realistic specifics; but ultimately what they asked for
was a new system, a new recognition for this group. If one
seriously listened, what they were saying was simply that the
Chicano wanted no more of a society inspired, oriented and
dominated by the Anglo; he whom they accused of denying
them their culture and language and distorting their history
and identity without a viable or an acceptable substitution.

While an anxiously precarious School Board negotiated
publicly and in chambers with various committees and power
structures, the Chicano militants agreed to call off their
activist demonstrations and instead plunged into orthodox
political activity behind a Mexican-American candidate to the
state legislature. With the crucial California law-and-order
primary but a fortnight away, and while a roaring heat/smog
summer taunted the *Batos Locos* (crazy guys) in East L.A. to

fantasize of their own 'Watts,' the seemingly cool prosecutorial officers of this bombastically flamboyant city of seven million transplants got uptight and nearly blew it.

Singling out thirteen of the Chicano "leaders," D.A. Younger and Police Chief Reddin—both rumored to be in line for the Nixon administration at the time—went for broke: Despite the School Board's grant of amnesty to all students and teachers involved in the walkouts on May 27th of '68, the Grand Jury returned shotgun indictments against The East L.A. 13 on fifteen (15) separate counts of conspiracies to disrupt the public schools; felonies, punishable by up to forty-five (45) years in the state penitentiary...in effect, a life sentence!

With the Grand Jury's recommendation of ten-thousand dollars bail for each of the thirteen defendants, and with the dramatic, coordinated roundup in their homes and in their organizational offices the last weekend of the primary, the fight was on: Immediately the traditional political activity ceased; the issues were no longer discriminatory education. Now it was abusive and excessive prosecutorial power by an unrepresentative government—a tailor-made issue for these young, Chicano nationalists.

More Mexicans are concentrated in the city of Los Angeles than anywhere else, with the exception of Mexico City. Fully cognizant of the political significance and consequences of their actions, The East L.A. 13 did what had not been done by any Mexican American: They challenged the jurisdictional power of the indicting body (the Grand Jury) on grounds of its discriminatory selection and resultant unrepresentative character by the very judicial officers, the Superior Court judges, who would not inquire into their allegedly criminal conduct.

Laying the groundwork for appeals to the Supreme Court, they retained expert witnesses and used cardboard boxes full of documentary and statistical evidence to legally establish their identity as a people separate and distinct from the majority, thereby meeting the constitutional requirement of "classification" which is a pre-condition to a demand for consideration and representation from within their group upon the Grand Jury.

An expert urban sociologist lectured to a singularly silent court and counsel that the defendants did *indeed* belong to a separate and distinct group of persons despite their anthropological classification as Caucasians and their legal recognition as citizens. Throwing statistics to the winds while the thirteen defendants took notes, the lady expert told a lady judge that the Mexican had been isolated, counted and analyzed by every level of American government... As a heterogeneous group they meet all accepted criteria of ethnic classification, including internal and external identification; that this group contains a communality of values and behavior patterns even more amply than the Anglo-Caucasian majority and the unquestioned "Negro" minority. While "Mexican Americans" compromise the vast majority of this self-identifying group, members of other Hispanic/Indio cultures, too few in number and disparate for separate integrity, also consistently link themselves with the "Spanish Surnamed" identity. All of these peoples have been victimized in the areas of education, employment, housing and the judicial process, resulting in a more alienated and a more impoverished group than even the Black person, at last in the Southwest where they are by far the largest single minority...

They call themselves members of *La Raza*, connoting a sense of peoplehood—much as the Jews identify with *chosen people*—which binds together the meanest with the most virtuous, the most humble with the richest. The vast majority are bilingual and Catholic. They tend to live in highly clustered *barrios*, residentially the most segregated of all the minorities, where they share a communality of ideals and *costumbres* distinct from the Anglo. Family roles, folk beliefs, incessant interest in themselves and in Mexican/Latin affairs all play off the omnipotent and omnipresent central theme to their lifestyle: *Machismo*, that instinctual and mystical source of manhood, honor and pride that alone justifies all behavior.

Had the witness not been a lady, perhaps the defendants and their supporters would have carried her off the stand on their shoulders, for they emotionally and intellectually knew the potential implications of the testimony. Coming from an articulate, academic Anglo, as it did, they swallowed it whole cloth into a nationalistic/revolutionary jargon posing as ideology. The staccatoed, computerized, analytical statistics "justified" their very existence; what had been but an inchoate propaganda of their own now became a rational truth to serve them not only in their confrontations with the Anglo establishment, but more importantly with their painful attempts at the proselytizing of a Mexican community which condemned the walkouts along with their patent nationalism and which winced at the racial rancor in their verbosity. The older, passive/fatalistic Mexican had become threatened by this sudden public attention now given to his race by the walkouts. His ancient fear of identification with the peon—translated "Black" in '68—supported his need for anonymity, and brooding had become a way of life; the exposure would surely lead to retribution and a return to yesterday's problems... And now this Grand Jury challenge accusing Superior Court judges of bigotry!

In Los Angeles County, the Grand Jurors are nominated by the Superior Court Judges. Over a ten-year period, 178 judges nominated a total of 1,501 nominees, of which only twenty were Spanish Surnamed. Of these judges, 91.6% never once nominated a Spanish Surnamed person. The actual Grand Juror is then selected at random from the list of nominees, and, understandably, the result has been a mere token representation of ALL the minorities. Specifically, only four (4) out of total of 210 Grand Jurors, or 1.9%, has been a person with a Spanish Surname, and one of these is in fact a Negro.

From the testimony of the thirty-three judges subpoenaed to testify, at times vague if not downright hostile, a reasonable composite of the 1959-1968 "grand juror" was constructed: (1) He is comparatively advanced in years. (2) He is wealthy, of independent financial means. (3) He is, or was, a business owner, executive, or professional—or married to one. (4) He is a close personal friend, occasionally once removed, of a Superior Court Judge. (5) He is of the White race... In a word, as characterized by an appellate Judge: WASP.

With but one or two exceptions, each of the judge/witnesses stated under oath that he neither asked nor nominated a Mexican because he knew none who were qualified and/or able to accept the nomination, and further, that he did not feel personally obligated to affirmatively seek out and consider potential nominees from the various identifiable minority groups within the community.

The trial court denied the motion to quash because in its opinion there was no showing of intentional discrimination, since in each of the ten years *at least one Mexican was nominated.*

Racial exclusion was prohibited in jury selection as early as the Civil Rights Act of 1875. Five years later, the United States Supreme Court held that racial exclusion in the selection process violated the equal protection clause of the Fourteenth Amendment. This constitutional prohibition is not limited to discrimination against Negroes, although the defendant in nearly every important case has been of that class; it applies to any reasonably distinct classification of persons which may be excluded from consideration solely on the basis of race or any other irrelevant factor. Obviously it does not prohibit the state from setting reasonable standards for qualification, nor does it require that any particular jury contain a specific or proportional representation. No individual citizen has a right to consideration for jury services; on the contrary, one has a duty to respond if summoned. And, finally, no criminal defendant may demand that the particular Grand Jury which indicted him or the specific trial jury which tried him have even one member of his class thereon. The rule of law is simply a practical and logical recognition that these fact-finding bodies should be democratically constituted institutions, selected from a representative grouping; drawn from a cross section of the community—not an elitist, stacked body summoned to protect the interest of the most wealthy, the most intelligent, the most successful or the most...

But, as in every constitutional principle, the problem is that of proof. Where, by governmental edict, a class is peremptorily excluded or where a class is admittedly denied consideration, the rule is violated per se, and no further proof is required for reversal.

But what of token or symbolic representation? And what is the constitutional significance of patent or admitted proportional representation? Most significantly, what if the selection process, whatever the result, was admittedly carried out innocently and in good faith?

For nearly a hundred years now, the rule of law has remained constant. Equal protection of the laws is more than an abstract principle. It is a legal right which every citizen may demand and which each state must provide. The Supreme Court has consistently declared that limitation of a class no less than its exclusion is an evil to be condemned, whatever its form or whatever its motivation.

To reiterate, the problem is that of proof!—the *raison d'etre* of the legal profession. As direct evidence that discrimination almost universally exists in the minds or in the exclusive possession of the court official whose very conduct is being publicly challenged, the Supreme Court has relied heavily on expert opinion and statistical data as circumstantial evidence of class discrimination. A long-standing and significant disparity between the proportion of the defendant's class in the community as compared with the percentage nominated for jury duty will of itself raise a presumption of the class discrimination prohibited by the federal constitution. But it is only a presumption; i.e. a rational deduction from an observable fact. The burden is then cast upon the jury selector to explain, contradict or disprove the assumed fact of discrimination by other facts. He may, for example, show that he in fact considered the "excluded" class, or that the class does not exist, or that the class refused the nomination, or that none within the class are qualified.

But none of these "explanations" may simply be assumed or merely asserted, they must be proven. Specifically, protestations of innocence and/or good faith will not suffice. The constitutional imperative requires the official to affirmatively seek out and familiarize himself with the qualifications of all the recognizable classes within the community with the goal of reasonable and rational consideration; for "if there has been discrimination, whether accomplished ingeniously or ingenuously, the conviction cannot stand." (Justice Black, Smith v. Texas, (1940) 311 U.S. 218)

In the recent case of The East L.A. 13, (Salvador Castro v. Superior Court, (April, 1969) 2d App Dist No. 34718), the district attorney presented no proof whatsoever to rebut the asserted presumption. Instead, he merely argued to the three-judge court that the statistics and the judges' testimony did not show any intentional discrimination against the Mexican and that the seeming disparity could be attributed to the fact that eligibility depends upon qualification and availability. He argued that since the Mexican population was disproportionately young, alien, non-English speaking, economically disadvantaged and educationally inferior, "the raw population figures and percentages [would be] utterly meaningless."

While numerous Mexican partisans listened, the district attorney reminded the appellate judges that the modern grand jury's function included "highly sophisticated duties, such as accounting and business transactions." In response, counsel for the defense quoted Justice Brown of the Fifth Circuit Court—the court most frequently confronted with the issue—speaking in Brooks v. Beto [1966] 366 F2d 1:

"...the courts have consistently held that statistics speak louder than the Jury Commissioners...the law has never contented itself with any such hollow, shallow ignorance... It is not enough to choose from those they see... Innocent ignorance is no excuse. It neither shields the jury's action from scrutiny, nor does it justify the half-hearted, obviously incomplete performance of duty by the officials... The court has long been aware of this see-no-evil-hear-no-evil-find-no-evil approach."

Neither side to the controversy was unaware of the potential significance of the case. Studies made by the California Rural Legal Assistance indicate that nearly all California counties contain the same statistical racial disparity in their Grand Juries as does Los Angeles. Equally important is the fact that the issue may be raised by defendants other than racial minority group members, as it was in the recent trial of Sirhan B. Sirhan, whose attorneys used the evidence and arguments produced by the Chicano defendants. Why this defense has not been previously raised, either by Mexicans or any other excluded class, unfortunately reflects upon the legal profession. That it requires imagination and hard work is understandably a contributing factor; but perhaps the most compelling reason for their failure to raise the issue is that ultimately what the lawyer says in such a motion is an indictment of the profession which he professes and a castigation of the society to which he belongs.

True or not, the Chicano militants interpreted the D.A.'s argument to say that the Mexican was perhaps too stupid and too poor for service on the Grand Jury of Los Angeles. This "explanation" will simply serve as further evidence of the racist society which he seeks to destroy and which has compelled him to seek his destiny in an identity and a rage that this society can ill afford. Presently, the court has enjoined the trial. It may be months before the decision is pronounced.

But what of the Chicano radicals-becoming-revolutionaries? It is much too early to say in what direction their nationalism will travel; too soon to even suggest that their actions will be governed by the society's response to their claims for equality.

The concepts of integration, assimilation and acculturation describe historical relationships between Africans, Orientals and Europeans, persons all foreign to this land. Despite the lack of organization or of truly national leaders, despite the inability to articulate his rage, the Mexican-American claims the Southwest by right of prior possession, by right of ancestry. His most distinctive, prominent characteristic is his *Indio-Mestizo* blood; that is the deeper meaning of *La Raza*. And whether we speak of historical or Einsteinian time, it was but a few moons ago that this Southwest was inhabited exclusively by the Indians.

One thing is certain, this we can say: The Mexican will not perish for lack of dreams; for whatever the outcome, the young Chicano presently dreams of Zapata while reading his Che.

[1969]

UNA CARTA DE ZETA AL BARRIO

Estimada Raza:

Hace tres años que llegué al este de Los Angeles en busca de una historia sobre las actividades de La Raza. Pero en su lugar encontré mi propia identidad como un verdadero hijo de La Raza Cósmica. Vine de visita y como escritor, pero como me lo pidieron ustedes, Raza, y contra mis deseos personales, me he quedado en esta metrópolis, infestada por el smog y el racismo, como Abogado Chicano. (Asumo que este comentario es sobre las necesidades de nuestra gente, y no crítica de mis habilidades como escritor.)

Trabajé por un mes en la oficina del Defensor Público, por un mes, hasta que me corrieron por mi participación en actividades de la Raza y mis críticas del sistema judicial, que nos condena sin conocernos y nos sentencia sin permitir que nos defendamos con nuestro estilo propio.

Después del arresto de "Los 13 de East Los Angeles", Comité Chicano de Defensa Legal financió mis actividades hasta que algunos de sus miembros decidieron que no había suficientes fondos para continuar nuestras relaciones; decidieron que el poco dinero que había era más importante para marranos de fianzas (bail bond) que para el licenciado.

A razón de los esfuerzos de la redacción de la Revista *La Raza*, y otros Chicanos in East Los Angeles, el Fondo México-Americano para Defensa Legal, financiado por la Sociedad Ford (Ford Foundation), decidió emplearme como abogado bajo la dirección de su Jefe Salchicha en San Antonio y sus lambiscones en East Los Angeles, esos valientes avariciosos que se autollaman defensores de la fé.

Después de 6 meses, en enero 1970, estos abogados maricones me pidieron que renunciara, y para callar sus remordimientos, me pagaron suficiente dinero sangriento para mantenerme vivo...y para mantenerse vivos a sí mismos.

En agosto de 1970, el Programa Reggie (O.E.O) me dió una beca para continuar mi trabajo en el barrio. Expresamente me dijeron que aunque las reglas del programa contra la pobreza no permitían mi participación en casos "criminales", ellos se asegurarían que yo fuera pagado. También acordaron venir a mi defensa si se me atacaba por mis actividades.

Como ustedes saben, "Cara de Marrano Nixon" ha decidido destruir todos los programas de Ayuda Legal en el país; al menos esos que él cree le dan ayuda y albergue al "enemigo" (la gente). El "cowboy" Reagan ya ha empezado la destrucción del programa de Cruz Reynoso de Asistencia Rural Legal de California (CRLA). Juntos en menos de un año acabarán con cualquier oportunidad del Chicano para encontrar representación legal adecuada.

Recientemente los abogados Hugh Manes y Dick Weinstock de la Sociedad de Ayuda Legal de Los Angeles (L.A.N.L.S.S.), me informaron que sus programas y sus trabajos, por supuesto, podrían ser salvados si, (1) yo resignaba, o (2) debaja de defender criminales. Siendo el Búfalo Moreno que ustedes me han hecho, les dije que se metieran su trabajo.

En estos días represento a los "Biltmore 6", 6 Chicanos acusados de conspirar para incendiar el Hotel Biltmore mientras que el "cowboy" Reagan vomitaba su racismo sobre los problemas educacionales del Chicano en abril 1969.

El 23 de marzo comenzaré con la defensa de Rodolfo "Corky" Gonzales, que será procesado por segunda vez, por el mismo delito—su participación en la Moratoria Chicana del 29. Y en mayo, representaré a Raúl "Papus" Martínez, en su juicio por asesinato. El incidente resultó de un atentado contra su vida por ciertos "tapados" y bajo la dirección de ciertas "ratas".

Mi opinión es que la presente revolución sólo tendrá éxito cuando dejemos de engañarnos de que todavía hay esperanza de sobrevivir en este sistema racista.

La esperanza que nos da la Ayuda Legal es un paso en dirección equivocada. A pesar de las buenas intenciones de los "gabachos" liberales que nos defienden a su manera, estoy convencido que ultimadamente estaremos mejor cuando la Ayuda Legal, y otros programas del gobierno, se salgan del barrio. Si debemos sufrir, hagámoslo solos, sin miedo y con la dignidad de los que prefieren libertad a limosnas. Si estos "gabachos" liberales estuvieran seriamente trabajando para la Raza, tomando órdenes de la Raza, y realmente haciendo algo de valor, tal vez mi conclusión fuera diferente...pero la realidad es que todavía nos ven como "los prietitos" que necesitan su ayuda y actúan como los patroncitos de ayer—arrogantes y paternalistas.

Raza: a pesar de los constantes chismes sobre mi personalidad y vanidad, me presento ante ustedes como cualquier soldado que ha aprendido a tomar lecciones del pasado. Estoy listo a tomar órdenes de mi comunidad de La Raza Unida.

Específicamente: ¿Resigno? ¿Debo de parar de defender criminales? ¿Les digo a Nixon, Reagan y La Ayuda Legal que se vayan a la chingada?

Espero su respuesta. Espero su apoyo.

[1970]

DECLARATION OF CANDIDACY

The history of Los Angeles County is one of violence, vice and corruption in high places. Neither the expenditure of huge sums of money nor an increase in the personnel of all the law enforcement agencies throughout the county has diminished the decay inherent in our communities. On the contrary, history is replete with examples to prove that the privilege of bearing guns and their use under color of law has in all probability increased the incidence of violence. There can therefore be no justification for the continued waste of millions of taxpayers' dollars in the maintenance of a militancy within the confines of the county.

Because the forces of oppression and suppression—the law enforcement agencies continue to harass, brutalize, illegally confine and psychologically damage the Chicano, the black, the poor and the unrepresented, I hereby declare my candidacy for the office of Sheriff of Los Angeles County, and pledge myself, my friends and associates to the following:

1. The ultimate dissolution of the Sheriff's Department.
2. The interim actual and symbolic demilitarization of deputies.
3. The immediate withdrawal of concentrated forces in the barrios and ghettos.
4. The immediate investigation into criminal activities of law enforcement officers.
5. The implementation of community review boards from the various areas.
6. The immediate use of personnel, equipment and facilities for utilitarian and socially beneficial programs as recommended and approved by community review boards.
7. Equality of treatment and justice for all.

I would like to interest you in working for our campaign of The People. I am convinced that we are in the final years of a relatively peaceful society, that the next few campaigns will be the final gasp before all hell breaks lose throughout the country and indeed throughout the world. The present forms of government on the national, state and local level seem totally inadequate to meet the needs of the citizenry. Political parties and labels have become meaningless and irrelevant to the issues that plague our society. Structures, philosophies, ideologies, rules of law and procedure are simply not working, and it is apparent to me that they will no longer work in a society such as we have created in between our numerous wars. It seems to me that if we are to survive the holocaust of imminent disintegration and destruction, that we must prepare now for a structure, a way of life that might hopefully turn back the tide.

I personally do not choose to run for the office of Sheriff. But I do not see any other man who is willing to take on the responsibility of telling the people the facts of life and to propose to them the radical solutions to the radical problems. With this attitude, I have been endorsed to run for that office by the Congress of Mexican American Unity which is the single socio-political organization in Los Angeles County that is representative of my community.

We propose some very immediate plans which realistically cannot be more specific for the simple reason that the final solution must come from The People, and that cannot occur unless and until we are elected to that post. When I propose the ultimate dissolution of law enforcement agencies, I recognize that such a proposal will be misinterpreted by the average person. But that is because the average person has been totally brainwashed into believing that violence and the threat of violence is instinctive to our nature. From a purely pragmatic point of view, the increase in armaments and personnel has not decreased the violence in men nor the incidence of crime. Under the present concept of law enforcement agencies, there can be no hope for the decrease of crime. Instead, there is every reason to believe that crime and violence will continue to increase under our present system, and that the one single source of this friction is the very arm of the law which was originally conceived as a means of lessening conflict in society. Of more importance to our platform is the realistic implementation of various programs at the outset. The disarmament of deputies, except for those specifically engaged in apprehending violent criminals, and the withdrawal of such a heavy concentration of forces—with machine guns, tanks and helicopters, etc.—would produce an immediate beneficial effect. All symbols of brute force, including uniforms and armaments would further serve as a means of lessening the hostility between the forces of oppression and The People.

The election and utilization of citizen review boards throughout the entire jurisdiction of the County Sheriff's substations would serve as the basis for the implantation of any, all or none of these proposals. Ultimately, what our campaign hopes to do is to give fair-minded people an opportunity of choice. If we are elected it will serve as a warning to all those forces of reaction throughout the country that seem intent on killing every form of dissent and dissenter. Our People, the Chicano, and our brothers, the Black, the poor and the unrepresented, can unite under this concept without conceding one iota of power, interest or the dissolution of their own specific interests and issues which are of more concern to them.

Since we are running a campaign of The People, it is not for me or for any of my associates to determine to what extent or in what manner you or any group with whom you associate should take up the banner. The responsibility and obligation must be yours and yours alone. If we are to be successful, it must come from the desire of The People to be free, totally free from those who oppress them. No man can tell another how, or even if he should be free. Therefore, we will not make any attempt to have on organization for this campaign. As the saying goes, you've got to Do Your Own Thing!

Justicia y Libertad.

[23 February 1970]

TESTAMENT

I, Oscar Acosta, being of sound mind, hereby declare: I revoke all former wills, and specifically the one of Dec. 1973 in which I bequeathed the major portion of my estate to my former spouse; I bequeath and devise and dispose and give all of my estate, all my earthly belongings, both real and personal, choses in action, accounts receivables, and all royalties from all my publications, all memorabilia, files and unpublished works, in short: everything that I possess at the time of my death is for my only son, Marco F. M. Acosta. If any person should contest this will or make any attempt to share in the proceeds of my estate, to that person I give ten dollars and may my wrath abide in her forever. I suggest that Neil Herring, Esq., of Los Angeles County, be appointed administrator of my estate.

[13 January 1974]

SELECTED BIBLIOGRAPHY

Acosta, Oscar "Zeta." "The Autobiography of a Brown Buffalo," *Con Safos* 2, no. 7 (1971): 34-46.

_____. *The Autobiography of a Brown Buffalo*. San Francisco: Straight Arrow Books, 1972; reprint. New York: Vintage, 1989.

_____. "The Autobiography of a Brown Buffalo," in *Growing Up Latino: Memoirs and Stories*, edited by Harold Augenbraum and Ilan Stavans. Boston: Houghton Mifflin, 1993: 193-207.

_____. "Perla Is a Pig," *Con Safos* 2, no. 5 (1970): 5-14; reprinted in *Voices of Aztlán: Chicano Literature Today*, edited by Dorothy E. Harth and Lewis M. Baldwin (New York: Mentor, 1974): 28-48.

_____. "The Revolt of the Cockroach People," *La Gente* (November-December 1973): 4-5, 12.

_____. *The Revolt of the Cockroach People*. San Francisco: Straight Arrow Books, 1973; reprint. New York: Vintage, 1989.

_____. "Tres Cartas de Zeta," *Con Safos* 2, no. 6 (1970): 29-31.

Acuña, Rodolfo. *Occupied America: A History of Chicanos*. 3rd ed. New York: HarperCollins, 1988.

Alurista. "Alienación e ironía en los personajes de Arlt y Acosta," *Grito del Sol* 2, no. 4 (1977): 69-80.

_____. *Oscar Zeta Acosta: In Context*, Ph.D. Dissertation, Ann Arbor, MI, 1983.

Blazer, Sam. "Review of *The Revolt of the Cockroach People*," The Nation (13 April 1974): 469-71.

Bruce-Novoa, John. "Fear and Loathing on the Buffalo Trail," *MELUS* 6, no. 4 (1979): 39-50.

Calderón, Héctor. *Criticism in the Borderlands. Studies in Chicano Literature, Culture, and Ideology*. Durham: Duke University Press, 1991.

_____. "To Read Chicano Narrative: Commentary and Metacommentary," *Mester* (1983): 3-14.

_____, and Ramón Saldívar, eds. *Chicano Criticism in Social Context*. Durham: Duke University Press, 1989.

____. *The Hispanic Condition: Reflections on Culture and Identity in America*. New York: HarperCollins, 1995.

____. "The Latin Phallus," *Transition* 65 (Spring 1995): 34-53.

____. *Bandido. Oscar "Zeta" Acosta and the Chicano Experience*. New York: HarperCollins, 1995.

Steadman, Ralph. "Gonzo Goes to Hollywood. The Strange and Terrible Saga of *Where the Buffalo Roam*," *Rolling Stone Magazine* (29 May 1980): 38-40.

Thompson, Hunter S. "Fear and Loathing in the Graveyard of the Weird: The Banshee Screams for Buffalo Meat," *Rolling Stone Magazine* (15 December 1977); anthologized in *The Great Shark Hunt: Strange Tales from a Strange Time; Gonzo Papers*, vol 1. New York: Summit Books, 1979: 495-516.

____. *Fear and Loathing in Las Vegas*. New York: Random House, 1972; reprint. Vintage, 1989.

____. "Strange Rumblings in Aztlán," *Rolling Stone Magazine* (29 April 1971): anthologized in *The Great Shark Hunt*. New York: Summit Books, 1979: 119-51.

Thwaitasn, Joanna. "The Uses of Irony in Oscar Zeta Acosta's *Autobiography of a Brown Buffalo*," *The Americas Review* 20, no. 1 (1992): 73-92.

Whitmer, Peter O. *When the Going Gets Weird: The Twisted Life and Times of Hunter S. Thompson. A Very Unauthorized Biography*. New York: Hyperion, 1993.

[Reprinted from *Bandido*.]